Video Marketing

Video Marketing

*Create engaging video campaigns to drive
brand growth and sales*

SECOND EDITION

Jon Mowat

KoganPage

First published in Great Britain and the United States in 2018 by Kogan Page Limited as *Video Marketing Strategy*
Second edition 2021

2nd Floor, 45 Gee Street
London
EC1V 3RS
United Kingdom
www.koganpage.com

122 W 27th St, 10th Floor
New York, NY 10001
USA

4737/23 Ansari Road
Daryaganj
New Delhi 110002
India

Kogan Page books are printed on paper from sustainable forests.

© Jon Mowat 2021

The right of Jon Mowat to be identified as the author of this work has been asserted by him in accordance with the Copyright, Designs and Patents Act 1988.

ISBNs

Hardback   9781398601161
Paperback   9781398601147
Ebook   9781398601154

British Library Cataloguing-in-Publication Data

A CIP record for this book is available from the British Library.

Library of Congress Control Number

2021940693

Typeset by Integra Software Services Pondicherry
Print production managed by Jellyfish
Printed and bound by CPI Group (UK) Ltd, Croydon CR0 4YY

For Florence and Spencer
You still rule

A NOTE ABOUT ONLINE VIDEOS

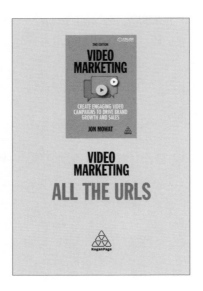

I mention a lot of online videos in this book. You can download this PDF containing all their URLs from the book's webpage: www.kogan.page.com/vm2.

When you see the ▶ symbol in the book, you can look the video up in the PDF and click on the link there.

CONTENTS

LIST OF FIGURES

LIST OF TABLES

ABOUT THE AUTHOR

Jon Mowat is an award-winning content creator, video strategy expert and public speaker. His career started at the BBC where he spent 12 years as producer and director on documentaries screened internationally on BBC1, BBC2 and BBC Worldwide. He's made films on topics ranging from cheetahs to drug addicts and spent six months embedded with the Royal Marines in the Gulf War. He has won numerous TV industry and marketing awards, including three from the Royal Television Society.

Since 2005 Jon has been Managing Director at Hurricane Media, one of the UK's leading video marketing agencies. Hurricane creates TV commercials, video content and social media campaigns for brands across all verticals, with specialisms in FMCG, not for profit, technology, leisure and medical. The agency has delivered work for AXA, ASDA, Airbus, Barclaycard, BMW, Fred Olson Cruises, Mazda, National Grid, Peugeot, Shelter, Sykes Holiday Cottages, Volvo, World Food Programme, World Health Organization and many more.

Jon is a regular writer and speaker on video marketing and has been published in a range of marketing publications including *Adweek*, *Brandwatch*, *CIM*, *Smart Insights*, *Social Media Today* and many more in the sector-specific trade press. He lives in the southwest of England with his two children Spencer and Florence and finds writing about himself in the third person very odd indeed.

PREFACE

Well, here we are again... a second edition! First time around, I wrote knowing that the marketing world was heading towards video in a big way. The industry knew that video was a core tool for growth, it knew that video would increase in both reach and volume, and there was even the blossoming notion of a 'video first world'. But the extent to which this came true has proven to be quite staggering, even for evangelists like myself. Leaps in technology, changes in the marketplace and a vast increase in the quantity of videos online have been matched only by the enthusiasm of brands and consumers to embrace it.

We are first-hand witnesses to a period of seismic shift in the advertising and marketing world. Paradigms that have stood for 50 years are being shaken to their foundations, and video marketing is at the forefront of the charge towards a new order.

Video has proven itself to be *the* key tool for effecting behaviour change; technology has advanced to the point where video has become ubiquitous and techniques to ensure success have been honed to perfection. The medium impacts on every part of marketing and sales, and has a huge influence over society as a whole. The shift is supported by the biggest brands and social media platforms in the world. Hundreds of millions of people now watch online video, and global advertising spend has moved with them.

But videos need production (which needs budget) and the volume of available content means that videos can sink from view without a trace. In short, the rewards have increased but so too have the risks of failure.

The same social media teams, which just five short years ago were using tiny percentages of marketing budgets to write and seed blogs and short pieces of video content, are now burning through the substantial chunks of money needed to create and activate videos. On top of this, brands that used to spend millions on television adverts have turned to video as traditional TV spots have lost their effectiveness. This has attracted the focus of senior players in all businesses, which in turn has led to video becoming more strategic in approach. In short, marketing, sales, brand and PR teams need to understand how the medium works, what it can do for them and how to roll out, achieve and measure... and that's why I've written this book.

Video Marketing takes the wonderfully creative, terribly powerful, pretty expensive and hugely complex world of online video and makes it work for you. In this edition I've updated the theories I used to explain video and included practical strategies that you can put in place for your brand straight away. I hope you enjoy learning from it as much as I've enjoyed writing it.

ACKNOWLEDGEMENTS

Top of the list of acknowledgements has to be my wonderful publisher Kogan Page and the just as wonderful Jenny Volich, who surprisingly trusted me on the first edition, Chris Cudmore who saw me through my first release and Stephen Dunnel, who even more surprisingly trusted me a second time around! The rest of the team at Kogan Page are equally as important in the process and the support of Heather Wood, Charlotte Owen, Rebecca Bush and Natasha Tulett cannot be overstated.

Without Carolyn Hair at Hurricane this book would literally not have happened... thank you!

John Lanyon, Creative Director at Hurricane, is the creative power at the heart of what we do and his support over the years has helped us to grow by delivering outstanding work.

Thanks to every one of the lovely, creative and dedicated people in Team Hurricane... Alex, Dan, Rob, Joe, Emma, Laura, Dawn and John Hopkins (who has done a fantastic job creating the figures for this book), who make going to work a totally enjoyable and rewarding experience.

Thanks to all the brand and marketing managers who let me use their case studies and imagery to bring the theory to life: Michael Ballard at Lenovo, the team at Kleenex, Steve at Vidyard, and Steve at Wirewax. A real note of thanks here goes to Joe Weston at We Are Social for the valuable insights into video strategy at the sharp end... I will repay the favour with more beer one day.

Jackie, I look forward to seeing how you put the book to good use!

Also, a big shout out goes to the wonderful team at TwentyThree who are great allies in the world of video; thanks to Thomas for letting me interview him and to Casper for sorting out my life!

Thanks to the other great people that I get to share my working life with. Magnus at Bespoke, the team at Yours Sincerely, all the camera operators, producers, planners, directors, sound ops, designers and editors that do such great work, and finally the amazing clients that I am so proud to make content for.

Lots of love goes out to Catherine, Danny, Elliot, Dad, Jean and the extended Mowat clan.

Oh, and finally... thanks to Florence and Spencer, who did as little towards the second edition of this book as they did towards the first... but they waited patiently for me to finish so get a big mention anyway!

Video marketing strategy: an introduction

01

What is video marketing?

It's 2014 in Skillman, New Jersey, in an unremarkable business park just 45 minutes' commute from the hustle and bustle of New York City. The marketing team for Johnson & Johnson's Clean & Clear are facing a tough reality.[1] Despite a substantial spend on TV advertising, the brand is not engaging with its target consumers and its market share is in danger. The team realizes it is time for a new approach.

After extensive audience research, they discover that the brand is not putting content where the audience is watching. And they certainly aren't talking to their audience in the right way (they are in fact still talking to teenage girls in the same way they have been since 1992, through TV spots linked to key demographics).

In a decisive and bold move, the team develops a strategy that engages the brand's elusive teen audience in relevant and timely conversations. At the centre of this strategy is a video marketing campaign unlike anything the brand has attempted before. The team is to create over 120 pieces of video content in less than a year, taking on board input from bloggers and end users. It's a bold move, and one that could have serious implications for the team if it doesn't work.

By the summer of 2015 it has become clear that the decisions made by the marketing team just 12 months before were a turning point for the brand. The campaign on which they had embarked has earned the brand millions of views for its anchor series, *See the Real Me* and, more importantly, has driven double-digit increases in market share.[2]

This is a real story, and one that will resonate with many marketers, as it is being repeated across the world's brand landscape.

TV advertising is a weakening force in the modern world; it's still effective and it's still going, but it's not what it was. What's more, the entire industrial advertising complex is being shaken up to the point where it is barely recognizable. The old certainty was that the biggest player spent the most on media, would therefore get biggest market share, and would dictate the playbook of all other brands. This is what kept the likes of Procter & Gamble and Unilever at the front of the supermarket line for over 50 years. TV is not dead yet, indeed brands that tried ditching it have found this to their cost (a 5 per cent decline in sales wasn't what Pepsi was hoping for when it went digital only), but the model is changing beyond recognition.

The decline in TV isn't the only seismic change on the horizon. Ad blockers (a way to automatically prevent ads from appearing in your social streams and on visited sites) are here to stay. This is being driven heavily by well-off millennials born between 1980 and 2000 (which is a major worry for brands looking to reach this market especially). I say 'well-off' here as ad blockers and ad-free subscriptions are normally a paid service, which leaves the less well-off more likely to receive ads in their streams (especially worrying for those selling luxury goods to an affluent market). In 2019, 47 per cent of consumers were using ad blockers.[3] This target market is more likely to turn to content that they can engage with or to influencers such as bloggers or people they follow on social.

Being a brand that comes to mind both quickly and fluently to customers is what matters, and a massive TV spend alone is no longer the best way to achieve this. The market share of brands that have been safe for a generation is being chewed away by upstarts with online digital budgets and a hot product to talk about. The brands on the best growth curve are nimble, responsive to consumers and backed by a highly targeted online and social ad focus. So, TV ads are losing their potency, and the increasing use of ad blockers is stopping display and online ads… it all sounds pretty bleak for advertisers. And it certainly is if you are not finding something to replace these channels.

Nowhere can this be seen more clearly than in the 'Razor Wars' between Gillette and new subscription-based upstarts. Gillette (P&G), the global behemoth of shaving, poured millions of dollars into fending off rival Unilever with traditional TV spots. But they both suddenly started losing share to an unexpected rival, run by two guys who reportedly came up with the idea at a family barbeque. The start-up was the Dollar Shave Club, which, with its now infamous online video campaigns, has grown beyond anyone's expectations. Here was a brand with a fresh offering and a mean line in viral videos giving the big boys a run for their money.

In March 2012 the Dollar Shave Club started selling subscriptions and released a YouTube video starring founder Michael Dubin. Not only was this a new way to sell razorblades, but the video was a new paradigm for attitude. Michael himself took viewers on a tour of the company warehouse and boldly exclaimed that the blades were 'f***ing great' and 'so gentle a toddler could use them'.

DollarShaveClub.com – our blades are f***ing great
6 March 2012, Dollar Shave Club YouTube channel
 Video 1

Dollar Shave Club's meteoric rise culminated in it being bought by Unilever for $1 billion. There was no technical advantage or innovative thought in the blades themselves. In fact, the Dollar Shave Club blades are arguably not as good as Gillette, but by using innovative marketing techniques they changed the playing field and built a massive brand in just four years. This was something too big for Unilever to miss so they bought it. It also didn't hurt Unilever to keep arch rival P&G from snapping up the company.

This story has one final swing in its narrative. Since being bought by Unilever, the brand faces the challenge of avoiding the old ways of doing things. They now run TV ads, which might be seen by some as going back to the old school. It could be a great idea, or it may be proof that the biggest companies have yet to leave the idea of mass TV advertising behind them. What is also interesting is that Gillette is hitting back, not only creating its own subscription product but taking the marketing fight online.

SCOTT GALLOWAY: DEATH OF THE INDUSTRIAL ADVERTISING COMPLEX

Scott Galloway, a clinical Professor of Marketing at NYU Stern School of Business, has been making waves in the minds of advertising execs by proposing a simple position: the systems of marketing and advertising that kept the big players on their thrones for over 50 years are coming to an abrupt halt.

Galloway's presentation has sent a shiver down the spines of hundreds of advertising execs that have had the good fortune to see him talk at Cannes or elsewhere. Watching someone eruditely and categorically introduce the impending death of one's chosen career industry is not a comfortable experience.

The radical changes that are happening around marketing technology negatively affect brands' ability to broadcast their messages through advertising. As consumers now get user reviews around their product choices they do not rely solely on brand communications to make their decisions.

The industry that is most going to feel the effects of this is traditional TV ads and print. This is driven by the fact that consumers, especially young wealthy ones, are paying to watch ad-free services such as Netflix or Amazon Prime, and are dumping ad-rich channels like MTV (which is seeing its market share plummet).

Galloway has a wonderful way of describing TV adverts:

> Broadcast television is cursed with being a swimmer, and every 11 minutes someone takes a dump in the pool... you literally get interrupted by something that is shocking, is ugly, makes no sense, is disturbing, is totally out of context, and you literally have to stop swimming and go, 'what is going on here, what is happening here' and two minutes later you start swimming again.

When you describe it like that you can see why people are leaving ads behind.

To find out more, why not watch one of Scott's presentations:

Death of the industrial advertising complex
22 July 2016, L2inc YouTube channel
 Video 2

It doesn't take an expert to point to the fact that social media and the internet have changed the landscape forever. And into this tumultuous world comes online video, something with the power to emotionally connect just like TV ads, but backed by highly targetable technology with data analytics and interactivity. It's held in the hands of 1.3 billion people and backed by the giants of Facebook and Google. So the rewards are there for brands nimble enough to break the shackles of old models. Now, having the biggest spend will certainly ensure success but won't guarantee continual category dominance. The democratization of the internet means the door is open for smaller brands as well as big ones.

The content soup

Having established that old models of advertising are in decline, and that social and video are the routes to consumers (especially young and affluent ones), we are in danger of seeing content as the magic bullet for our brands and clients. But sheer ad spend and its associated volume of content is becoming a massive problem of its own making. Marketplaces are increasingly fragmented, and with that fragmentation comes extreme competition for people's attention. The biggest enemy of truly great content is the truly awful content all around it.

FIGURE 1.1 The internet minute

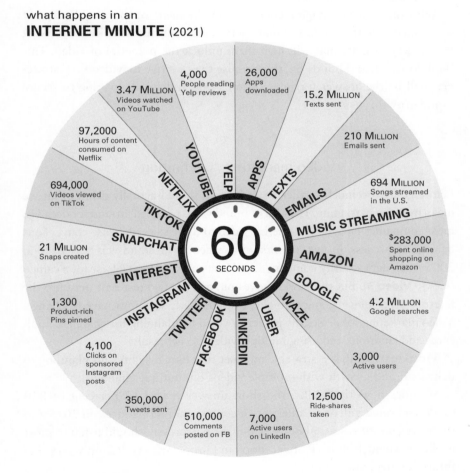

what happens in an
INTERNET MINUTE (2021)

SOURCE www.visualcapitalist.com

There is simply too much content reaching our target consumers. Around us is a gloopy mix of words and pictures that sparkles at our attention like a mirror in the sunshine. Some is sticky, some tasteless and some instantly forgettable, but it is all content vying for attention. Brands trying to grow share, increase audience engagement or even just maintain relevance are competing in a world of 'infobesity'. At Hurricane, we know this problem as the 'content soup'.

How do brands cut through this content soup to deliver effective campaigns that have solid ROI? For brand managers and owners looking to stand out, there needs to be a number of clear strategies, from developing nimble products that hit the market's zeitgeist, to fast feedback of reviews and more. But the ones we are interested in for this book are the ones that help brands in their marketing.

With the moving image increasingly at the heart of the world's biggest social media platforms, brand managers and agency teams alike are looking for the key insights that will help them unlock the potential of video. This book looks at, and builds on, the premise that a move to 'video first' strategies will be the answer for many brands (big and small) looking to secure brand growth.

Video marketing: a definition

Before going too much further, I suppose we should actually define what we mean by video marketing. The idea of brand video has been around for decades; most companies have used a one-off video to drive sales, increase conversions or raise awareness. In fact, the first viral video for a brand was way back in 2005 when data security company Live Vault roped in John Cleese for a cameo (see ▶ **Video 3**). But the world moves on, and a video just sent out onto the internet is no longer going to make a difference... so things have to change. Video marketing harnesses the power of video by planning for channels, audiences and emotions and using multiple videos to get results.

Video marketing is a strategic mindset that uses insights and planning to delivers brand growth with multiple videos on multiple channels.

So, does it work? Well... the short answer is yes! 62 per cent of B2B marketers rated videos as an effective content marketing tactic in 2016 and there are countless stats about it... but the person you should listen to most is Nicola Mendelsohn, VP of Facebook in Europe, who very simply says ' the future is video, video, video'.

STATS – HOW BIG IS VIDEO IN MARKETING?

- 62 per cent of 18- to 32-year-olds prefer to check their smartphone if they have any 'downtime' rather than just sit and think.[4]

- 37 per cent even check their smartphone if there's a short lull in conversation with friends.[4]

- In 2021, a million minutes of video content crossed the internet every second.[5]

- Video will be 82 per cent of all IP traffic (both business and consumer) by 2022, up from 75 per cent in 2017.[6]

- Content delivery network (CDN) traffic carried 71 per cent of all internet traffic in 2021.[5]

- More than 60 per cent of marketers and small business owners said they planned to increase investment in video marketing in 2017.[7]

- Live video will grow 15-fold from 2016 to 2021.[8]

The Clean & Clear case study that opens this book is one of many examples of the growth in brands using video, and more specifically using planned video campaigns to grow. A quick Google search for 'Why should I use video?' throws up countless statistics. These range from the obvious – 'Show off your company'[8] – to the insightful – 'Adding a product video on your landing page can increase conversions by 80 per cent'[9] – onto the impressive – 'Companies using video grow revenue 49 per cent faster year over year than companies that do not use video'[8] – and even to the outlandish – 'one minute of video is worth 2.5 million words' (see the box on dodgy statistics later in this chapter).

But why did this all start? How did we get to the point where video stands astride the marketing world like a behemoth and controls hundreds of millions of dollars in advertising revenue? One thing to consider is the power of the search engines, because the changes they make to search algorithms make a huge difference to what eventually becomes popular. If engines say mobile video is taking off, it quickly becomes a self-fulfilling prophecy. In 2014, Facebook changed its algorithms[9] to prioritize video search, and within months the first viral sensation happened. The 'Ice Bucket Challenge' was a fundraising campaign for amyotrophic lateral sclerosis (ALS) that quickly saw 2.4 million tagged videos circulating on Facebook. The campaign raised more than US $100 million in a 30-day period, and was able to fully fund a number of research projects. The challenge also gave us an excuse to watch George W Bush having ice poured on his head. Reality TV star and 45th US President Donald Trump also took part, and in his own inimitable style chose to have the water poured over him by Miss Universe and Miss America.[10]

ALS Ice Bucket Challenge – George W Bush
20 August 2014, ALS YouTube channel
▶ **Video 4**

Donald Trump ALS Ice Bucket Challenge
28 August 2014, The Trump Organization YouTube channel
▶ **Video 5**

The Ice Bucket Challenge proved the long-held hypothesis that video would become the dominant online medium of the future, and that the largest platforms were eager backers. Mark Zuckerberg stated: 'We see a world that is video first – with video at the heart of all our apps and services'.[11] And when Mr Zuckerberg says video first, he means it – across the entire FB family from the main platform itself to Messenger, WhatsApp, Instagram, Oculus and more.

How to get the most from this book

I was once discussing business books with a client and he noted that everything he read seemed to follow a rule of thirds. He found that a third of the book's content he already knew, a third was not that exciting and a third was actually really useful stuff. This (non-scientific but useful) analysis has stayed with me during the writing process and I've done my best to help you navigate past the third you may already know, keep the non-exciting third to a minimum and make the useful third as useful as I can.

I'm also aware that people of vastly different experiences will be reading this book, some just starting on a marketing journey and others who are senior players in well-developed marketing departments with considerable resources and staffing. With that in mind I cover a fair breadth of information to help you find the right level for your needs. To help you get the most from this book in as quick a time as possible, it's divided into four sections. Signposts will point you to where you can go if you already know some of the topics, and also where you can go if you would like to find out more.

Section One is a dive into the state of contemporary marketing and the place of video strategy within it. We look at how marketing is changing in a socially driven world, why video is such a significant channel, and how it works. I suggest that all readers start here to get grounding in the psychology that underpins successful video marketing as well as its history, forms and potential.

Before exploring how to construct wide-ranging, multichannel strategies we need to explore what makes great video content, and Section Two does just that. Here we focus on what makes powerful and effective single videos. It includes an introductory chapter for those new to marketing or for those wanting to make sure they have no knowledge gaps. It then moves into a three-step plan for creating powerful, effective individual pieces of content.

Almost everyone at some stage will be faced with the challenge of making a video themselves, whether it's a talking head on their iPhone for a conference or something more advanced for the public to watch. Section Three answers the immediate issues you will face.

Finally, Section Four builds on the success of individual films and develops them into series, cross-platform campaigns and content hubs. It leads you by the hand through the process of building an effective video marketing strategy that complements your wider marketing activity. This section is for those in larger brands looking to push ROI across multiple channels or smaller brands that see real value in moving their marketing to a video-heavy strategy.

Just before you get started, here is something to make your life easier. Setting out to write a physical and virtual book about video presents a unique challenge, as much of it requires readers to be able to watch examples and case studies. Unless someone has invented a book with a built-in TV this is going to be hard. I could ask you to type in a lot of URLs on your laptop, but getting 45 characters correct first time is always going to be tricky. With that in mind this book has a downloadable PDF that keeps all the videos, references, links and template documents you will need in one place. This is the link: www.koganpage.com/vm2

The web is always changing and some links may disappear, but if this happens I will update the links on the PDF so you should be able to see the content. If you do spot any links to videos that don't work as you read the book, let me know so the PDF can be updated.

References

1 Google
March 2015
Video marketing lessons from Clean & Clear®
www.thinkwithgoogle.com/marketing-resources/content-marketing/clean-and-clear-video-marketing-lessons (archived at https://perma.cc/F4G9-KM86)

2 Clean & Clear
12 April 2016
See the real me, *YouTube*,
www.youtube.com/watch?v=rPNZc0rYZqA (archived at https://perma.cc/D8J4-ZSFP)

3 TJ McCue 19
March 2019
47 percent of consumers are blocking ads
Forbes
www.forbes.com/sites/tjmccue/2019/03/19/47-percent-of-consumers-are-blocking-ads/ (archived at https://perma.cc/R37K-UVVU)

4 Internet Advertising Bureau UK
18 October 2013
Always on: a global perspective of mobile consumer experience
www.iab.com/insights/2017globalmobileperspective/ (archived at https://perma.cc/3MGT-DFWB)

5 Cisco
9 March 2020
Cisco annual internet report (2018–2023) white paper
Networking Solutions White Paper
www.cisco.com/c/en/us/solutions/collateral/executive-perspectives/annual-internet-report/white-paper-c11-741490.html (archived at https://perma.cc/9EQW-CAN8)

6 Megan O'Neill
22 June 2016
The 2016 social video forecast [infographic]
Animoto
https://animoto.com/blog/business/2016-social-video-forecast-infographic/ (archived at https://perma.cc/2QFY-XE4E)

7 Bubba Page
1 July 2015
6 reasons you need to use video marketing
Inc.com
www.inc.com/bubba-page/6-reasons-to-use-video-marketing.html (archived at https://perma.cc/X7XP-FDRT)

8 Liis Hainla
10 October 2017
8 powerful reasons you need to use video marketing
Dreamgrow
www.dreamgrow.com/8-reasons-why-your-business-should-use-video-marketing/ (archived at https://perma.cc/D96X-CRKK)

9 Wallaroo
9 December 2020
Facebook newsfeed algorithm history
http://wallaroomedia.com/facebook-newsfeed-algorithm-change-history/ (archived at https://perma.cc/5UTT-MMMR)

10 Eb Adeyeri
27 August 2014
Ice bucket challenge: what are the lessons for marketers?
Guardian
 www.theguardian.com/media-network/media-network-blog/2014/aug/27/ice-bucket-challenge-lessons-marketing (archived at https://perma.cc/RS7E-XMVL)

11 Facebook
27 July 2016
Facebook reports second quarter 2016 results
https://investor.fb.com/investor-news/press-release-details/2016/facebook-reports-second-quarter-2016-results/default.aspx (archived at https://perma.cc/JCZ7-49P2)

02

Why video marketing works

So far, we've explored video's growth into a global phenomenon and how it offers a powerful, if not rather complex, new tool for brands. But why has it become such a dominant force? The short answer is that well-planned video on mobile is arguably the most effective mass communication format ever. If used correctly it's the best platform marketers have ever had to change people's opinions. Video is not a magic solution to every marketing problem but it's a substantial part of the solution, and an understanding of how to get the best from it will improve results. In this chapter we will look at the four core reasons for video's power so you can create better marketing. We will look at how moving images grab our attention, how the action of holding a phone makes us more connected to content we watch, how highly targeted ads allow for precision marketing, and finally how emotional stories change behaviour.

1 Moving image

Since we first removed ourselves from the food chain, we've not had to spend our commute to work worrying about being something else's breakfast. A commute past a hungry lion would certainly liven up the morning conversation at the day's first meeting. Our distant ancestors, however, were not so lucky. They needed every advantage that nature could give them to avoid becoming prey, and an ability to detect motion was key to sensing the presence of predators. For those of you that are into this area there is a fascinating topic called the Snake Detection Theory. This theory proposes that we owe our amazing sight to these reptiles as they forced us to get better or get eaten. Snakes are arguably our oldest adversary (having been

FIGURE 2.1   Why video is so effective

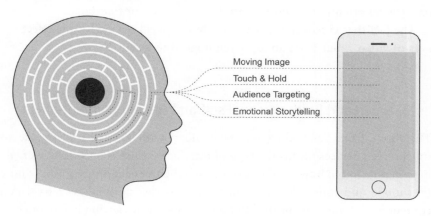

eating mammals for the best part of 100 million years), so they have been instrumental in helping us to evolve our visual defences.[1]

The brain doesn't see light, it merely interprets information coming from the retina via electrical signals from cells. There are about 90 cells in the retina, and we don't know what most of them do. However, studies at the University of Washington have found the cells in our eyes that enable to us to see motion.[2] A specific subtype of amacrine cell excites the ganglion cells, signalling the brain to be aware that an object is moving. What is interesting is that if the whole scene that we are looking at moves, the cells remain silent (which occurs when we move our head). But if only part of the scene moves, they signal to the brain that there is movement. Thus, we are tuned into small, sudden movements, like those of a predator.

This ability has obvious applications for those of us whose jobs involve catching people's attention, and a good understanding of how it works can be very useful. So what happens to people when we detect motion? Scientific tests at the University of Delaware showed subjects both moving and non-moving images, and took a range of measurements that included skin conductance and heart rate. The results showed that:

> Picture motion significantly increased arousal. Picture motion also tended to
> prompt more heart-rate deceleration, most likely reflecting a greater allocation
> of attention to the more arousing images. For multimedia producers concerned
> with the cost of using video clips or creating animations in their products, the
> results suggest that the endeavour may be well worth the effort.[3]

In summary, when we see moving images our attention is aroused and we pay greater attention… and we can thank a snake for that one.

The fact that videos move is a neat physiological reason for the effectiveness of video… but what about psychological reasons?

2 Touch and hold: personal self and the endowment effect

The move from controlling our technology with keypad and mouse to touchscreen devices means the type of interface we use is becoming increasingly significant in how we relate to content. 60 per cent of net traffic is now on mobile and touch devices, and what was the 'normal' way to watch content is no longer the norm.[4] But why this shift in viewing behaviour?

I have no doubt that, as you read this, you are within 5 foot of your mobile phone. If you're like me, it's probably right beside you. Boy, do we love to hang on to our mobile devices. So much so that we generally spend an average of three hours and 15 minutes on our phones every day, picking up our phones 58 times in 24 hours, with the top 20 per cent of smartphone users spending upwards of four and a half hours glued to the screen.[5]

This behaviour directly affects how we think. 62 per cent of us prefer to check our smartphone if we have any 'downtime' rather than just sit and think, and 37 per cent check their smartphone if there's a short lull in conversation.[6] People's inability to leave their phones alone is the newest addition to common 'displacement' behaviours such as smoking, doodling, fiddling with objects and picking at food.

So what is it that we find alluring? The answer is shown in Figure 2.2. The scientists amongst you may know what this is straight away… but for the rest of you, it's guess time.

FIGURE 2.2 The reason we can't put our phones down!

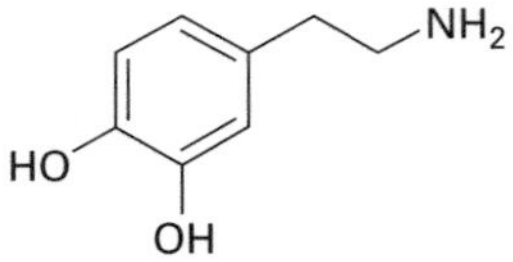

Figure 2.2 shows the chemical symbol for dopamine. Dopamine is a neurochemical that signals to our brain when we need to be paid attention. It makes us feel good when we do things, so we keep doing them. It was a necessary part of evolution as it encouraged us to find food, helped us to

focus on remembering things, and gave us the motivation to complete tasks. Without it, humanity simply wouldn't have been that bothered to get things done.

However, dopamine is more than just a task-master – it makes us feel great. It's sometimes known as the 'love drug' because it creates a sense of belonging and attachment. Dopamine levels rise when parents look lovingly at their child, when two lovers gaze into each other's eyes and when we feel part of a group. Basically, dopamine makes us feel great, naturally. But mankind has started to use it in less-than-natural ways.

Your phone is a dopamine pump, and every time you use it, you get a little bump of the good feelings that keep you going back for more. Hunting for, and finding, new information provides a dopamine high. So does being validated, liked by others and feeling accepted in a wider group. Basically, all things that we look to our phone for.

There is a debate as to whether we are literally addicted to the dopamine that is activated by our phones... but we sure do love it. It's why there is a clear pattern of mobile phones being carried in people's hands, even when they aren't using them. 30 per cent of men and 37 per cent of women walk outside holding 'inactive' smartphones... just waiting for something to happen.[7]

However, our bond with our phone goes way beyond a simple dopamine kick. Our behaviour is driven by deeper psychological forces. In this section we are going to look at two separate principles, the extension of personal self, then the endowment effect, and we will explore how they interact with each other in a way that makes video a great tool to drive changes in behaviour.

Personal self

Philosophers Andy Clark and David Chalmers first posited the 'extended mind' hypothesis about mobile devices in a 1998 paper.[8] Personal self is the sum total of all that a person can call 'who they are'. It's more than just our body, it's how we think, our clothes, home, partner, friends, children and beliefs. The key characteristic that marks things as part of our personal self is that losing them leads to a sense of great loss. Losing our home will cause a sense of loss, losing the jacket that we feel great in will, having a terrible hair cut will... and to this list we can now add our mobile phones.

Clark and Chalmers put forward that our mental states (including beliefs and memories) aren't just 'in our heads'. They are now stored in the digital world. As examples of this, we no longer know the birthdays or contact details of people (as they are all stored on our phone); we plan our clothing on Pinterest and map out our social lives on Facebook. Their theory is that we increasingly see our phones, and the digital lives that we lead on them, as part of who we are psychologically. Since the late 1990s this intertwining of our devices and our psychology has increased. We can now customize our devices, allowing our lives to be shared with some and not others, to reflect who we are and to make a statement of our beliefs. Whether we are sports fans, gamers or socialites, the phone can be constructed to become a reflection of ourselves. For those of you wanting to look further into how our psyche is interlinking with technology it is worth reading Sherry Turkle's *The Second Self: Computers and the human spirit*, which has now been updated for a 20th anniversary edition.[9]

The implications of our devices as an extension of our perceived selves are varied, but a key impact for marketers to understand is that people view their phones (or at least the data and content on them) as part of their psychological make-up. Things that appear on a person's device appear 'closer' to them than messages that appear elsewhere. People trust their emotional response to content on their mobile, as it is part of their extended self, and this takes us neatly onto the endowment effect

The endowment effect

Getting things costs time, money, effort, and often all three. It's because of this that we value things we already own more highly. By the age of two children understand what possessions are, and by the age of six children exhibit the 'endowment effect', where they place significant value on an object that belongs to them.[10]

If something is already 'ours', we want to keep it, which seems logical as, after all, we went through the effort of getting it. When we don't have something we want, getting one is a transaction cost to us. Once we do have it, however, it represents an opportunity, as we don't have to do any more to get it. We therefore think that things we have already are worth more. This observation is called the 'endowment effect' and has been explored by psychologist Richard Thaler, who looked at how it can explain many things, such as why free trials of things work so well. Thaler summarizes this particular example thus:

> Consider the case of a two-week trial period with a money-back guarantee. At the first decision point the consumer thinks he can lose at most the transactions costs of taking the good home and back. The second decision point comes two weeks later. If the consumer has fully adapted to the purchase, he views the cost of keeping the good as an opportunity cost. Once this happens the sale is more likely.[11]

The endowment effect has been seen in hundreds of experiments. The most famous of these was when students were shown to be reluctant to trade a coffee mug they had only just been given for a bar of chocolate. This was the case even if they did not prefer coffee mugs to chocolate when given a straight choice between the two. Owning a mug was simply better than giving it up.[12]

So how does the endowment effect impact on video marketing? The crux of the research is that we value an item more highly when we have it. But when we are shopping on a handheld device, we are going some way to thinking that we already have it in our hands. Holding the images in our hand and touching the screen tricks the mind into thinking that we (in some way) already own it and we therefore value it more highly. This is especially true if we are swiping the images or rotating them with touch gestures – a great advantage for e-commerce brands whose products can be marketed on touch devices. This is underlined by the fact that test subjects have proven willing to pay more for goods they are buying on a handheld touch device than they would when purchasing on a desktop or other remote screen. S. Adam Brasel and co-author James Gips have tested the hypothesis of endowment in the digital world by comparing how shoppers behaved when using touch devices compared with non-touch devices such as laptops.[13,14] Test subjects ran through a number of purchasing scenarios on both mobile devices and laptops. In line with the hypothesis, Brasel and Gips proved the endowment effect was greater on touchscreens. In fact, they got so many data points that they were able to put specific numbers to it. People who purchased items on touch devices were only willing to sell them if they received far greater sums of money than people who bought items on laptops. Although the 'consumers' never got the actual items, those people that had purchased using touch wanted an average of $68 to sell their possessions. This compared to a much lower average of $47 with people using laptops. These effects were especially pronounced when subjects were buying items with a tactile nature (such as a soft sweatshirt).[14]

Brasel and Gips went further in a second set of tests, exploring what would happen if people purchased things using devices that they already owned, rather than on a device that they had borrowed. The assumption was that high levels of salience with the tech would lead to a greater sense of ownership and the endowment of more value onto the items they were buying. The second tests ran as before, with the additional element of buying things both on borrowed devices and ones that test subjects already owned. It was discovered that the levels of perceived psychological ownership and endowment were again greater on touchscreens. This was even more pronounced when subjects purchased items on a touch device that they actually owned. It is interesting that device ownership didn't affect results for laptops; it would appear we are ownership-neutral on devices we don't touch. In conclusion to this study, we can say that the highest levels of endowment arise when shoppers are buying items with 'tangible' qualities, on a mobile device that they already own. The implications for marketing are clear – spend your ad dollars on mobile devices to get higher returns.

Personal self + the endowment effect

Things get interesting when we put the two psychological ideas we've talked about together. We feel like we already partly own the things we see on our phone, and what we already own we value more highly. This gives us a killer marketing potential, as objects and services we show to people via their mobile device are automatically valued more highly than if they were told about them in another way. This area of psychology is increasingly big business, and we could talk about it for hours, but for now we just need to have an awareness of it, and we can move onto more practical reasons for the power of video.

3 Audience targeting

We've had a look at some quite abstract ideas up to this point. Now we move onto something more practical... the power of targeting content at people by the specifics of who, and where, they are. Our digital lives leave a footprint that's actively collected by all the major tech companies. Our data is a commodity created as a by-product of everything we do online, which is bought and sold for a profit. Data sets are generated by trackers and apps that cover everything we do, from purchases, searches and messages to locations, communication patterns, interests, faces, emotions and illnesses. This data, known as behavioural surplus,[15] enables us to know not only who is currently thinking what, when and why but, more importantly, what they *will* be thinking, when and why. When we know this, we can target ads and messages at highly selective groups of people.

To illustrate how targeting works, let's take a moment to see it in action with a project I've worked on at Hurricane for Sykes Holiday Cottages, a UK-based holiday cottage rental company. We created a 30-second TV spot that played on broadcast TV nationally with the core message of 'This is your time' – a message around spending your holiday time well. Although this was targeted at timeslots in which we believed there were rich seams of prospective customers, the nature of TV is that targeting has to be broad and fairly unscientific. Things really got exciting when we also created social media versions of the ad that were tailored to, and focused on, the four key audiences for the brand: couples, groups, families and pet owners. These went out as a paid campaign on Facebook and Instagram and sat on the brands' social channels. The data captured, and the specificity of the targeting, delivered real value for the brand, who saw increased website enquires, social mentions and bookings.

This is only an introduction to how this is done, but it shows that it is video's ability to be targeted at specific audiences that makes it so effective. You can read more about this in Section Three.

4 Emotional storytelling: the two-system mind

Storytelling

So far, we've covered psychology, physiology and ad targeting. The final piece in the puzzle (and I've saved the big one for last) is to understand how videos can drive behaviour change in audiences by talking to them at an emotional level. Emotional storytelling is the single biggest thing that video has going for it. It's easy to make a video that is emotionless and ineffective, but when you get it right you can sit back and watch your campaign results soar.

I opened this book with a story, the story of a marketing team facing falling share and engagement. They stepped out of their comfort zone and overcame the challenge to deliver a wild success. It was a classic three-part structure, often referred to as the 'Hero's Journey' (which we will discuss later). I included the story for a simple reason: you were more likely to connect with what I was saying if I brought it to life through a story of people you would empathize with. I could have opened the book with some dry theory… but that would not have engaged you as well.

Humans have evolved telling and listening to stories. It's how we have always communicated and how we understand the world around us. Indeed, when humans see or hear a story, a lot happens. Firstly, our brain waves change, the amygdala and hippocampus kick in to remember things, our language centres spark up ready to understand the world, and our brain is flooded with neurotransmitters and hormones like vasopressin, serotonin, endorphins, oxytocin and our favourite… dopamine. These chemicals cause emotion to kick in, which hijacks our cortex … making us forget about using our observant, considered judgements, instead moving to a reliance on emotional decision making.

Make someone feel something, and you have their attention. Telling a story engages a bigger part of our brain than facts and statistics. During the listening to (and telling of) stories, vast amounts of the human brain become active. The part of the brain that deals with the theory of the mind (or how we understand others) comes alive, along with sources of oxytocin that cause empathy,[16] the amygdala hippocampus system (which processes many memory types) and the left perisylvian region (responsible for languages). This chemical reaction underlines the fact that humans have a predilection for narrative, with a psychological and neurological basis born from millions of years of evolution. Narrative engages the entire human brain. It can change the opinion of even the most stubborn of minds using pathos (an appeal to emotion), and is a way of convincing an audience of an argument by creating an emotional response.

A story is when one person tries to pass knowledge, feelings and visions from their own mind into that of someone else. Uri Hasson from Princeton has done a fascinating TEDx talk on how the brains of the storyteller and the listener try to get in sync as we talk and listen. At the university's lab they used fMRI scanners to show that stories activate a wide range of responses in our mind. He sums it up as follows:

> Imagine I invented a device which can record my memories, my dreams, my ideas, and transmit them to your brain. That would be a game-changing technology? But in fact we already possess this device, and it's called the human communication system and effective storytelling.[17]

There are several engaging groups of theories on why humans have developed stories. Some think that we developed them to help navigate life's complex social problems – just as flight simulators prepare pilots for difficult situations.[18] Some evolutionists believe storytelling evolved as a form of displaying sexual prowess, with storytellers who showed skill and intelligence around the campfire having more success in attracting a long-term mate.[19] Still others take the more practical approach that we used stories to ensure the exchange of knowledge, culture and morals. This can still be seen in the oral tradition of Dreamtime Stories amongst tribes of Australian Aborigines. These tribes tell expansive stores that can take 10 minutes to recite, cover up to 20 wide-ranging topics each, and reflect the accumulated knowledge, spirituality and wisdom of the people themselves.[20]

The exact anthropomorphic origins of storytelling are not, however, as important as the mere fact that stories are hardwired into our souls. The human propensity for emotional narrative was noted as far back as Aristotle, who wrote: 'The orator persuades his hearers, when they are aroused to emotion to his speech; for the judgments we deliver are not the same when we are influenced by joy or sorrow, love or hate.'[21] It sounds right, but we had to wait over 2,000 years for this to be scientifically proven in a fascinating experiment by Fritz Heider and Marianne Simmel (1944). They conducted a test that showed a random selection of people a series of animated shapes and observed their reactions.[22]

Before explaining the results of the Heider Simmel experiment you may like to try it for yourself, in which case watch the link here and think about how you would explain to someone else what is happening:

Experimental study of apparent behavior. Fritz Heider & Marianne Simmel. 1944
26 December 2010, Yann Leroux YouTube channel
▶ **Video 6**

What do you see?

When I watched this film I saw a large triangle bullying a smaller one, while a scared circle tried to stay out of the way. In the end the two smaller shapes work together to trap the bully and escape. My reaction to the experiment was identical to that of the original subjects. In that group, everyone shown the experiment credited the shapes with human characteristics (with the famous exception of one person – who noted that they had arrived late and in a bad mood. They felt they would have come to an alternate conclusion in different circumstances). This experiment was the first conclusive proof that humans make sense of the world around them by attributing stories to it. If you enjoy this subject, a very interesting five minutes can be spent watching the live reactions of comedians to this experiment on the link below:

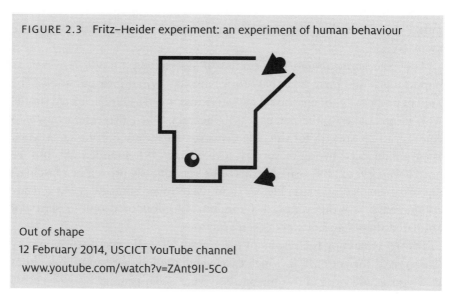

FIGURE 2.3   Fritz–Heider experiment: an experiment of human behaviour

Out of shape
12 February 2014, USCICT YouTube channel
www.youtube.com/watch?v=ZAnt9II-5Co

So, it can be proven that humans are hardwired to see a story, thus underlining their significance in our thinking. But how do stories motivate behaviour? This is where things start to get really interesting. A study by Dr Paul Zak at Berkeley University has shown that emotional videos release chemicals in the brain. They have reported their findings into a fascinating video called 'Empathy, neurochemistry, and the dramatic arc' (I've put a link below). Viewers were shown the animated story of a small boy called Ben who has brain cancer and does not have long to live. The tests showed that the story elicited two main emotions: distress and empathy. It was also noted that two chemicals were released during the watching of the film: cortisol (which causes us to pay more attention to a stimulus) and oxytocin (connected with care, connection and empathy). Results showed that the more oxytocin that was released, the more empathetic viewers felt towards the subject of the video, and this was a driver of behaviour. The study went even further and was able to predict the amount of money people would donate to a charity based on how much cortisol and oxytocin had been released. The higher the levels of oxytocin, the more people were willing to donate to charity. Thus it could be proven that people's behaviour was changed by altered brain chemistry, driven by an emotional story. In effect, the videos were changing behaviours by changing brain chemistry. This is incredibly important to marketers as we know that, to change behaviour, we have to make the audience feel something.

Empathy, neurochemistry, and the dramatic arc: Paul Zak at the Future of StoryTelling 2012

3 October 2012, Future of StoryTelling YouTube channel

 Video 7

But how do these drivers get used in practice? At Hurricane we harnessed emotional drivers similar to those in the experiment in a video for the UK-based charity Together for Short Lives. This charity, which does amazing work with the families of children diagnosed with life-limiting illnesses, asked Hurricane Media to produce a film as a brand piece to raise their profile and, importantly, to speak to the children and families that they are here to help. The ambition was to communicate the needs of families when they hear the news of their child's diagnosis and to also reassure families that there are specialist children's palliative care services to support them. The film speaks to families who care for the UK's 49, 000 children and young people with life-limiting and life-threatening conditions. The film has won three awards and has accumulated 29,000 views on YouTube.

FIGURE 2.4   Together for Short Lives

We're having a baby
14 October 2014, Together4ShortLives YouTube channel
▶ **Video 8**

The video has been a massive driver for engagement and fundraising for the charity. This work underlines how theoretical insights can have impact in the real world. The impact of emotion goes way beyond simple brain chemistry. We are now going to take a short while to look at a theory that is core to modern marketing, one that you should always be considering when planning your video content.

The two-system mind

In their book *The Long and the Short of It*, Les Binet and Peter Field summarize the power of emotion perfectly: 'Emotional campaigns, and in particular those that are highly creative... produce considerably more powerful long-term business effects than rational persuasion campaigns.'[23]

In essence, emotional drivers are the key to unlocking behaviour change, but why do emotions drive behaviour? To explain this, we can turn to the behavioural psychologists behind much of contemporary marketing theory.

Economist Daniel Kahneman has demonstrated that people think much less than they think they do, and that they rely on a large amount of subconscious decision making. In a nutshell, our brains make decisions using two systems running in parallel. We have the subconscious 'System 1' brain that makes decisions quickly with little effort, and indeed with little thought. We also have a 'System 2' brain which is what we would normally think of as 'thinking', ie it makes decisions based on conscious pondering of data.[24]

This field of study is key to understanding how to change behaviour, but this is not a psychology book and it's a well-studied area that you can follow up if you are interested. However, to really understand video marketing you would ideally have some grounding in the topic. Therefore, what follows is a simple explanation of the two-system brain. This is going to paraphrase lots of amazing behavioural psychologists and it's not a definitive resource, but it will lay out current thinking in sufficient detail to help put later chapters in context.

The System 1 mind: emotional video, marketing and consumer behaviour

Fundamentally, the brain has too many decisions to make. It simply can't give every one of the 35,000 remotely conscious decisions we face each day[25] the same amount of attention and effort. If we wanted to go outside but before doing so had to weigh up all available routes with the same level of attention that we give to deciding a career change, we would never leave home. Researchers at Cornell found that people make an average of 226.7 decisions a day about food alone.[26] To save our poor minds from exploding under the pressure, we have evolved to allow much of our decision making to be done automatically at low energy cost using what we call the System 1 brain.

System 1 evolved in the limbic system of our brains when the human species was in its infancy, and it was there to keep us alive. This part of our mind handles basic emotional responses and helps us to react quickly to the world around us. If we step out into traffic, it is System 1 that quickly gets us back to the pavement. System 1 also handles basic emotions that are key to our survival. Being scared, angry, happy or forgiving are all driven by this part of the mind, as we need to make those decisions quickly. But it also works on less obvious things to keep us alive, such as who we should trust (which it does by analyzing people's faces and demeanours for trustworthiness). This is why first impressions can be made so quickly and are very hard to undo.

System 1 is designed not only to make big decisions about danger quickly but also to save effort. We are all familiar with the sensation of decision overload, when after an intense day we become less accurate and more muddled in our thinking. Thinking hard does use up slightly more glucose,[27] but increases in the burn rate of glucose by the brain are minuscule compared to the total drain on the brain. So it is not the case that we avoid thinking to save actual energy. But making decisions does lead to decision fatigue; the more we think across the course of a day the worse our insight and decision making becomes.[28] So it is not surprising that we avoid making conscious decisions by using System 1 when we can.

> Human beings are to independent thinking as cats are to swimming. We can do it, but we prefer not to.
>
> Daniel Kahneman

Look out for the book *The Long and the Short of It: Balancing short and long-term marketing strategies*, written by Les Binet, Head of Effectiveness at adam&eve DDB, and Peter Field, Marketing Consultant. This book, published by the Institute of Practitioners in Advertising (IPA), should (along with a few others discussed in this chapter) be in the bag of every CMO for easy reference at all times. It's short and to the point, so I would recommend a thorough read; however, its key points can be summarized as follows:

- The ways in which long-term (brand) and short-term (activation) effects are generated are fundamentally different.
- Long-term brand effects (such as awareness) always produce short-term effects (eg sales growth), but the reverse is not true.
- Focusing on short-term activation such as sales targets will not grow a brand as well as a long-term, well-planned brand growth strategy.
- The best growth effects come from a balance of short-term activation (eg price promotions) and long-term brand building. By far the best effects come when these two are combined into a single campaign (known as 'brand response campaigns').
- The IPA data points to a ratio of 60:40 of brand to activation as being the most productive.
- Emotional campaigns (aimed at the System 1 mind) produce powerful long-term brand building.

- Rational campaigns (aimed at the System 2 mind) produce the biggest short-term gains, such as increases in sales. They will not, however, lead to long-term advantage. Brands should ensure they develop ways of measuring the long-term growth caused by their campaigns as well as short-term uplift in sales.

As a species we are pretty lazy, and very often if System 1 makes a decision we will go with it. To change our minds takes a lot of effort, and that's why we are reluctant to do it. If System 1 can't or won't make a decision (maybe the problem is too complex or simply impossible) it's bumped up the chain of command to our System 2 brain. System 2 thinking is a much more deliberate and conscious affair than System 1 and deals with things that are not immediate reactions to emotions, and processes that do not affect our immediate wellbeing. Traditional roles assigned to System 2 are things like mortgage applications, assembling a dinner from a tricky set of leftover ingredients, or fixing a complex piece of machinery.

It is much less effort for the brain to deal with data on a subconscious level than to have it move up into our conscious mind. Therefore, System 2

FIGURE 2.5   System 1/System 2

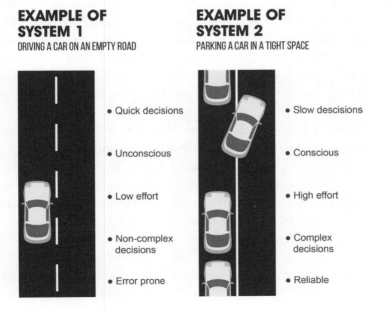

EXAMPLE OF SYSTEM 1
DRIVING A CAR ON AN EMPTY ROAD

- Quick decisions
- Unconscious
- Low effort
- Non-complex decisions
- Error prone

EXAMPLE OF SYSTEM 2
PARKING A CAR IN A TIGHT SPACE

- Slow descisions
- Conscious
- High effort
- Complex decisions
- Reliable

is inherently avoided if the decision can be made by System 1. In fact, we can go for long periods with all functions being avoided by our conscious mind – for example, we have all had the odd realization after driving for 30 minutes that we haven't been consciously aware of how we got where we are.

Some choices are made by our System 1 mind but flagged as needing conscious approval. On these occasions it is also less energy for the System 2 brain to agree with decisions that have already been made by System 1, merely rubber-stamping them for approval. Later we will see how this can impact on marketing tactics, as getting emotional buy-in can avoid having to persuade people with logic.

At this point it is important to note that System 1 and System 2 are not real things; they are not physical parts of the brain nor are they a single identifiable system. Although many of the processes can be mapped to independent parts of the brain, the mind is incredibly interconnected. It is better to view the two-mind system as a context around how we explain behaviour and behaviour change.

So, we now we have a framework for understanding how people make decisions. For those of us who spend our lives trying to change people's minds, what can we take from it? Well, we can market things to people by talking to their System 2 mind, but we will have to be ready to answer a lot of questions (which may not be possible in increasingly brief, social media-driven conversations). And even if we achieve that we may not get the result we are looking for. If we want to drastically change behaviours without a lot of dialogue we need to be talking directly to System 1 and thus effecting change at an emotional level. This is a level at which viewers may not even be aware of their thoughts changing. Fundamentally, emotion leads to action, logic leads to conclusions… and, being honest, we want our viewers to act, not to reach decisions. Decisions may, after all, not be made in our favour.

Marketing is becoming increasingly focused on System 1 and getting things done by firing an emotional response that people simply act on. It is possible, however, that System 2 might notice the emotional effect and choose to step in, analyze what's going on and make a decision. Most of the time it simply doesn't get involved, though, as to do so takes effort and quite frankly it has bigger things to be thinking about. If we can get the System 1 brain to make decisions without people being conscious of them, we can sneak in our agendas without having to persuade anyone of anything. Later we will be exploring how to directly affect System 2 with a straight-on charge of logic. But for now, let's stick with System 1 and how to affect behavioural change with emotion.

SYSTEM 1 AND EMOTIVE MARKETING

In this chapter so far we've discussed how we market to the System 1 brain, including how to use video to drive long-term brand growth with emotion. We covered the fact that stories are a fundamental part of how humans communicate and how harnessing them can affect behaviour. We looked at how moving images can attract attention and how this is part of our evolutionary development. We covered how the very essence of the medium itself, that we hold the phone in our hands, can drive connections through principles such as the extension of personal self and the endowment effect. All of these give marketers things to think about, most notably that we are always looking for an edge to raise an emotion.

Before launching into the next section (which looks at how we can engage with the System 2 part of our mind to further increase brand persuasiveness) I thought it was time for a quick note of caution on using emotions to sell. Marketing is increasingly becoming about emotional connections with people, and about leveraging those connections to get people to buy things. And do you know what... sometimes people don't really like that very much. Yes, we must connect on an emotional level, but when building a campaign, it really is worth challenging yourself to make sure you are not overdoing it.

Recently I had an experience that made this balance real for me, and gave me an insight into what can go wrong when emotions are squeezed with no real connection to a brand. Britain's cinema-going audiences are a typically reserved bunch; not for them the applauding and cheering of other nations. No, in Blighty, the end of a film is met with nothing more than a slow trudge to the exit sign, accompanied by the quiet crunch of discarded toffee popcorn underfoot. The idea that these theatre-goers should engage in a shared event is unheard of – which makes what I saw stand out in my mind.

Over the summer I took my kids to a movie (*Trolls* – it was pretty good) and before it began we were shown the usual ads for high street brands and local restaurants, most of which passed without incident. Then the final ad came on screen. Its opening shot was a slow-motion child sitting on a swing, backlit by the sun. This was accompanied by the simple sound of a solemn but heartwarming solo piano (that type of piano used when some brands want us to 'feel something'). The advert grabbed people's attention and the theatre settled to a hush. We were then treated to a montage of superbly generic emotional imagery: 'troubled' children looking happy, disabled people laughing, lifeboats rescuing grateful people and more. It went on for a full five minutes and not once did anyone in the audience have a clue what it was advertising. You could hear people start to whisper, 'What's this for?' and I overheard and least two people try to guess a brand. The film built to its emotional peak and as it did so the whole cinema, which was by now thoroughly confused, waited to see what brand was behind the emotional overload. Then the brand logo came on screen and there was a moment of silence. It took a while but eventually the reality sunk in that the film was for no more than a low-range high street supermarket... and the whole theatre laughed out loud. Even more than that, as people laughed, they realized that they were not alone in thinking this was utter rubbish and people even started shouting at the screen. To say this is unheard of in a British cinema is an understatement. This video was obviously trying to get the audience to 'feel' by connecting with the System 1 mind. But the cynicism of the ad men had been revealed and the brand was a laughing stock. Yes, emotions are the way to go, but please take care not to overcook it.

Another brand that got it pretty wrong was Pepsi, in a now infamous video that was pulled within days of being launched. In the same way as the audience in the cinema, viewers of this film could feel that they were having their emotions manipulated, and they didn't respond well. This was made worse by the inclusion of a celebrity and its somewhat ambitious claims that a soft drink could solve most of society's problems:

Full Pepsi commercial starring Kendall Jenner
6 April 2017, Yash Yadav YouTube channel
 Video 9

So that I don't end this section on a negative note, I wanted to show you a brand that did get emotion right. The idea that Pepsi had was to construct a campaign around the vision of people coming together for a better society. It was a great campaigning position but one that lacked authenticity; it was a constructed narrative that fell flat in its execution. But this campaigning angle can be successful in video when done well, as underlined by Heineken. When they tried it they picked up plenty of acclaim and over 12 million views. As part of the campaign (created by agency Publicis London) the beer company worked with a not-for-profit organization, The Human Library, that uses conversation to challenge stereotypes. The film makers took real people from different political worlds and started a conversation over a beer. It is a wonderful example of emotional video marketing at its best, with honesty and openness based on a powerful creative idea.

Heineken Worlds Apart OpenYourWorld 1
26 April 2017, Aaron Whittier YouTube channel
(▶) **Video 10**

The System 2 mind: logical discussions and mobile video

Up to this point we've looked at long-term brand growth and how it is driven by emotional connections between customers and brands. Much of this has centred on motivating our System 1 mind to affect decision making. Ideally, our emotional message is so powerful that we have got System 1 to drive our consumer's decision. But what if there are niggling doubts? Maybe it's a complex issue. Maybe the campaign's goal is to drive short-term activation targets, so we are discussing issues like price that are mostly unaffected by emotion (something that is especially common in B2B marketing). In these situations, we will need to enter into discussion with the conscious (System 2) mind. Video can be a powerful tool to communicate with System 2, as it is able to quickly and succinctly convey complex messaging, allowing detailed or price-based conversations to be had.

USING THE SYSTEM 2 MIND TO CREATE EFFECTIVE B2B VIDEOS

In the B2B world, there is often a need to engage at a logical level. Films still need to be emotive and inspiring but business people (working with someone else's money) are held accountable for their decisions. It's rare that people sign million-dollar contracts related to their life at home, but contracts of this size are common in business. As we will discuss in Section Two, there are still emotional drivers for business that can be leveraged, but let's take a look at an example showing how video is well suited to explaining facts in a B2B context. At Hurricane we have made many B2B films for the engineering market; I'm keen not to litter this book with our agency's work, as this is not supposed to be a brochure... but this is particularity relevant so I've made a small exception. The video for UK engineering firm Geo Kingsbury shows how complex discussions can be had in a very short period of time with video. The key is to carefully prioritize messages and give just enough information to answer questions without too much detail (while not creating any confusion because things are missed). It really boils down to a well-planned script that balances what is said with what is not said.

Kingsbury – Index – MS16 CNC Turned Parts – Multi-Spindle Series 21
September 2016, Kingsbury UK YouTube channel
(▶) **Video 11**

Summary

So we are at the end of the chapter on why video marketing works; let's take a moment to review the key points to take away:

- Brands grow best by focusing both on long-term brand goals and short-term activation targets. Video is a powerful tool to do both.

- Long-term brand growth is built best with videos that create emotional connections, appealing to our System 1 mind.

- Short-term goals are best met with logical, to-the-point messages and video can be used effectively for this by talking to the System 2 mind.

- We can understand why video is so good at emotional engagement by looking at 'stories that move, held in our hand'.

- Stories are a powerful tool used by humans throughout history to share knowledge and influence behaviour.

- We are hardwired to engage with moving imagery.

- We listen to our mobiles as they form part of who we are (extension of self).

- The physical qualities of touchscreens make us value things more (the endowment effect).

- Video is a powerful tool for short-term sales activation as it is a direct route into consumers' daily lives and can quickly put across logical, System 2-focused messaging such as pricing and promotions.

References

1 Kelly Servick
28 October 2013
Did snakes help build the primate brain?
Science
www.sciencemag.org/news/2013/10/did-snakes-help-build-primate-brain
(archived at https://perma.cc/CAC5-UBGV)

2 Daniel Kerschensteiner
16 June 2015
Eye's motion detection sensors identified
The Source, Washington University in St Louis
https://source.wustl.edu/2015/06/eye-motion-detection-sensors-identified/
(archived at https://perma.cc/J5FT-RVRT)

3 Benjamin Detenber, Robert Simons and Gary Bennett
1998
Roll 'em!: the effects of picture motion on emotional responses
Journal of Broadcasting and Electronic Media
http://rsimons.psych.udel.edu/rollem.htm (archived at https://perma.cc/
RPN8-RDUN)

4 S Adam Brasel and James Gips
9 January 2011
Media multitasking behavior: concurrent television and computer usage
Cyberpsychology, Behavior, and Social Networking
www.ncbi.nlm.nih.gov/pmc/articles/PMC3171998/ (archived at https://perma.
cc/83W8-LTYH)

5 Jory MacKay
21 March 2019
Screen time stats 2019: here's how much you use your phone during the
workday
Rescue Time
https://blog.rescuetime.com/screen-time-stats-2018/ (archived at https://perma.
cc/RB5P-PU4M)

6 Internet Advertising Bureau UK
18 October 2013
Always on: a global perspective of mobile consumer experience
www.iab.com/insights/2017globalmobileperspective/ (archived at https://
perma.cc/B534-FSHM)

7 Laura P Schaposnik and James Unwin
23 April 2018
The phone walkers: a study of human dependence on inactive mobile devices
Cornell University
https://arxiv.org/abs/1804.08753 (archived at https://perma.cc/6LP7-GQ2D)

8 Andy Clark and David Chalmers
January 1998
'The extended mind'
Wikipedia
https://en.wikipedia.org/wiki/The_Extended_Mind (archived at https://perma.
cc/7JMC-EMFP)

9 Sherry Turkle
2005
The Second Self: computers and the human spirit, 20th anniversary edition
MIT Press

10 Susan A Gelman, Erika M Manczak and Nicholaus S Noles
October 2012
The nonobvious basis of ownership: preschool children trace the history and
value of owned objects
Journal of Child Development
www.jstor.org/stable/23321193?seq=1 (archived at https://perma.cc/
JS4V-ZRSP)

11 Richard Thaler
June 1979
Toward a positive theory of consumer choice
Journal of Economic Band Organization
www.eief.it/butler/files/2009/11/thaler80.pdf (archived at https://perma.cc/
G2EN-8NDM)

12 *The Economist*
19 June 2008
The endowment effect: it's mine, I tell you
www.economist.com/science-and-technology/2008/06/19/its-mine-i-tell-you
(archived at https://perma.cc/S3CW-ET3J)

13 S Adam Brasel and James Gips
April 2014
Tablets, touchscreens, and touchpads: how varying touch interfaces trigger
psychological ownership and endowment
Journal of Consumer Psychology
www.sciencedirect.com/science/article/pii/S1057740813000934 (archived at
https://perma.cc/528H-HXXJ)

14 S Adam Brasel and James Gips
September 2015
Interface psychology: touchscreens change attribute importance, decision
criteria, and behavior in online choice
Cyberpsychology, Behavior, and Social Networking
 www.ncbi.nlm.nih.gov/pubmed/26348814 (archived at https://perma.cc/
W5RR-XBG4)

15 Shoshana Zuboff
2019
The Age of Surveillance Capitalism
Profile Books

16 Jeffrey Kluger
2 May 2010
Study: a dose of oxytocin increases the cuddles
Time
http://content.time.com/time/health/article/0,8599,1986318,00.html (archived
at https://perma.cc/922L-WZ2A)

17 Uri Hasson
February 2016
This is your brain on communication
TED Talks
www.ted.com/talks/uri_hasson_this_is_your_brain_on_communication
(archived at https://perma.cc/PP85-KTZS)

18 Jonathan Gottschall
2013
The Storytelling Animal: How stories make us human
Mariner Books

19 The Conversation
20 May 2016
Can being a good storyteller lead to love?
http://theconversation.com/can-being-a-good-storyteller-lead-to-love-58827
(archived at https://perma.cc/VVS4-C8FZ)

20 Helen McKay
Australian Aboriginal storytelling
Australian StoryTelling,
https://australianstorytelling.org.au/storytelling-articles/australian-aboriginal-
storytelling-helen-mckay (archived at https://perma.cc/9GS4-RQ4V)

21 Wikipedia
Rhetoric (Aristotle)
https://en.wikipedia.org/wiki/Rhetoric_(Aristotle) (archived at https://perma.
cc/Z5R9-PCJP)

22 Fritz Heider and Marianne Simmel
1944
An experimental study of apparent behaviour
American Journal of Psychology
www.jstor.org/stable/1416950?seq=1 (archived at https://perma.cc/EP5Q-
ZQ4U)
Experiment film can be viewed on YouTube at www.youtube.com/
watch?v=ZAnt9II-5Co (archived at https://perma.cc/2ZQF-JE7H)

23 Les Binet and Peter Field
2016
*The Long and the Short of It: Balancing short and long-term marketing
strategies*
IPA

24 Daniel Kahneman
2012
Thinking, Fast and Slow
Penguin

25 Dr Joel Hoomans
20 March 2015
35,000 decisions: the great choices of strategic leaders
Leading Edge Journal, Roberts Wesleyan College
https://go.roberts.edu/leadingedge/the-great-choices-of-strategic-leaders
(archived at https://perma.cc/SX3D-BRJC)

26 Brian Wansink and Jeffery Sobal
1 January 2007
Mindless eating: the 200 daily food decisions we overlook
Environment and Behaviour
http://journals.sagepub.com/doi/abs/10.1177/0013916506295573 (archived at
https://perma.cc/AS59-6X98)

27 Ferris Jabr
18 July 2012
Does thinking really hard burn more calories?
Scientific American
www.scientificamerican.com/article/thinking-hard-calories/ (archived at https://
perma.cc/V2ND-S62R)

28 On Amir
22 July 2008
Tough choices: how making decisions tires your brain
Scientific American
www.scientificamerican.com/article/tough-choices-how-making/ (archived at
https://perma.cc/LZ7F-8X3U)

Further reading

On Amir
22 July 2008
Tough choices: how making decisions tires your brain
Scientific American
www.scientificamerican.com/article/tough-choices-how-making/ (archived at
https://perma.cc/LZ7F-8X3U)
John Tierney
Do you suffer from decision fatigue?
17 August 2011
New York Times
www.nytimes.com/2011/08/21/magazine/do-you-suffer-from-decision-fatigue.
html (archived at https://perma.cc/K52V-YBLC)

03

Video types and approaches

We saw in previous chapters that video motivates both the System 1 and System 2 minds (remembering this is more of a construct to help us think about how we think, rather than a rigid psychological or psychological reality). As we start looking at how exactly we will use video to motivate people's behaviours, what types of videos do we have in our armoury? And what considerations are there to use them in the best way?

When brand films first hit online consumers, they were little more than online TV ads with big budgets and big media spend. In many ways these were simply the traditional TV ad model moved online. Brands invested heavily in expensive production, promoted it, waited and repeated. Ford's 'Evil Ka'[1] was a classic example of this. But, as we will discover in this chapter, the world has moved to a model of 'always-on marketing' and brands are moving to the creation of a steady stream of content that is activated in a different way. Initially this applied to blogs, forums and posts, but as technology has made creation cheaper and brand benefits have been proven, the techniques have been applied to the powerful medium of video.

Thinking like a publisher

In over a decade of working at the BBC I made a wide range of programmes, and indeed worked in development, where we came up with new ideas and tried to get them commissioned. I made documentaries about marines in Iraq, cheetahs in Africa and myriad other topics from history to drug addiction and science. When I was making these programmes, I was always thinking about how best to structure a story, how to make an attention-grabbing opening, how to craft peaks and troughs in narratives, and how to encourage viewers to come back. In fact, all TV directors, producers, writers and editors think in a specific way about their output, and it is very different from the mindset of an advertiser. Broadcasters think in a way that 'pulls' in viewers. When I moved into the marketing world I was struck by how different the mindset was – it was instead all based around 'push'. Yes, the big-ticket TV ads liked to see themselves as entertainment with a logo at the end but, on the whole, marketing content was neither entertaining nor useful.

How publishers think – pull:

- How can we attract viewers to our content?
- How can we keep viewers coming back with regular schedules and growth of content identity?
- How do we get people to recommend our content?
- How do we entertain?
- How do we make people feel?

How marketers think – push:

- How can we get our message in front of people?
- How can we get into people's lives?
- How many messages can we send to people?
- How do we inform?

'Always-on' marketing

In a marketing world pulled along by online content creators who broadcast multiple times a day, pushed along by ad blockers that are stopping people seeing messages, and at the mercy of ad-free streaming services, marketing has had to change. Brands wanting to reach their audiences are moving to the 'always-on' mentality that allows viewers to connect when they are ready. This is much more of a broadcaster or publisher mindset, with emotional, useful and regular content at its heart. Always-on does not replace the cyclical nature of ad campaigns; it augments them so that the needs of a social media audience are met. Typically, brands are smoothing out the sharp peaks in interest and engagement of traditional TV campaigns by extending content around them or using stand-alone content that is always available (hence the term 'always-on'). A campaign by Evian called

'Roller babies' was a classic example of this. The campaign (developed by Euro RSCG) built the hype around the large-piece film (which, as we will explain later, would be known as a Hero film) with smaller, socially seeded teasers.

After the content was launched it was backed up with further 'making of' films and related content. All this was designed to build anticipation for the launch, provide a smoother rise to the peak of activity, and create a longer tail of interest. Some brands are going further and abandoning TV altogether in favour of small, more regular pieces of content that build a steady diet of help and information-giving.

All amazing Evian singing dancing surfing rolling babies and making of commercials ever

6 August 2019, Funny Commercials YouTube channel

 Video 12

As 'always-on' has developed, the industry has needed a system of thought to help frame goals and styles. Driven by YouTube's thinking, marketers have come to see the online world as comprising three overarching types of content. These are based not on creative execution but on intended use, and we know them as Hero, Hub and Hygiene (HHH). As the biggest driver of this mindset is Google/YouTube, it has pretty quickly been accepted as a de facto standard. However, it does not cover every aspect of video outside the YouTube platform so I have changed 'Hygiene' to 'Help' and added a further type of content: 'Go!' Go! content is something that came to prominence quite recently, but it is important as it is the last step in the marketing funnel when we look to drive conversion into sales.

So, this gives us a framework of Hero, Hub, Help and Go! (HHHG), covering the creation of big brand viral, but also focusing the mind on the creation of long-running or chapterized content that keeps viewers coming back. In many ways, this is the evolution of brands from publishers as well as advertisers.

Getting attention with Hero content

Hero content is the name given to big set-pieces that drive long-term growth through awareness, or that will support a brand in breaking into a new segment. The content tends to be bold, emotional and pushed to a wide audience. Hero is by its nature emotional in form and therefore less likely to be aimed at short-term goals such as price promotions alone. Unlike other types of content, it is not normally something the audience is looking for, so it has to be able to attract, hold and reward attention and typically has a media spend behind it.

ALWAYS-ON

Figure 3.1 shows how these content types work over time to build audiences and grow engagement. It's worth noting the following:

- Hero content creates high peaks in engagement that get a lot of attention but that die off quickly (as they are typically driven by a short-lived paid ad campaign).

- After each Hero campaign the level of awareness is slightly higher than before – so it helps drive awareness in incremental steps.

- Hub content drives gradual growth in engagement and has fewer peaks; normally as this is self-discovered or activated in ways outside paid ads (see Chapter 8 on activation for more on this).

- Help content is the most 'always-on' of always-on content. As it is found via organic search it may not have a peak in views when it first launches, but you can expect it to deliver results for years rather than just months.

- Go! content runs across the funnel, waiting until customers are close to purchase and helping to close the deal.

FIGURE 3.1   Always-on marketing

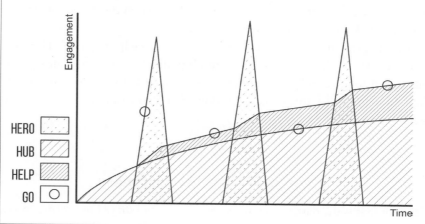

In later sections we will be discussing how to make great Hero, Hub, Help and Go! content and how they work at various stages of the digital sales funnel, but for now let's look at some examples of things that have worked for brands, to help understand what we will be discussing.

The trilogy of Hero, Hub and Hygiene is being driven by YouTube/ Google, and although I am renaming Hygiene as Help and adding another type (Go!) the Google definitions are of Hero and Hub are very useful:

> Hero content refers to the big, tent-pole events that provide a massive step change to your audience growth. A live-streamed event, a viral video… a cross-promotion with a YouTube influencer, or even a made-for-YouTube ad. It may revolve around a large cultural event… or it may be a major event that you instigate.[2]

As Hero content is the form most likely to be pushed into people's lives, if it fails to deliver on an emotional level or is perceived to be of low value it is likely to fail overall. As an example of how much people get upset with things they don't want being pushed onto them, just search online for 'unwanted U2 album'. It will reveal how the supposedly mutually beneficial relationship between U2 and iTunes became a public relations nightmare, turning the social media airwaves blue with vitriolic frustration.

Let's look at some Hero films. If you've previously read around this topic you will no doubt be slightly bored by the web's insistence on talking about Evian babies and Jean-Claude Van Damme's backwards Volvo trucks,[3] both of which are really just old-school TV spots put online. Let's instead cover some exciting examples starting with emotional Hero films, which in my opinion are always the best to watch.

B2C brand Hero film

Let's start with a straightforward enough style of Hero film. This short, created by Hurricane for Sykes Holiday Cottages in the UK, is interesting as it builds itself around the emotional idea of spending your holiday time carefully. The campaign centred around a 30 second short aimed at a wide audience with core messaging, which was then spun into numerous digital versions, each used as stand-alone Hero films at specific parts of the market. Consider how the film focuses on the emotions of people in the film, rather than a list of features and benefits.

This is your time for Sykes Holiday Cottages
Hurricane Media
 Video 13

B2B brand Hero film

Emotional storytelling isn't just restricted to consumer marketing. In this film for Cambridge University Press (again created by Hurricane) we tell the story of a young Spanish woman that dreams of becoming a pilot. To be an international pilot one has to be able to speak English, and this is her story.

Better learning for Cambridge University Press
Hurricane Media
 Video 14

Live-streamed event Hero film

When Virgin Holidays (never a brand to shirk from the big idea) wanted to own the Hero space, they embarked on an ambitious campaign centred on a live broadcast. Filmed in 18 locations around the world and edited into a live online ad, it was pushed out through a variety of paid and owned channels around the hashtag #Seizetheholiday. It attracted 16.9 million impressions from the promoted trend and peaked at 838 searches per minute. Like all good live streams, most of the noise came before and after, with a good build-up of anticipation and a long tail. I cover this in much more detail in Section Four, where you can find practical advice on getting the best from live-streamed video.

Seize the holiday. Virgin Holidays live TV ad
10 September 2016, Virgin Holidays YouTube channel
 Video 15

Campaigning Hero film

Dove are often at the top of the viral video charts with their Real Beauty campaign, and they have come to own the 'female empowerment' message. In the #MyBeautyMySay campaign, they continued the narrative that women should choose how they want to be perceived, rather than being limited by societal pressures and perceptions. It reached 13 million views in six weeks, a testament to the quality of the creative and activation strategy put behind it.

Dove beauty on your own terms #MyBeautyMySay
28 June 2016, Dove US YouTube channel
▶ **Video 16**

Shelter is a UK based charity that fights to end homelessness and the issues around it. Hurricane has had the honour of working with the charity for successive Christmas campaigns. In this film we tell the story of Rhys who was living on the streets but, thanks to Shelter, now has a safe home.

Back to a good place for Shelter
Hurricane Media
▶ **Video 17**

YouTube influencer Hero videos

Influencer marketing focuses on using key opinion leaders (KOLs), also known as influencers, to drive messages to market. It's an excellent tool for adding highly targeted audiences to the top of the sales funnel. Rather than marketing directly to consumers, brands inspire, hire or pay influencers to do it for them. To be true to the genre, the influencer should have their own clear online tone of voice, have a substantial following, be pushing the message out through their owned channels and should not adjust their tone or personality just to plug the product. As you read this book, you will see that influencer films come into both Hero and Hub content categories, with the former tending to use traditional celebrities (from the worlds of TV, film, sports and music) and the latter using more contemporary-styled digitally famous (mostly self-focused) individuals. They can be profile, working or niche influencers (which I discuss further on page 135).

Profile influencer marketing is especially good at reaching niche audiences that don't respond well to traditional paid placements. As an example of this let's look at Nicole Guerriero, an Argentinian fashion and beauty influencer on YouTube who vlogs on fashion and lifestyle. Nicole has promoted content for Clinique, bareMinerals, Audible and more. The link below is to a Clinique review and has over 650,000 views.

Easy summer night look

25 June 2016, Nicole Guerriero YouTube channel

 Video 18

Influencer marketing is often lumped in with celebrity endorsement as they are very similar in style and effect, although the latter is normally closer to an advert. This dynamic is clear in the campaign for Lagavulin whisky, in which they wanted to make their single malt more relevant to a younger demographic. To help them do this, they enlisted the help of well-known personality Nick Offerman as an influencer.[4] The choice was inspired as he is known for playing a straight-talking, whisky-loving character in the TV series *Parks and Recreation*, and has an online persona to match. Offerman was featured doing nothing more exciting than sipping whisky by a roaring fire and relaxing but what brought the idea to life was that he did this for an uninterrupted 45 minutes! It was an excellent creative execution and did well enough to get three million views and win a Shorty Award for Best Influencer and Celebrity Campaign.

Nick Offerman's 'yule log'

2 December 2015, Lagavulin: My Tails of Whisky Official YouTube channel

www.youtube.com/watch?v=LS-ErOKpO4E

Just to round off this part of influencer marketing it's worth sounding a note of caution. A bubble industry is growing up around influencers and they are often framed as a magic bullet to brand growth, and as the bubble grows their fees are increasing at a staggering rate. Choose your partner with care and make sure you know exactly what you are getting. Reports of brands paying $25,000 for a plug on a vlog that sits alongside three other similar products with no differentiation are unfortunately not uncommon and it's really a waste of advertising spend. Also, make sure that the influencer genuinely understands what you do and why you are different.

Flagpole event Hero videos

Flagpole content is interesting for being more of an issue of timing than form. As in all areas of marketing, video can be activated around specific events. Search traffic for particular seasons, holidays and events can spike massively over a short period of time. With Thanksgiving and Christmas, this runs for several months, whereas April Fool's Day is a short-lived yet hugely popular event. Leveraging search terms around these events can be an easy win for marketing teams. At Hurricane we made a film for Barclaycard (through lead agency Dare) that launched a new mobile payment service for dogs around the tag #paywag. Released on 1 April 2013, it was of course a spoof, but the noise around it attracted 260,000 views in one day alone. The campaign gained views from searches on 'April fools day' and further attention by featuring in numerous charts of top April Fool's Day jokes.

> Barclaycard PayWag – contactless payment device for dogs
> 1 April 2013, Barclaycard YouTube channel
> www.youtube.com/watch?v=luL_C0cGe9A

Growing engagement with Hub content

While Hero content is shouting from the rooftops, Hub is quietly getting on with things behind the scenes. Regularly scheduled videos encourage viewers to engage with the brand channel. Many brands, like Red Bull for example, are moving away from big Hero moments and increasingly focusing on their Hub content, ensuring a constant broadcast of engaging, fresh videos to deliver growth. As we will see in Chapter 5 when we look at the digital sales funnel, it's not only Hero content that attracts people to a brand, as well-placed, highly targeted Hub films can work just as well. Hub content keys into consumers' passion points to build brand following. Going back to Google's definition of HHH, Hub content is:

> The content you develop on a regular basis to give a fresh perspective on your target's passion points (eg verticalized content about a product line). This is often staggered throughout the year.[5]

RED BULL MOVES FROM HERO TO HUB

Over the years, Red Bull has thrown enormous sums of money behind its Hero campaigns. Not least of these was Felix Baumgartner's supersonic free fall from 128 km over the earth. It was first broadcast as a live stream and then packaged into highlights that by 2021 had had 47 million views.

> Felix Baumgartner's supersonic freefall from 128k – mission highlights
> 15 October 2012, Red Bull YouTube channel
> www.youtube.com/watch?v=FHtvDAOW34I

But these big stunts by the Red Bull brand have quietly been overtaken by a focus on smaller but still engaging hub content. The 'Who is JOB?' reality web series is now into its second season and functions just like a TV show. The series follows the life of a pro surfer called Jamie O'Brien and allows viewers to immerse themselves in their surfing passion through his life. With such an enthusiastic fan base it's no surprise it's driven viewer and subscriber numbers. Greg Jarboe from Tubular Insights has written a great piece on how Red Bull changed from Hero to Hub and if you like the topic it is well worth a read.[6]

> Who is JOB 2.0?
> Red Bull YouTube channel
> www.youtube.com/playlist?list=PL2DOBF08EEB83857A

Influencer marketing Hub videos

Content built around influencers appears in the Hero section above but when it comes to building consideration with regular engagement it can be key to a good Hub content strategy. Influencers will understand their own audience far better than a brand ever can and will be able to position what you are saying in the best way. Fashion brand ASOS uses Hub content effectively on its channel with a consistency in tone and style. The series 'ASOS supports talent' comprises eight films showcasing young creative people talking about their latest work and background, and harnesses influencers in exactly the right way.

ASOS supports talent: ELF kid – ASOS
19 December 2016, ASOS France YouTube channel
www.youtube.com/watch?v=nDhXuxObXuo

Organic search focused Hub content

This series of films created for Sykes Holiday cottages was designed to leverage organic search results around UK holiday destinations.

Experience more with Sykes Holiday Cottages
Hurricane Media
www.hurricanemedia.co.uk/portfolio/branded-content-sykes-experience/

Branded Hub documentary

As a documentary maker for well over a decade of my career, I've got a real soft spot for this type of content and it's always rewarding to see it done well. A genuine documentary tells the story of real people in their own voice or through the voice of a narrator. The magic in the form is an emotional reward from seeing real people overcoming real-life challenges. A powerful doc will take viewers on an emotional journey alongside the protagonist, so both parties finish somewhere new, whether for better or for worse.

A great branded documentary is simply a great documentary with a logo front and end. Although this sounds like a good idea to start with, brands often find that losing narrative control of a project can be an unnerving experience. This is especially the case if they are used to controlling everything down to the smallest detail on a shoot. But when documentaries are aligned too strictly to the needs of a brand they lose their magic and effectiveness. Brand teams can feel pressure to get involved in minute details and sometimes it is forgotten that people in documentaries are not actors but real people with real feelings. Adjusting small things may not affect the impact of film: 'We can't say that' or 'Can we get them to say this message?' can be fair enough and may not overly affect the film, but be careful not to push it. On one branded documentary I created about a very sensitive subject the client asked, 'Can they cry again but look to camera a bit more?'... suffice to say, that project did not go well in the end. Allowing great film makers to make great documentaries will be far more effective than watering it down. If you're going to use the format be brave and do it properly!

Häagen-Dazs is a brand that got it right, allowing film makers to make powerful, genuine content, with a hint of brand. The documentary film *Crafted*, directed by Morgan Spurlock and financed by the ice cream giant, was so good it was acquired by Amazon and ranked in their top 10 films for three weeks, resulting in a 10 per cent increase in sales.[7]

Crafted official trailer 1 (2015) – Morgan Spurlock short documentary HD
11 June 2015, Movieclips Indie YouTube channel
www.youtube.com/watch?v=O3SpWO3UJOk

PATAGONIA

Another brand that has nailed this approach is Patagonia, with their documentary highlighting the issues around Alaskan Oil. For hundreds of generations, the Gwich'in people of Alaska and northern Canada have depended on the Caribou that migrate through the Arctic Refuge. With their traditional culture now threatened by oil extraction and climate change, two Gwich'in women are fighting to protect their land, and this film tells their story beautifully. The brand name appears at the end and the film makers are left alone for the rest of the film to get on with telling the story. The key to the two working together is that the subject matter is so closely aligned with the goals of the brand.

FIGURE 3.2   Patagonia

The Refuge – fighting for a way of life
28 November 2016, Patagonia YouTube channel
www.youtube.com/watch?v=A4DH5cK37Y8

Building an audience with Help content

Next we move on to Help content (referred to by YouTube as Hygiene). Again, YouTube neatly sums this up the approach to this by asking, 'What is your audience actively searching for regarding your brand or industry? What can serve as your 365-day-relevant, always-on content programming?'[8]

Help content answers the questions that people are searching for. It appears in people's searches when they need to know something and drives both SEO and organic search ROI. Got a cooking brand? Then it's 'Films on how to cook'. Got an advanced medical laser treatment? Then it's 'How do medical lasers work?' I prefer the term Help to the term Hygiene used by YouTube, as 'Help' focuses the mind on the purpose of the content and keeps attention on what you are trying to do.

Help content is a powerful medium as it drives long-term brand growth but it can also drive short-term sales goals. Building timely Help content around specific events with the possible inclusion of a price-point narrative can be very effective. Think of people searching for 'How to cook turkey' videos at Christmas who find a grocery brand offering not only how to do it, but a single-click package containing all the ingredients with a discount.

On the UK grocer Tesco's YouTube channel there are numerous 'How to make...' recipe videos. These key into viewers' searches for online recipe guides such as the 'clean food' trend of using courgette (zucchini) as an alternative to pasta. Tesco have created a video that answers the high-volume search query 'How to make courgetti without a spiralizer'. Note how the video is titled exactly the same as the search term – driving organic search results (see page 126 for more about optimization). If you learn nothing else from this book, at least you will know how to make a healthy meal!

How to make courgetti without a spiraliser – Tesco Food
16 June 2015, Tesco YouTube channel
www.youtube.com/watch?v=a41vOD-VCc4

When thinking about help content you should examine viewer intent and develop relevant video content to meet those needs. There is a range of tools available to help you do this, including Google Keyword Planner, YouTube Trends and Answer the Public.

Driving conversions with Go! content

Finally we move into 'Go!' content, which helps convert interest and engagement into sales. This content appears less often in the sales funnel but can be key to reaching sales targets. If your brand has lots of engaged followers and a strong product but is not making sales, it is well worth considering Go! content as a solution. For me, Go! content does what it says: it drives people to act, whether that is to click a product into a basket, use an email form or pick up the phone. Of course, all other types of content can do this too – but these films are created with little else in mind and sit very close to the end of the sales process.

A classic example of this content type is product films that sit right next to products on a page. Brands that we have worked with have found that sales of specific products increase substantially when a video appears alongside them. The key here is to get the basket and video as close together as possible. Systems such as Wirewax add interactivity to the video itself and directly link clicks to a shopping basket (see page 235 for more on this).

Summary

- Brands are moving away from the old model of a few pieces of big content through the calendar, replacing it with an always-on model that reflects the thinking of a publisher as well as that of a more traditional advertiser.

- There are four categories of content that can be used across the sales funnel: Hero, Hub, Help and Go! Each has different benefits and strengths.

- Hero content needs to be emotionally engaging, but if the viewers feel these emotions are not authentic the campaign will fail.

- Large-scale Hero projects with significant media spend behind them can be used at intervals across the schedule to drive awareness.

- Always-on strategies rely on a body of Hub and Help content that forms a reason for viewers to stay engaged.

- Help content should reflect the audience's needs and be based on highly searched terms.

- Go! content can drive conversions at the final stages of the sales funnel.

References

1 Ford
29 April 2006
Evil Ka, *YouTube*,
www.youtube.com/watch?v=TvtzEgFBl3I (archived at https://perma.cc/6SBF-ARG6)
2 Google
October 2015
Schedule your content
www.thinkwithgoogle.com/marketing-resources/youtube/schedule-your-content/ (archived at https://perma.cc/9GG9-U2DL)
3 Volvo
13 November 2013
Volvo Trucks – the epic split feat Van Damme (live test), *YouTube*,
www.youtube.com/watch?v=M7FIvfx5J10 (archived at https://perma.cc/C73E-Y4GW)

4 Wikipedia
   Nick Offerman
   https://en.wikipedia.org/wiki/Nick_Offerman (archived at https://perma.cc/
   X4D7-ALPF)
5 Google
   October 2015
   Build a content plan
   www.thinkwithgoogle.com/marketing-resources/youtube/build-a-content-plan/
   (archived at https://perma.cc/Z9SB-THEP)
6 Jo-ann Fortune
   16 April 2015
   Is hub content the real hero?
   Econsultancy
   https://econsultancy.com/is-hub-content-the-real-hero/ (archived at https://
   perma.cc/ZH8T-3LRC)
7 Jeff Beer
   18 June 2015
   Why Morgan Spurlock partnered with Haagen-Dazs for his newest doc'Crafted'
   Fast Company
   www.fastcompany.com/3047555/why-morgan-spurlock-partnered-with-haagen-
   dazs-for-his-newest-doc-crafted (archived at https://perma.cc/6MZR-ZG2P)
8 Google
   October 2015
   Schedule your content
   www.thinkwithgoogle.com/marketing-resources/youtube/schedule-your-content/
   (archived at https://perma.cc/9GG9-U2DL)

04

Video platforms: what you need to know

Up to this point in the book we've outlined the types of content one might consider, along with some example executions, and we're nearly ready to look at the strategy of what films to make and how to activate them. The only missing piece of the puzzle is where to put them. Videos will have to be uploaded to online video platforms (OVPs). These packaged online services enable users to upload, convert, store and play back video content on the internet. But which platform will give us the best chance to make a brand famous?

OVPs are constantly evolving so it's foolish to go into too much detail in a printed work, but there are universal constants that are not going anywhere soon. An effective video strategy will understand the pros and cons of each, so you need a governing set of principles rather than a constantly changing list. One thing that will not change, though, is that despite some immediate similarities, each platform will engage with audiences in different ways and each has their own strengths and weaknesses. In 2005, video platforms were basically the same; brands uploaded a video and people watched it in landscape format on their desktop computer with the sound on. They commented on it, liked it and if you were lucky they shared it. But, like every technology, OVPs have developed at pace. The way people use them and the way that brands can harness them are constantly changing. We must now consider whether sound is on or off, what rotation the phone will be held in, how people use multiple channels at once and more. If we don't, our content simply won't be effective.

In this chapter we will go over some arching principles to consider when looking at platforms, then through all the major players in the space, and finally directly compare the two biggest ones (YouTube and Facebook). First, let's go into some governing principles of platforms and how they can be put into a number of categories: fluid vs fixed, short-form vs multi-form, social platforms vs video marketing platforms.

Fluid vs fixed

When we scroll through timelines on social platforms like Facebook, Instagram and Twitter we are, if we are honest, looking for the next bit of candy to grab our attention. I use 'we' in this context as I'm just like everyone else and can find myself scrolling aimlessly looking for something to add value to my experience. If something does catch our eye as we motor through our feed we watch, read or share it. And when that's done, we flow straight onto the next thing with a flick of a thumb; this is why we refer to these types of sites as 'fluid'.

Fluid sites are places where short conversations can easily be shared but long conversations are harder for brands to form. They are places where heavy ad spend will get you noticed quickly, but attention will tail off as viewers move on to the next thing. The videos that work well on these platforms are 'thumb bait' and will have a decent media spend behind them.

Conversely, there are other platforms like YouTube, Vimeo and Wikipedia where we are in absorption mode. We typically visit these sites to be entertained or learn rather than to socialize and are open to following a train of thought. There is much less motion with the thumb on these sites and pages will stay relatively static for a long time, so we refer to them as 'fixed'. Paid placements can be used to drive traffic just like on fluid, but further engagement can be gained by retaining viewers with more great content. Fixed platforms are where real engagement with video can be grown.

Short-form vs multi-form

When I was at the BBC we referred to short-form films as being half an hour long, and long-form films as being upwards of an hour. But in a sign of the times, long-form is now anything from two minutes upwards. Much has been said about decreasing attention spans, with some commentators suggesting that they are ever-decreasing and that viewers cannot concentrate for more than a minute. Other commentators say that we can concentrate just fine, pointing to the fact that many people watch entire box sets in only one or two sittings. Wherever you stand on society's attention span as a whole, the technology we live with allows those that want to move on to the next thing quickly to do just that.

Short-form video platforms such as Twitter, TikTok and Snapchat serve up a diet of bite-sized portions of content for snacking and sharing.

Multi-form platforms are those that do not focus just on the shortest of videos but are able to deal with both long- and short-form content. Typically, these sites carry content that is 20 seconds and upwards.

Social platforms vs video marketing platforms

Social video platforms are those that do not charge to host videos and instead make their money from advertising. They are either a social platform on their own with social tools built in (such as sharing or liking on YouTube) or they are integrated into a wider social media platform (like Facebook). Brands on social platforms have little or no say over what content is displayed alongside their own and can find themselves placed alongside competing messages.

Video marketing platforms in contrast are directly within a brand's control and are typically paid for as a subscription service. They are a walled garden of a brand's content although they often offer some form of integration with external social media channels. Video marketing platforms will often allow you to upload videos directly to social channels and provide some form of hub on which you can build content within an owned space. The main reason to embed videos using a video marketing platform rather than a free social channel is that it likely to integrate with your other sales and CRM software. Most decent platforms will plug into Salesforce, HubSpot, Google Analytics and others (depending on which you choose to use). This means that you can become far more sophisticated in your marketing efforts and even automate what content visitors to see your site see, depending on where they are in the sales funnel.

It's worth noting here that although a brand website is an 'owned' space you can lose control by embedding videos hosted on social platforms. Some brands that I have worked with have found that hosting videos on their site that are embedded from social platforms (like YouTube) can actually push viewers away from their site. Visitors to the main site click on the YouTube icon on embedded videos and disappear forever. Personally, I also think embedding from YouTube weakens the look of a brand page and there are many, better-looking alternatives. That said, you'll find that most of the paid platforms take longer to integrate on your site than a standard YouTube embed code. Some need code added to resize the window and many offer integration with your marketing and sales software that is useful but takes a bit of development time.

The issue of copyright is an ever-changing one and every platform has different T&Cs. Some say that when you upload a video you no longer have exclusive copyright, whereas others say that you hand them a royalty-free licence to show it. There is no point at all in a book going into the differences in terms across the various platforms as they change all the time. However, a quick look at their terms and copyrights is advisable if you are detail minded. So, we've covered some basics, now let's get into specifics and run through the biggest platform types.

Owned platforms

TwentyThree

▶ **Video 19**

Owned, multi-form, fixed, embeddable, integration into sales and marketing software.

TwentyThree is a really solid platform that allows deep integration with sales and marketing systems. You can build libraries of content, create playlists, add email gates, overlay interactions, do great webinars and generally use it to drive up data collection with what you create. It's the platform we use at Hurricane and they are nice to work with.

Vidyard

▶ **Video 20**

Owned, multi-form, fixed, embeddable, integration into sales and marketing software.

This well-established player has been listed as one of the market leaders by Forrester Research.[1] It's a cross-platform player, allowing embedding on owned and social sites with plenty of analytics. It offers email gates, interactive annotations and hyper-personalized videos with embedded text elements such as names, etc. It can also be integrated with common marketing platforms.

Brightcove

▶ **Video 21**

Owned, multi-form, fixed, embeddable, integration with sales and marketing software.

Another major player in the owned space is Brightcove, a cross-platform HTML 5 platform that delivers really good quality across desktop and mobile. It's a professional product used by a wide range of brands and agencies. Videos can be optimized for different devices and distributed directly onto social channels. It also offers a customizable video hub where you can build up an easy-to-use library. Brightcove offers a live streaming interface, lead generation tools, and email capture forms. The analytics are better than many and it can be integrated with marketing tools like HubSpot.

JW Player

▶ **Video 22**

Owned, multiform, fixed, embeddable.

This player manages, hosts, distributes and monetizes videos on the web and mobile apps. It's an HTML 5 and flash player offering tweaks to SEO and social sharing, live streaming and simulcast with Facebook. It integrates with video ad server, ad network or ad exchange and has support for Google Interactive Media Ads (IMA). It has all the analytics and account management backend that you would want in a player like this, but it is worth noting that customization can be tricky and would need brand-side development. I've never been as convinced with the quality of the video stream of JW Player versus some of its rivals but this can change at any point with new technology developments.

Dalet

▶ **Video 23**

Owned, multi-form, fixed, embeddable.

Another market-leading platform that works across media logistics and video delivery with detailed analytics and wide industry support. It supports live streams as well as audience insight, embeddable players and content hubs. This platform goes beyond a simple OVP and adds in the ability to capture and produce across multiple distribution channels.

Social platforms

Unlike owned platforms, social platforms are shared and are in the public space. The most obvious of these are YouTube and Facebook, so we will start there.

YouTube

(▶) **Video 24**

Social, multi-form, fixed, embeddable, live streaming.

The Google-owned big daddy of them all, with more than one billion users (which is almost a third of people on the internet). The second-biggest search engine on the net, it is closely linked to results on Google SERPS and is considered to be more or less essential as an ingredient in a video campaign. It's a free-to-use service that stays free even for business, although there are options to upgrade and personalize if required. YouTube allows interactive elements and for videos to be monetized by channel owners. It's also a major player in the video advertising arena, with enormous revenues being generated each year by its Pre-Roll and Display Network ads.

YouTube is the archetypal video content hub, offering increased engagement and attracting viewers to multiple pieces of video. The chance of being discovered by an enormous number of viewers plays a very important role in video strategy. The downside of the volume of videos on the site is that viewers can in fact be attracted away from a brand, so attention has to be paid to how the video is positioned.

The social aspect of YouTube is incredibly powerful, although the quality of the comments that videos attract is notoriously wide-ranging. Popular videos will often attract inappropriate or unpleasant comments, so many users disable comments and moderation is highly recommended.

Facebook

(▶) **Video 25**

Social, multi-form, fluid, embeddable, live streaming.

Facebook is the big challenger to YouTube, although its basic nature is to work in a very different way, so it is unlikely to ever replace it. In 2015, Facebook users watched over 100 million hours of video a day and 1.5 million small and medium businesses shared videos.[2]

Although Facebook is multiform, in that it aims to play short, medium and longer films, it is beginning to back longer content within its news feed and even to fund original programmes. Facebook has been going backwards and forwards on whether videos play with sound automatically, so it's important to be aware of how content shows when you launch a campaign.

Facebook's key value in a multi-film video campaign is its ability to reach a wide audience quickly when using paid placements. By its nature it creates a large buzz over a short period, but viewers are unlikely to engage with further pieces of content after viewing; instead they will typically be distracted by other items in their news feeds.

More than four billion video views take place on Facebook every day. But don't forget that over three-quarters of these are watched without the sound turned on![3]

TikTok

▶ **Video 26**

Social, short form, fluid.

The new giant on the block, TikTok was the most downloaded app of 2020 and is on a constant growth curve.[4] It's massive with Gen Z and Gen Y, and young people are a majority of the TikTok community. This kind of reach is obviously attractive to brands but TikTok is not an easy beast to tame and many brands are looking at it, scratching their heads and saying 'What do we do with this?!'. This is made harder by the fact that TikTok will only work if you make content that's unique for its audience. For brands looking to make videos that can be used across multiple social media platforms (with only minimal reskinning) this adds a layer of effort to create a bespoke content strategy.

It's also worth remembering that the TikTok audience can bite back… think back to their spectacular trolling of Trump's Tulsa rally when youngsters from around the globe booked thousands of tickets, giving the impression of a massive sell-out that collapsed into farce when no one showed up.[5]

One route to a successful TikTok campaign is to take part in an existing conversation and bring in influencers to leverage attention. During the Covid-19 pandemic, the #WipeItDown challenge became a popular meme with TikTok creators wiping their mirror to the 'Wipe It Down' song and revealing a different version of themselves on the third wipe. Fashion brands leveraged this challenge by partnering with influencers who wore their clothing during the third wipe.

Wipe it down TikTok compilation
15 May 2020, Oskar Kip YouTube channel
▶ **Video 27**

As well as joining in current memes, brands can create their own, with Sponsored TikTok challenges becoming increasingly popular. Makeup brand NYX created one around the #dollhousechallenge that encouraged people to flex their makeup skills by turning themselves into a doll. The hashtag was used three-quarters of a million times on TikTok and became a top trend of the year.

TikTok: what is the Dollhouse Challenge?
2020, Ellissa Bain, HITC
▶ **Video 28**

Vimeo

▶ **Video 29**
Social and owned, multi-form, fixed, embeddable.

Vimeo was launched in 2004 by a group of filmmakers and has grown to over 200 million users – most of them working in film, animation, music and other artistic media. It's a well-respected player and has been used by thousands of brands to embed video content. It's interesting as it can be used either as a free 'social player' with likes and community engagement or as a paid-for 'owned' platform that allows a high degree of control. Vimeo is really the best-value owned player in my opinion and if you don't need the sophisticated options of the platforms mentioned earlier it can do a great job. At Hurricane we now use a specialist player but previously we used a Vimeo pro account to host the videos on our site and it was really solid. A pro account allows users to rebrand the player as well as affect the look of the controls. YouTube videos, however well encoded, never look as good as those on the Vimeo player; this is especially true on longer-form content, as YouTube files must not exceed 2 GB and they can look compressed.

Vimeo is significantly smaller than other social platforms and while it's good for showing films to an engaged audience, note that it's not the place for your big Hero campaign. If you want to use Vimeo for wider campaigns it isn't integrated with Google Analytics so you might not get metrics of the same quality; however, in 2017 the developers added data capture functionality to its players, which can be unlocked by taking out a business account and used to provide sales leads.

A key feature of Vimeo is that channels (collections of videos on shared themes) are made by members and used as a way to discover related content. This is a great way to get your video out to a specialist audience, for example a brand film on rock climbing will get exposure to a specialist audience if it makes it onto an adventure channel full of interested people.

YouTube vs Facebook

Contrasting Facebook with YouTube opens up numerous lines of thought and is a useful exercise. Let's first cover a major difference that underlines the necessity of understanding the range of platforms. As discussed at the start of the chapter, YouTube is a fixed platform, whereas Facebook is fluid, and it is from this fundamental difference that other differences spring.

If a video is uploaded to both Facebook and YouTube on the same day, it will perform very differently on each platform over time. With a decent weight of media spend behind it a Facebook video will have immediate

FIGURE 4.1   Vimeo player

views and create a lot of social noise quickly. It will deliver higher viewer numbers for your budget than YouTube, but once the backing of the media spend stops, viewers will tail off. The YouTube version, however, will take longer to get viewers but once media spend dies off there will still be activity on the video and more importantly on the channel around it. YouTube will therefore have a longer tail of ROI, deliver higher levels of completed views for your budget, and is most likely to deliver higher levels of engagement.[6]

So what is the cause of these differences? Fundamentally people that arrive on YouTube do so to watch video; they are actively looking for content to watch and have the sound on. Facebook users arrive to socialize, not watch. Brands can use thumb bait to get them to watch a single video but once it has finished they will return to their feed. Further to that, Facebook users typically have the sound turned off and the phone in portrait. None of this makes users especially open to video.

The main thing to take away is that a well-balanced video campaign will use both Facebook and YouTube, getting the instant awareness-raising benefits of Facebook along with the higher engagement and longer activity tail of YouTube.

Short-form video

Snapchat

▶ **Video 30**

Social, short-form, fluid, embeddable.

Snapchat is a real-time messaging app and social platform available as a mobile app only. It has grown from niche photo-sharing app to a global player with a value in 2017 of around $16 billion.[7] The app allows users to share photos and videos, but 10 seconds after viewing, the content is deleted. It is this ephemeral, fleeting nature of Snapchat that creates such a distinct user experience. In 2016 the platform averaged 10 billion video views a day.[8]

If you're trying to reach a younger market, Snapchat can be the platform that makes the difference. Although the demographics of Snapchat are weighted towards teenagers and young adults, making it a goldmine for some brands, the fact that content self-destructs automatically has led to the app being used for dating, sexting and, unfortunately, online bullying. Brands need to be aware of the context in which their messages will appear.

The self-deleting nature of Snapchat has been changing and users can now post to news feeds. These 'stories' allow users to share their video in a feed, which lasts for 24 hours, to a group of friends rather than just as a direct message (DM) or private group message.

Another point to note with Snapchat is that campaigns can be costly to get going so it is really only an option for established advertisers with a decent media budget. In addition, the vertical video nature of the interface means that bespoke content is really the only way to go, so you will incur some additional production costs.

Brands to look at for inspiration on Snapchat:

Sour Patch ⏵ **Video 31**
Everlane ⏵ **Video 32**
Cisco ⏵ **Video 33**

Instagram

⏵ **Video 34**
Social, short-form, fluid, embeddable.

This Facebook-owned app allows users to post video between 3 and 60 seconds long and also allows live streaming. In 2016 it started to carry 60-second video ads and to count views on videos, giving marketers a better idea of how many people watch their clips. By 2017, Instagram users had viewed over 40 billion photos and were sharing an average of 95 million photos and videos per day.[9] All this makes Instagram a firm favourite on the video marketer's list.

As with all platforms, attention goes to people that master how to use it. One brand that nailed Instagram is home improvement retailer Lowe's. In their 'Flipside' campaign, viewers were presented with two realities playing in a video at the same time, one the right way up and the other flipped so it was upside down. The viewer could choose which one to watch by rotating their phone around. This worked because of the looping nature of Instagram and made a novelty into a narrative tool:

Lowe's ⏵ **Video 35**

Twitter

(▶) **Video 36**

Social, short-form, fluid, embeddable

Every second, around 6,000 tweets are tweeted on Twitter,[10] which corresponds to over 350,000 tweets per minute, 500 million tweets per day and 200 billion tweets per year. Which is quite a lot!

Brands can broadcast to their own following, react to conversations on current topics using hashtags, or pay for placements into user feeds. The best way to use video on Twitter is as an extension of your current Twitter strategy. Think about taking part in existing conversations with video. An example of this was when Great Britain's Olympic team hosted a Twitter chat and included video replies. Videos of well-known sports personalities responding to questions via Twitter created an engaged conversation and drew followers.

Linear vs interactive

Technology marches on, and video marketing is always changing. Traditionally, viewers are used to watching videos from start to finish, absorbing what happens and then moving on, in what we can call a 'linear' fashion. Interactive technology is changing all of that. Viewers can now be offered multiple videos and choose which one to watch and in what order ('branching'). Additional information can be called up at the click of a button ('hotspots'). Viewers can even click on items that they want to buy and put them straight into an ecommerce shopping basket for checkout ('shoppable'). And, finally, my favourite is that viewers can be sent a video that is entirely bespoke to them, using data from a spreadsheet, such as name and location ('personalized').

Which technology is right for your brand depends on the story you are trying to tell and where you are in the sales funnel. It is a lot easier to create emotional stories with a linear player as you control the pace, shots and narrative. On the other hand, if you want to put across lots of information or add an element of gamification to your content, interactive is a fantastic tool to work with.

Interactive players

WIREWAX

(▶) **Video 37**

Owned, multi-form, interactive.

Wirewax is a leader in interactive video, with tens of thousands of users, including Ted Baker, Disney and the BBC. It offers some really good technology including facial recognition, hotspots, interactive video cards and click-to-buy. It allows brands to monetize their video content by adding interactive hotspots that point to more videos or that place items directly into a shopping cart. It also supports 360 and multi-stream video and allows viewers to switch between two films on the fly with a pretty cool touch slider. You can use Wirewax as a stand-alone platform or integrate it with others. I feature an interview with the MD of Wirewax on page 237.

IDOMOO
(▶) **Video 38**
Owned, multi-form, interactive.

This personalized platform is a really exciting tool that enables brands to create films that are individual to each viewer. Hurricane has made several personalized films based on the Idomoo platform and results have been great. View rates and conversions are really high on these films as people love watching things that are personal to them. These films are typically sent via email with a thumbnail that includes people's names, and it hugely drives up open rates. They can also be used as a data capture tool. People that input their email and details can be sent a film that is personal to them.

Summary

So there we have it, an introduction to platforms and what they have to offer. What has been interesting for me is just how much there is to cover on this; I really have only scratched the surface of difference in platforms and the approaches that work best on them. The key thing to remember is that every technical solution will have strengths and weaknesses, and it will require a conscious strategy to get the best out of them. A really successful video strategy will use a mix of platforms that reaches the right audience and answers the KPIs of the project.

References

1 Forrester
31 October 2016
The Forrester Wave™: online video platforms for sales and marketing, Q4 2016
www.forrester.com/report/The+Forrester+Wave+Online+Video+Platforms+For+
Sales+And+Marketing+Q4+2016/-/E-RES121294 (archived at https://perma.cc/
VNA9-S5HC)

2 Sarah Dawley
24 October 2016
A long list of Facebook statistics – and what they mean for your business
Rainmaker
https://rainmakermediany.com/long-list-facebook-statistics-mean-business
(archived at https://perma.cc/WW7Y-7UDM)

3 Salman Aslam
6 January 2021
Facebook by the numbers: stats, demographics and fun facts,
Omnicore Agency,
www.omnicoreagency.com/facebook-statistics (archived at https://perma.cc/
EH43-6BWP)

4 Lexi Sydow
2020: what happened in mobile and how to succeed in 2021
App Annie
www.appannie.com/en/insights/market-data/2020-mobile-recap-how-to-
succeed-in-2021/ (archived at https://perma.cc/4RRJ-ZQCD)

5 Donie O'Sullivan
21 June 2020
Trump's campaign was trolled by TikTok users in Tulsa
CNN
https://edition.cnn.com/2020/06/21/politics/tiktok-trump-tulsa-rally/index.html
(archived at https://perma.cc/VA5T-LFWF)

6 Carla Marshall
28 July 2015
Facebook video owns day one, but YouTube wins the long-term love,
Tubular Insights,
http://tubularinsights.com/facebook-video-day-one-youtube-long-term/
(archived at https://perma.cc/P68E-YLGV)

7 Maureen Farrell
16 February 2017
Snapchat parent Snap Inc sets valuation at $19.5 billion to $22.2 billion as
IPO approaches
Wall Street Journal
www.wsj.com/articles/snap-sets-valuation-at-19-5-billion-to-22-2-billion-
sources-say-1487221327 (archived at https://perma.cc/6NQK-RUZQ)

8 Sarah Frier
28 April 2016
Snapchat user 'stories' fuel 10 billion daily video views
Bloomberg
www.bloomberg.com/news/articles/2016-04-28/snapchat-user-content-fuels-jump-to-10-billion-daily-video-views (archived at https://perma.cc/LTR3-G5MP)
9 Christana Newberry
6 January 2021
44 Instagram Stats That Matter to Marketers in 2021,
Hootsuite, https://blog.hootsuite.com/instagram-statistics/ (archived at https://perma.cc/N5FP-RSB8)
10 David Sayce
The number of tweets per day in 2020
www.dsayce.com/social-media/tweets-day/ (archived at https://perma.cc/U58A-DLHK)

Creating great videos

SECTION TWO

Creating great videos

05

The basics of video marketing

We've taken the time in the first section of the book to look at the context, psychology and impact of mobile on video. You made it through the theory and you're still with me, which is great. Now that we've taken that journey together it's time to put theory into practice. So how do we make content that engages, emotes and challenges behaviour? In short, how we do make it great?

Making a great video campaign boils down to three simple steps… planning, production, activation. There you go, all sorted! It's simple enough on paper, but obviously each one of those steps is a big endeavour that you need to get right. Over the next four chapters we will break each of these fundamentals down into component parts and help you to build a powerful, effective video marketing strategy. Before we do that, though, let's just put everything into the marketing context.

I do a lot of speaking at events for marketing professionals and I often come across people who are not from a marketing background that have somehow found themselves as the lead, if not sole, marketing person within a business. This seems most common in verticals, where a detailed knowledge of the industry, such as engineering or medicine, is key. If this is you, it's likely that you have a vast amount of experience in the industry and great knowledge of the product. But it's also likely no one has ever said, 'This is the process to market what we do.' If this statement rings true, this is the chapter that's going to change all that; we will take an overview of the modern marketing and sales funnel and make it relevant to video with lots of case studies.

Let's start by summarizing the marketing process with a specific focus on video. There's a truism that brands only ever have two goals: long-term brand growth and short-term sales uplift. It might be phrased in slightly different ways, but it will always boil down to this. To achieve this, brands need to push people through a sales funnel that takes in a mass audience and converts as many as possible of them to customers. First, we will look at the classic model of the marketing funnel, then show how this isn't relevant in a video first, digital age, before we bring ourselves up to date.

When I left the BBC and set up Hurricane, I knew a lot about making great TV shows but zero about how marketing works. I sat down in a café with a small business advisor called Chris and he drew on the back of a napkin (literally) the classic 'sales funnel'. I learned that it was wide at the top, and this was where one shovelled in one's prospects; it then tapered to the end, with prospects falling away as they became excluded or lost interest. The theory was that through mass communication such as TV ads, paid

FIGURE 5.1   The classic sales funnel

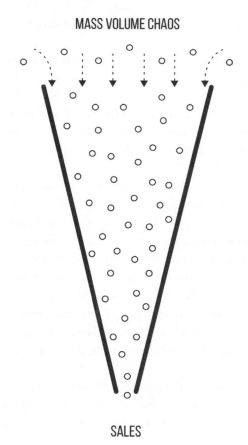

MASS VOLUME CHAOS

SALES

placements, PR, etc, companies could grab the attention of a vast number of people and drop them into the top of the funnel. Once potential customers were in touch with the brand it was simply a case of presenting enough information so that eventually enough of them could be encouraged to make a purchase at the bottom. It seemed like a lovely model, and while for some brands we can make an argument that it holds some relevance, for most it is now totally archaic.

The sales funnel in the digital marketplace is completely different.

The top part of the funnel is when people first become aware of a brand, product or service. The entrance to the modern sales funnel is much narrower than it has been before, and there are two main reasons for this. First, the 'power of X' is driving a decline in the effectiveness of mass advertising, and second, people now find brands and products directly themselves. This happens either through a web search or from recommendations via social or actual physical conversations. Let's refer to this part of the sales funnel as 'Awareness'.

Further down the funnel, people now take the time to have a good look around before deciding to purchase. They may compare your product with

FIGURE 5.2   The digital sales funnel

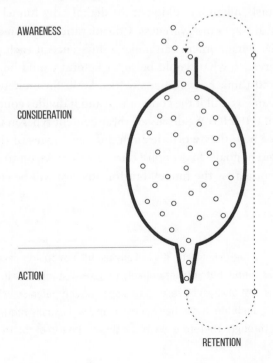

others or just want to get to know more about it. That is, unless you are a 'high I' on the DISC personality model like me and just crash on through to the purchase page without reading anything. At this stage of the funnel marketers can provide information but will struggle to motivate an action or change behaviour as people are consuming content, not buying. We can call this section of the funnel 'Consideration'.

Next, we move on to the business end of the funnel. There will be a point in the consideration process where people are ready to purchase, and with a nudge in the right direction you can push them over the line. This is called the 'Action' phase and is the end of the funnel most like its ageing relative, in that it is a narrow point where brands will be focused on closing the deal.

Finally, we have to remember that a sale is not the end of the job; it is up to the marketing team to drive customers back to the top of the funnel so that the sales process can repeat. I call this 'Retention'.

One man who has influenced my thinking around the digital sales funnel is a fellow author on the Kogan Page publishing label. Grant Leboff's book *Digital Selling*[1] is a confident repositioning of how sales teams must work in the digital age and is well worth a read.

Content can be used throughout the sales funnel to drive customers forward, with different content types having different strengths and weaknesses for the task in hand. Looking at the digital sales funnel and taking on board the critical stages of Awareness, Consideration, Action and Retention, we can consider what content can make a difference at each point. But this is a complex area, so what would be super helpful would be a construct to help explain and think how content works. Well, fortunately we have just that. At Hurricane we call it the content tree and it divides content into Hero, Hub, Help, Go! (HHHG) We discussed these content types in Chapter 3, and now we can see how they work through different stages of the sales funnel to achieve different goals. In Section Four we will move on to using multiple pieces of content across the funnel, but for now we will be considering one film at a time.

Hero content is a big-ticket item; it's a really useful way to add people at the top of the sales funnel but you are unlikely to have that much of it. Hero will often (although not always) be related to a specific campaign so will probably not have a long shelf life. It can be expensive and will usually require a media budget to cut through. Therefore, we place this at the top of the tree.

FIGURE 5.3   Hero, Hub, Help, Go content tree

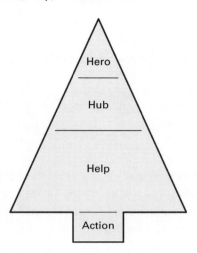

Hub content will be something that brands typically have more of, so it sits underneath Hero. Hub content is typically evergreen and over time will build up into a library of brand resources.

At the wide base of the tree is cheap-to-produce Help content. This is detailed granular stuff like white papers, extended interviews, 'how to' films and more. It's likely that a good content calendar will be churning this out all the time, so it sits at the base of everything. It's Hub and Help content that will keep customers retained and push them back into the top of the funnel.

Finally, people often need a little nudge to get them over the purchase finishing line. So at the base of the tree we have added a Go! section where we refer to films designed with closing a purchase in mind.

The content tree helps visualize what kind of content we have access to. As this book explores later, you should be using a range of content across a campaign to get things done. Key to successful video campaigns is to use the four content types as tools across the stages of the digital sales funnel, capitalizing on opportunities when people are looking for content.

iKamper: A case study of video marketing

CASE STUDY
The use of video across a sales funnel: Skycamp by iKamper

18 November 2016, Soon Park YouTube Channel
 Video 39

Let's bring things to life by looking at a young brand that has successfully used video content to drive its business. The Skycamp (www.ikamper.com) is a product close to my heart. It's pretty much the only thing I've been excited about buying for a few years, and I must even confess to waiting on Kickstarter, 15 minutes before it launched, and was fourth in line to buy. I ended up in this salivating purchase mode for a reason – the video strategy run by iKamper worked perfectly, combining a great product with informative videos and social sharing.

The Skycamp is a hard-shell pop-up tent that sits on top of a campervan or car. For a father of two like me that likes to head into the countryside biking and exploring, it's the perfect accessory. I don't need to convert my van to a pop-top and I get a massive extra bedroom for the kids.

My journey to purchase with the brand started when I was outside my house tinkering with the van. My neighbour Paul popped round holding his phone aloft like a trophy. 'Hey Jon, you're gonna love this!' he said as he handed over his device and pointed me to a video in his Facebook feed. It was a Hero-type film running as a paid Facebook advert. As soon as I saw the opening section of the video I knew this was the thing for me. In the film, a van drives through beautiful countryside with a cool-looking black box on its roof. After pulling over into some woods we see mum and a couple of kids happily relaxing while dad gives a quick flick of the wrist and hey presto, an amazing family tent is ready to go. Shot on a DSLR, it was functional but did its job perfectly. It made an emotional connection – I wanted the product and I was hooked.

For me, this was a perfect example of social video in action. The video that was on a paid Facebook placement did its job at the Awareness end of the funnel. My neighbour had been served a video and although it wasn't relevant to him, he got the pleasure of sharing it with someone else who he knew would like it. He could have sent it to me online but he went old school and came round in person.

With the product fresh in my mind, I went to the site and started stalking the brand. At this point I was in the Consideration phase. Although I liked the product I'd

FIGURE 5.4   Skycamp by iKamper: Spencer and Flo in their home away from home

never heard of the manufacturer and had lots of questions. Will it be well made? It's got to ship across the Atlantic so can I trust them? Will it fit on my van? This is where iKamper got the strategy just right. With a series of videos released over time they built up a library that answered all potential questions. These videos proved that there was real research behind the product and with titles like 'iKamper Hydrostatic Pressure Test' you didn't even need to watch anything to know that it was being thoroughly tested. Finally, help topics like 'Packing up Skycamp' and 'Loading and unloading' answered all the little niggles.

Eventually it was time for me to make the purchase in the Action phase of the sales funnel. This is where brands need to motivate people to input credit card details, and iKamper had the perfect tool. The product was released on Kickstarter at a precise time with good awareness through their network of when that was going to be. The homepage pointed straight to a countdown clock to when you could buy it. By this point people around the world were hungry to buy and there's nothing like a countdown and shipping on a first-come, first-served basis to close the deal. I wasn't the only one who was attracted by the product videos; iKamper had a Kickstarter target of $100,000, which it reached within eight minutes, and it went on to raise over $2 million before the campaign ended. It was the perfect mix of great product and effective videos.

Summary

So there we have it, a quick overview of the basics of video in marketing – in essence, it's a wide-ranging tool that works across the sales funnel. The four video types of HHHG can be used to drive awareness at the top, to encourage engagement in the middle, help convert to sales at the bottom and maintain retention rates by keeping people engaged.

We can now move onto look at the three key phases of creating a video marketing campaign: Planning, Production and Activation.

Reference

1   Grant Leboff
    Digital Selling: How to use social media and the web to generate leads and sell more
    2016
    Kogan Page

06

Step 1: planning

The first of my three steps to building a successful video campaign is planning. The very phrase 'planning' means so much to so many people. A TV agency, engineering firm and accountancy practice will all have a very different idea of what a planner does. So, what do I mean by planning in the context of this book? In short, I mean *making a plan to grow your business with video*. Creating a plan before you jump into the fun creative stuff is essential, as imaginative ideas without direction or goals will fail to generate profit or grow brands. In this chapter I will look at the steps needed to make a good video plan and the information you need to start getting one together. Before launching into how to plan for video, though, I have to make it clear that video is only one marketing channel. It's a very powerful channel, but any video planning must sit within your wider marketing plans and goals, so avoid thinking of it in isolation.

By planning, you are doing what some people do full-time. Those of you inside agencies or companies with larger marketing departments will be well versed in the dark arts of the 'planner'. These immensely clever people bring insight and results to the creative process. There haven't always been planners in agencies, and indeed agencies have been very successful in making decent profits without them. But it is fair to say that before the 1980s many areas of advertising lacked intellectual rigour. This changed when Stephen King of JWT and Stanley Pollitt of BMP (the undisputed forefathers of account planning) became unhappy with the basis of decision making within the advertising industry. They felt that creative teams had little actual insight behind their decision making and also that marketing departments (clients) and the agency account managers of the agency were not interacting as well as they could. In answer to this they developed teams that used market research and other data to add intellectual rigour to the development of ideas. The manipulation and analysis of data has grown up a lot since those initial days, and now that the discipline has reached maturity planners are using ever more precise (or at least, more complicated) tools and basing their thoughts on proven scientific principles drawn from behavioural economics and psychology.

In this book, we're going to streamline the planning process, and I give you a practical approach to building your own campaign. It's built around a seven-question process that will generate all the details you need to build a killer video campaign.

SEVEN QUESTIONS FOR SUCCESS

I've been planning videos and the campaigns around them for 20 years, and along the way I've come up with some good systems and practices to make it work. To help you, I've created a template 'video marketing planner' (VMP), which you can download and fill in. The VMP reflects the seven questions in this chapter, and it's a super practical way for you to start building a complete strategy. You can use it for one video or to build a multi video monster that works across multiple channel (see more on this in Section Four).

The VMP prompts you through the seven questions that are at the heart of video marketing:

1 What are your campaign objectives?

2 Who are you talking to?

3 When are you talking to viewers?

4 Where is your audience?

5 What are you saying?

6 How will you activate?

7 What are your campaign KPIs and metrics?

You can download the template VMP at www.koganpage.com/vm2

---

1 What are your campaign objectives?

Let's start at the very beginning... what are you actually trying to achieve? This seems like it should be an easy enough question, but answering it precisely almost always raises interesting dynamics. The normal dynamic for a brand project is to have multiple stakeholders from across the business, and these people invariable have slightly different objectives. The head of sales will want something very different from the CTO, who in turn will want something different from someone on the customer support team. In the middle of all of this is you! At the very start of the process, it's worth visiting all the stakeholders in your project to understand what they are expecting, then combine these into a single document, simplify them, and reflect them back. If nothing else, this will give you insights into stakeholders that are destined to be disappointed so you can manage their expectations. The main mantra with campaign objectives is that 'less is more'. One specific thing is going to be much easier to achieve than a catch-all solution. Get agreement on what it is you actually want to do, and you are off to a great start. It's worth having your allies lined up at this point to help you keep on track, and a top tip from me is that multiple stakeholders can be offered different versions of videos (or other video projects entirely) to meet their needs. I've found that as long as people know they will get the tools they require in the end they tend to go along with the overall plan.

The things that are most hotly contested in brand team meetings are the list below. Once you know them, you are in a good place to start:

- What is the business need for this film?
- If there is more than one need, which is the most important?
- What is the best outcome for the film?
- Who has sign-off on the project (and who is paying for it)?
- What are the measures of success? (We will cover this more in question 7)
- What timescales are you working to?

If you are thinking of using my downloadable VMP template, now is a good time to start. You will see that it includes space to put your project and company goals. Don't worry if there appear to be a lot of boxes that you cannot fill in yet, as that is what the rest of this chapter is about.

Planning for short- and long-term goals

Optimum campaign strategy will be different depending on whether you set long-term or short-term goals. Short-term goals are best served by behavioural triggers that are immediate, for example dealing with simple logic such as pricing, new products or specific timed events. Long-term goals (such as growing market share) will need a brand-building element that is more suited to emotional drivers aimed at the System 1 mind (which we talk about at length in Chapter 2). Knowing your goals will directly affect the kinds of video content you choose to create.

A lot of marketing activity goes into growing current customers, be that loyalty campaigns, regular content, newsletters and so forth. Yes, this is important, but radical improvements in turnover and sales will *only* come from a heavy focus on new customers. A central tenet of your marketing strategy should therefore be to grow the fame of the brand. For more on this you should read the IPA's book *The Long and the Short of It*, but for now here is a key paragraph from the publication:

> Across the board, in terms of metrics used, campaigns targeting new customers outperform those targeting existing customers. In terms of the business effects reported, the former are almost three times as effective as those targeting existing customers; in terms of total effects, they are more than twice as effective.[1]

This means that brands looking to grow must reach beyond existing social channels.[2] A nice video that is sent to people that already know you will not grow your business as much as getting something, of any level, in front of new people. It seems obvious but many times it's easy to go for the shortest route of talking to people you already know, rather than striking up a new conversation. A good video strategy will work for you across the sales funnel with a truly win–win goal being a strategy that balances long-term brand goals with short-term sales targets.

2 Who are you talking to?

Now that you know what it is your business is trying to achieve, it's time to clarify who you are talking to. What are the personas of your customers? What are the emotions that are going to encourage them to take action? Unless you can really say what your audience looks like, you're going to be stuck. All great videos start with an understanding of what makes the audience tick.

A good place to kick this process off is with your customer's personas. If you have well-developed personas for your customers, you can skip a few paragraphs here, but if you don't… you have a bit of homework to do first.

A customer persona (sometimes known as a buyer persona) is a semi-fictional character who reflects a specific subdivision of a market segment.

Customer personas differ between market segments (which represent a collection of customers with a shared need) as they add layers of detail around common demographic and purchasing characteristics, personifying a collection of customers.

The classic things that people include in personas are straight demographics like age, education, social status and profession, but don't forget that you are talking to a person, not a statistic. Understanding the pressures that your customers face, along with knowing their hopes and dreams, will be far more useful than knowing someone's age. Take some time to map out the main customer groups that you have and assign the key characteristic for each. If you want to get into the process of defining personas in detail, there are loads of resources just a quick web search away, and most good marketing agencies can help you through the process.

With your personas defined, all you need to do is to apply them to your video project. Which of your personas are you targeting with your video campaign? Which is the primary audience? And which is the secondary? If you have multiple audiences do you need to talk to them in different ways? For example, if you are in medical marketing you will probably talk to healthcare professionals in totally different ways than you would to patients (even though it's the same product). Later on, we'll be talking about messaging, but at this time, if you have any key messages or emotional motivators relevant to each persona, it is worth noting them alongside your personas. If you are using the VMS planner you can add those in as you go.

Once you have a broad definition of your audiences, you can start to consider the things that are most likely to make them engage with you, and it is this that you'll be putting in your videos. A good way to think about this is to consider a person's emotional drivers. 'Personal drivers' are the levers you can pull to resonate with an audience at an emotional level. This includes their hopes and fears as well as their goals in life, both public and private. For me, private goals are always more effective things to talk to than public ones. As an example, assume you're talking to a medical professional such as a surgeon. Their public goal could well be to provide patients with better treatments, but in private they may actually be motivated by how much kudos they will get if they use a shiny new product, or a low rate of complications so their average results go up, or they may even just want to finish work early and get to the golf course.

When I'm running workshops around this, I ask brands to think of the things that will make their customers care about or want their product. We start with the optimistic, that is to say the things that you would hope your customers care about, such as saving the planet, making the world better, delivering a better service, all those things. We are looking to find the one big driver that will make people sit up and think because it engages them emotionally. This is not the time for a huge list of services and benefits; that comes later. For now, think about the one big thing that your customers really care about.

Next, I ask the workshop to be a little more cynical in what benefits their customers want. As an example, they might want to look great to their boss and get a promotion, they may want an easy life, or they may just need to keep their job. It's really good to put a list of positive and negative drivers in a list and start to play around with which one you think is mostly likely to make an impact with your audience.

As a thinking aid, here is a list of the emotional drivers to consider:

- *Fear of missing out (FOMO):* Some people are motivated by the fact that others are already doing something – a useful motivator to drive behaviour change.

- *Laziness:* 'Our product will make your life easy' is a very powerful motivator.

- *Loss aversion:* People will put more effort into avoiding losing something they already have than they will to gain something new. Suggesting that not taking action will mean they lose something can be enough to get viewers to engage.

- *Vanity:* You can look better than everyone else with our product!

- *Social proof:* People's behaviour is influenced by social norms about what they perceive is 'acceptable', popular or trending. Content that reminds viewers of the wider success of a product can sway behaviour.

- *Goal dilution:* People are more likely to maintain focus on (and achieve) single goals rather than multiple goals, so focus your messaging on one thing.

- *Control or 'help my life run smoothly':* We all live in a busy world; giving consumers the idea that their life will become less hassle can be a powerful motivator. Videos with this driver should consistently prove benefits such as saving time and money.

- *Desire for a life that is about more than just 'surviving':* Allowing consumers to accept that life is about more than just fulfilling basic needs is key to persuading people to use luxury items. Viewers should be made to feel free to gratify any urges that make them feel happy.

- *Belonging or 'You know who I am':* Content that proves a brand is closely aligned with the self-orientation and beliefs of its audience will help foster a shared identity and build engagement.

This is a non-exhaustive list of motivators that you can look to leverage in your content, but it gives a good springboard for your thinking – which do you think would motivate your audience to change its behaviour?

CASE STUDY
How Kleenex® embraced emotional storytelling to drive brand growth by 'making caring contagious'

I have spoken to many brands in the process of writing this book, and one discussion that stood out as adding insight to the topic of emotive marketing was with Kleenex. I've included here a conversation with them that drills into their approach.

JM: How does emotive video fit into the brand's marketing strategy?

K: Since inventing the tissue category 90 years ago, Kleenex brand has been its leader and innovator. The category, however, was declining because consumers were only using tissues when they had a cold. In 2016 we used consumer insights around what the benefit of Kleenex tissue was for them – a gesture of care – and this allowed us to expand the notion of the brand and, by default, the category, by equating it beyond just a tool to wipe a nose or dry an eye. Along with our agency partners, we came up with a common goal for our 2016 programme: to uplift millions of people every day during timely moments in their lives with real stories showing meaningful gestures of care whenever 'Someone Needs One'.

JM: What's the importance of emotional storytelling for the brand?

K: For the Kleenex brand, emotional storytelling was an obvious match, as the brand has always been rooted in care. With this video content series and our larger 2016 'Someone Needs One' programme, we were challenging people to be aware of the often overlooked, everyday opportunities to show they care. Our hope was to inspire people to overcome indifference and make a connection with a friend, loved one or stranger in a moment of need; and sometimes, one soft Kleenex tissue is all it takes to break down those barriers to expressing care for yourself or someone in need.

Additionally, our target – which consisted largely of women aged 25–54 – had a high affinity for 'feel good' uplifting and emotional content, especially as it relates to moments in their life. We targeted our videos based on moments such as when they were celebrating life milestones (engagement, wedding, new baby), when they were travelling on a long commute, and when their relationship changed. So, this video series met them in the moments in which they were looking for this emotional connection with content from a brand they trust. The 'Someone Needs One' programme was about showcasing the impact of a gesture of care – big or small – in an effort to honour people who have made a difference. We identified stories and amplified those moments with a larger audience in the hopes of inspiring others to make care contagious.

You can see examples of this approach being put into action in the link below:

Time for a change
4 June 2015, Kleenex Brand YouTube channel
 Video 40

At this point it's worth noting research that shows motivators can be different between men and women. Jane Cunningham and Philippa Roberts argue in their book *Inside Her Pretty Little Head* that men and women have different motivations, many of which are hard-wired through evolutionary psychology.[3] They put forward that men are driven by the 'Achievement Impulse', and women by the 'Utopian Impulse'. From this starting point they establish a number of motivators that are specific to female markets:

- The Altruism Code: women are naturally nurturing and 'others' focused.
- The Aesthetic Code: women are attuned to appearance and enhanced environment.

- The Ordering Code: women take on varied responsibilities for others, take care with detail, and plan ahead.
- The Connecting Code: women are relationship-driven in order to survive.

Many companies have nailed the emotional driver that is right for their audience and have proven that no matter what your product or service there is a driver that will work. Sometimes people say to me that their product is too boring to have any emotion around it, and that they can only talk about benefits and features. To these people I show a video created by Taulia which can be seen on the link below. Now, I mean no disrespect to Taulia when I say this, but their product is insanely dull. That said, they have still found an emotional driver to engage people and they've had some fun along the way.

eInvoicing – Taulia
21 March 2014, Taulia YouTube channel
▶ **Video 41**

The final step in finding the right emotional driver for your audience is to look back at the list and find the most realistic, engaging and original one that you can get away with saying. You might find you have two or three really strong ones; if one doesn't leap out as a clear winner it's worth A/B testing your messages in some test films, print or digital output. At Hurricane we created a video for an investment app, which was basically an online tool that gave insights about investment decisions. We started the project with a session that gave us two potential emotional motivators. The first was that the app gave you great insight to make better decisions, the second was that the app was super cool and would make users look like they had the best investment tools. We didn't know which would work and A/B tested the results. Which would you think would resonate with investors better? The results showed that the driver that got the best results was not the one that promised better results, but the one that showed off how cool users would look if they adapted the technology.

So, you can see that you are now moving forward with your plan. You now know what job you need your videos to do and whom they are targeted at. The next step is to think about when you should talk to your audience.

3 When are you talking to viewers?

In this section we will be looking at when you are talking to your customers. By 'when', we are actually looking at a few things: not only what part of their day they are in, but also where they are in the sales funnel. It might be that they've never heard of you, or maybe they know your product but are not making the step to purchase. Knowing which of these you are dealing with will help you to create effective videos.

In Chapter 5 we talked about the digital sales funnel, and this is the model that we can use to think about when we are talking to viewers. Are you unknown in the marketplace? Well, then, start at the *Awareness* stage and consider what might grab some of the limelight (Hero films and paid ads are the order of the day here). Do people know about you but not have a good understanding of what you do? You need to focus attention on the *Consideration* phase with 'how to' videos, behind the scenes, meet the team and explainers. Or do you have loads of followers and engaged views but need to boost sales? You will need to focus on the *Action* stage of the funnel with short, punchy messages via social, paid and even email helping to give that final nudge.

Again, remember that less is more. Video is powerful, but it's not a miracle worker! Stick to one part of the sales funnel at a time. A video that works as a social ad for awareness raising is not the right tool for use in the middle of the funnel when you want to create deep conversations. As an insightful marketer, you will already know where the overall brand strategy is headed. The role of planning your video campaign is to help you get there quicker. Let's revisit the digital marketing funnel, bearing in mind your brand objectives. We are going to look again at the stages of the funnel from Awareness through Consideration, Action and Retention, and think about how the Hero, Hub, Help, Go! model can get you to your destination.

Video strategies to raise awareness

Awareness is how we make brands famous and drive new leads into the top of the sales funnel. It looks beyond existing networks and pushes the brand to new people. Awareness videos can be Hero content with large advertising spend or Help content that answers specific questions. It might even be a viral campaign relying on sharing (although these are becoming increasingly hard to activate).

Shareable videos – or virals – are in some ways the holy grail of fame campaigns to drive awareness. A viral view is a view that comes from the video being shared. It is organic and is considered to be free (although it is very rarely free, as we will discuss in the Activation theme of Chapter 8). One agency that has totally nailed the creation of shareable content is based in the same city as my agency and is run by the lovely people of Rubber Republic. Rubber has created hugely shareable videos for the likes of Mercedes, Audi, Google and more. One of my favourites was created for Fiat; it has received over 4.8 million views, been shared 428,000 times and has a share ratio of 1:10.

FIGURE 6.1   Fiat: The Motherhood

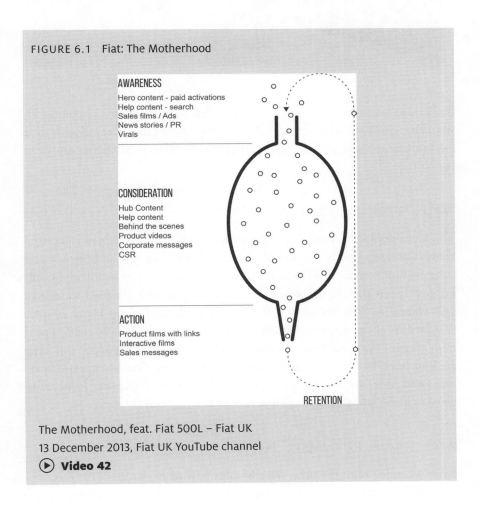

The Motherhood, feat. Fiat 500L – Fiat UK

13 December 2013, Fiat UK YouTube channel

▶ Video 42

FIGURE 6.2 Digital sales funnel and content

But raising awareness does not have to come from big Hero content with shareable content and heavy seeding budgets. One of the most cost-effective methods of picking up site or social channel traffic is SEO-friendly Help content.

Video strategies to encourage consideration

The Consideration phase is key to video strategy and is where interested viewers are engaged by the brand. It builds brand salience and fluency and is key to long-term brand growth. Consideration is where people are mulling over what they think of you, so content should be designed to inform and entertain. This section of the funnel could use some Hero content designed to elicit emotional responses, but it is more typically made up of Hub content that entertains people and Help content that people will keep coming back to for more information. Content for Consideration can be measured in terms of how many people subscribe to a channel, how many viewers move from video to video, and total engagement times.

Video strategies to motivate action

Now we move onto the most overtly sales part of the process, the business end where brands are looking to translate engagement into a purchase decision. It's where behaviour is changed from the consumption of information to the consumption of a product. It may be necessary to overcome some final doubts in the consumer's mind, in which case you could have videos on payment security, privacy or other trust-building issues. Action content might also introduce psychology motivators like the 'fear of missing out' or 'loss aversion' to persuade people that they need to act now. I cover these motivators in more detail later in this chapter.

Video strategies to improve retention

So the viewer has followed all your videos and become a customer; now is not the time to let them go. Although brands need to constantly expand the pool, it's not worth losing a customer. The fact of the matter is that people are not brand loyal, and in a competitive marketplace you need to work to retain your brand's place in their consciousness. Hub and Help content can be vital in this battle for attention. Providing guides on how to use your product as well as content that will encourage people to remain engaged is vital for keeping your brand in the mind of consumers.

Time of day

Once you know where people are in their journey, think about where they are in their day. You will need to communicate in ways that reflect key phases of people's day and adapt messaging to how they feel. Getting up, leaving the house and travelling to work is an interesting time. If you have short, punchy brand messages and can keep things eye-catching, then this is a good time for brand awareness. Just don't expect people to give anything other than a passing interest, they aren't going to engage with complexity or for a long duration. Instead, consider paid ads on Facebook, Instagram, LinkedIn and so on. Just make sure that anything you do works without sound.

If you have a more complex message to put across then visit people at work. Here they will often consume relevant information for a longer and will be looking for deeper answers. Just remember that even people at work need to be engaged with emotional messages and a clarity of voice. LinkedIn ads and posts work well in this stage, and videos via email sent at 10 in the morning have a good chance of getting looked at.

When people get home and start looking for entertainment, things change totally. They will spend longer on fixed platforms, moving from things like Instagram to platforms like Netflix and YouTube. They are also more likely to be wearing headphones so you can deliver more emotive messages with audio.

One final aspect to consider can actually happen at any time, at work or at home, but it's a very specific state of mind. It's when people want to find answers. Make sure you have a video ready to answer the big questions they are looking for on search engines. People looking for answers online are a cost-effective way to draw attention to your brand. A deep collection of organic search focused Help content on your site will make a massive difference to your performance.

Let's take a moment to look at an example of how to attract people looking for answers, as seeing it in real life is the easiest way to talk about best practice.

Hurricane worked with pet pharmaceutical company Beaphar on a project to raise awareness of an anti-flea product built around using only organic search with no paid. After looking for a search term that was used a lot, but that created a limited amount of competition, we decided to directly answer the question 'How to get rid of fleas for good'. We planned that someone who has searched for a similar term will find our video and immediately know it is what they are looking for. Because the whole film is in line with what potential customers are looking for, it has really high engagement and low bounce rates. The best thing about this approach is that it sits on video channels for years, just sucking up viewers and driving people to the brand. To date, the Beaphar film has clocked up over 120,000 (organic) views.

How to get rid of fleas for good!
20 August 2019, Beaphar UK YouTube channel
 Video 43

It's time again to fill in your VMP. Head to the 'audience persona' section. You'll see that there is a column where you can include the audience persona for each film you are thinking of making – fill in your primary audience, and secondary and tertiary audiences if you have them. Also fill in the emotional driver for each audience. It doesn't matter if you haven't decided what kind of film you will make yet, just get in the information you have about your audience.

At the moment we are only thinking of making one film, but you can do this step for each film that you are planning, from the Awareness phase, through Consideration and into Conversion and Retention (I cover multi video campaigns in Section Four). You may well use a different motivator for each step of the funnel, because what gets someone interested may not be the same thing that converts them to a sale.

4 Where is your audience?

Where do the people that you want to talk to live their digital lives? Are they elderly males that watch history TV channels? Are they GenZ'rs that can't put down their TikTok feed? Or are they high-level business executives that only look at their LinkedIn messages once a fortnight? These are the things that you need to understand before finalizing a video marketing plan. If I were to start down the route of explaining every channel you could use and when, this book would never end! It's likely you already know where they are as you would have looked at this when defining audience personas. However, if you are unsure where to find your audiences, I would suggest starting with the summary of platforms in Chapter 4. After that, you would be well served by searching 'best social media platforms for business', which will give you lots of additional information.

Consider not only which channels your audience will spend their time on, but also what implications those channels will have on the films you make. How will you adapt duration and structure? Do the channels you want to use have a fluid or a fixed structure? Do they give best results with paid activity, or are they best for shared or user-generated content? My main advice at this point is that this is not a 'one size fits all' situation. Creating one type of content and using that in multiple places could prove to be a waste of effort, time and money. Instead, think carefully about what needs to be created for each channel and how to maximize results. Using fewer channels to their full potential is a much better approach than spreading efforts too thinly across multiple channels and activating it badly.

If you are using the VMS planner, you will see a column called 'channel thoughts'. Make some initial notes here on the platforms that you are thinking of using and add anything you think may be useful in the production phase. At the start of the process you can put plenty in here; you can always strip it back later as your plans become more developed.

5 What are you saying?

Now we can get into a more traditional part of marketing: what is it you're actually saying?! It doesn't matter how clever your video strategy is, or how creative your videos are, if you're not communicating the right message to viewers, or you are saying too much or too little your campaign simply isn't going to work. To set the scene for this section, let's look at a simple

FIGURE 6.3 Durations study

DURATIONS STUDY

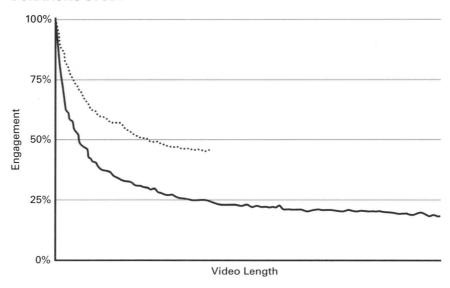

SOURCE Wistia

principle… less is more. Video is great for connecting at an emotional level, it is also brilliant at telling stories and communicating messages. But people are busy, and they are becoming less likely to give you their attention for long, especially if they are not engaged from the start. To demonstrate this, let's take a look at a study done by Wistia (Figure 6.3).[4]

The graph shows two films; the dotted line is a film that is 30 seconds long, and the solid line is a film that is 60 seconds long. Looking first at the shorter film (the dotted line), we can see that there is a fairly fast drop-off once the film starts. This is the bounce rate of viewers who realize this isn't a film they want to watch. Within five seconds the film has lost 25 per cent of viewers, and this is followed by a steady drop-off until the end of the film. The completion rate is just below 50 per cent, which is a solid performance, and as an assessment this is not a bad curve at all.

If we then look at the solid line (the 60 second film), we can see that the initial bounce rate is much higher than for the first film. Within five seconds we have lost half the audience, and this continues to plummet down. Drop-off then goes down to 25 per cent and this continues to decline until the end of the film, where it ends with only 23 per cent of the initial audience.

We can see the two curves, well-so what? The crazy thing here is that the first 30 seconds of both of these films are exactly the same. They are performing differently not because of the content but because of their duration. People are literally starting the longer film, seeing that it is 60 seconds in length, and not bothering to stay around.

There is one simple thing to take from this test, and that is 'less is more'.

In the next chapter we will be discussing how to run messaging sessions that enable you to build your messaging into powerful structures. For now, just collate all the potential messages (both factual and emotional) that could be used in your film. If you can go some way to prioritizing these in your head or with the team it will be of great use further down the line.

6 How will you activate?

Things are getting pretty advanced and your video is nearly ready to go into production. Now is the time to think about how you will activate your campaign. For me, activation is the process by which you take your final masterpiece, and you get it out into the world with maximum attention. The question of activating your film is complex and has lots of moving parts. It covers everything from paid placements on social through to internal PR, your own social channels and what the public say about you.

The easiest way to think about the activation of your film is to use three different categories; paid, earned and owned.

Paid

The classic way of activating your film is to use paid placements. Traditionally these might have been TV commercials or print. However, in our social media focused world these are more likely to be paid placements on Facebook, YouTube or Instagram. The key feature of paid activity is that people are not choosing to watch it. Whether it's programmatic ads through the Google Display Network or Facebook ads in a feed, we are pushing our content into people's lives. Because of this, expect engagement rates to be low, simply because people are not choosing to watch it.

At this stage of the planning process, you just need to consider the scale of your paid activity, rather than what specifically you are going to do. If you are creating a film that is designed to sit at the top of the sales funnel in awareness and you are looking to reach a new audience, a substantial amount of your budget should be put behind paid placements. If you are making an on-site conversation piece you won't need any at all. As someone that runs a company that makes videos I shouldn't really be saying this, but sometimes it's much better to make a cheap film with more paid activity behind it than it is to make an expensive film that you can't afford to get anybody to see. Be careful, though, as there's a delicate balance between costs savings and your brand's image. Other things to think about around paid at this point are whether you should A/B test multiple different messages. This can be really helpful and should be planned for now, as it might need to be built into your production and film creation at the next stage. A good tip on paid placements is to start small, test your messages, test your imagery, see what works and then scale up the campaign from there.

MEDIA NETWORKS

You can buy media space yourself, and it's pretty easy on social channels. However, consider whether you should use a media network (also called an ad network) that can place your film in front of a wider audience. If you read online publications like the *Financial Times* or the *New York Times* and see video ads, you are looking at the work of a media network. You can buy direct from publications, but networks will give you a greater reach, and the good ones will help you be more targeted. There are loads of networks that can do this. Google Display Network is an obvious choice, but other social channels have media networks as well, including LinkedIn, which has a pretty good business network, and there are numerous third-party players in the space. All networks will reach a slightly different audience, so look for a partner that works best for your brand.

Earned

The next method of activation is earned. Unlike paid (where you're letting the money do the talking), earned activation is about content being found through search, PR or social sharing. Earned activation is useful at the top of the sales funnel as it allows you to reach your audience without having to spend cash on media placements and is really good in the middle of the funnel as it is a great way to take part in longer conversations with prospective customers. Always remember that with earned activation you're not forcing your brand into people's lives, instead they are voluntarily watching your content. This means it needs to be genuinely watchable, it needs to be engaging and above all else it needs to be highly searchable by engines. It is because of this that the planning stage should consider how to attract people to find and watch it with strong tags, relevant titles and punchy thumbnails. Think back to the Beaphar flea treatment example we discussed earlier in this chapter. This was a piece of content specifically designed to leverage earned activation, with the whole film built around a high-value search term.

As an example of how successful earned content can be, take a look at the cooking video in the link below. It has nearly 14 million views, all of which have been achieved completely organically (that is to say, with no paid media behind it). The success of the film lies in having the highly searchable title 'how to make pancakes – fluffy pancake recipe', which is backed up with an incredible depth of copy explaining what's happening in the video. It has loads of tags, it's got back links to other places, it's got other resources… it even goes into detail as to what cameras were used to film it! Search engines inevitably think this is a wonderful piece of content and serve it right at the top of searches. What could 14 million organic views do for your brand?

How to make pancakes – fluffy pancake recipe
7 January 2017, Recipes by Carina YouTube channel
 Video 44

INFLUENCERS

Influencer marketing is a massive growth area and I cover it here although it falls into both the paid and earned categories. There are dozens of books and online courses that deal specifically with influencer marketing so I'm not going to cover too much here, but it's good to think about whether you will use influencers in the activation of your campaign as you may need to adjust your video slightly for their needs. There are lots of sites out there that will connect brands with influencers, including ghostlamp.com, upfluence.com, postforrent.com and socialbakers.com, all of whom will pay influencers relatively small sums of money to talk about the film that you have made and get it talked about. They also provide tools and platforms to find the right influencers to grow your brand. The great thing about using influencers in this way is that you can target your video at very niche markets and adjust your messages to fit. Every niche has a blogger or influencer talking about it, from tiny hobbies like finger knitting, through topics like cooking and into mass appeal areas like sports... enlisting influencers can really get your film out there.

Owned

With owned activation you are putting content out onto channels over which you have direct control. This includes your own website, social channels and internal team. Owned media is a very cost-effective way of activating content, but its benefits to brand growth are limited. Real brand growth comes from expanding your audience, not just talking to the one you already have. That said, for mid-funnel, conversion and retention content, owned media is a strong and proven way of taking you content to viewers.

Bear in mind that just because people follow you on social already it doesn't mean that they're going to give you attention if your content doesn't deserve it. Make sure that your videos have got great titles, punchy thumbnails and are engaging right from the opening or people just won't engage.

And there you have it – a top line overview of how you will activate your film. For me, successful campaigns will always use a combination of these three methods with different weighting for the activation type depending on the goal of the project. At one end of the scale are awareness campaigns, which will rely heavily on paid, and at the other end of the scale are conversion campaigns, which will talk more to owned audiences.

If you are filling in the VMS planner, now is a good time to make notes on your approach to activation. Start to map out the activation techniques you're going to use. I've added in some notes of my own, but the more detail you can add in, the more effective your video will be.

For paid activation, start to think about what audiences you might go after and which social you're going to use. As an example of why this matters, if you're running paid placements on Instagram your film will have a very different feel to it than if you are running them on LinkedIn. Knowing where your films will activate will inform the structure and tone of what you do.

If you are looking to leverage earned activation, it's also worth thinking about search terms, tags and keywords, and consider ways of attracting people to watch the content. The more detail you can put in at this point, the better your video marketing will be further down the line. Take a look at Chapter 8 for more detail on optimizing your films.

7 What are your campaign KPIs and metrics?

Up to this point in our section on planning we've discussed how to consider who you are, who your audience is and some thoughts on how to get to your goals. But how do you measure the impact when you've arrived? And how do you measure progress? Despite the modern world being full of data, it can be hard to tie video campaigns to results. While measuring engagement is straightforward, proving how views directly relate to sales is impossible (anyone who tells you otherwise should be treated with high levels of suspicion). Success should be measured in as wide a variety of ways as possible, certainly not only against total view count. Consider the following two scenarios... which is a viral sensation and which one is an actual success for the business that created it?

1 25 million people watch a viral video made by a brand. These people will never be in a position to buy what the brand is selling.

2 A product in a high-value and very specific marketplace has a potential customer base of 20 people. A functional brand video is sent to five of them and they each share it once, to another in the potential purchaser group.

That's a bit of an extreme example but it makes the point. Views are important and will always be a key metric, but setting wider KPIs that directly link to your overall goals is key to success. Set the most appropriate KPIs and metrics that you can. Equally, make sure you set up KPIs that are not too sales specific. CSOs and sales teams will always be asking what click-through rate (CTR) a video will get them and exactly what conversion rates will be, but these focus only on short-term goals and ignore the much greater long-term brand-building effects of good video, so make sure you use a balance of metrics.

Let's go back to the digital sales funnel, where we looked at the behaviours that you might want to be influencing – Awareness, Consideration, Action and Retention. In Table 6.1 I've set out the four stages of the funnel and laid out KPIs to consider; it's not an exhaustive list but it will get you thinking about which metrics to consider for proving effectiveness.

The key to KPIs being useful is to make sure that everyone on the team knows what is being measured and why, before the campaign begins. Sharing and agreeing your KPIs with internal stakeholders and agency partners as soon as you can will mean that you can hold people to the progress of the campaign. This not only focuses everyone on the job in hand but it stops

TABLE 6.1 Setting KPIs

KPIs for	Awareness goals	Consideration goals	Action goals	Retention goals
Views	Y	Y	Y	Y
Impressions	Y			
Share ratio	Y			
Unique users	Y			
Brand awareness uplift	Y			
Ad recall lift	Y			
PR inchage	Y	Y		
View-through rate		Y		
Engagement (watch time, sharing)		Y		Y
Subscriptions		Y		
Click to brand page			Y	
Uplift in sales during campaign period			Y	
Newsletter signup		Y		Y

someone from the senior team looking at the film's results and getting annoyed that a KPI they perceive to be significant has not done as well as they wanted (often if this happens it is someone from the sales team who has not understood that the campaign is about long-term brand growth, not immediate click-through to sales pages).

Benchmarking the success of your video

What does success look like? At Hurricane we've had clients ask us what specific results they can expect from a campaign before it is under way. I wish there was a short answer and that we could reel off guaranteed stats, but unfortunately it is never that simple. There are best-case forecasts, but until research and testing get under way it is impossible to be precise. There is a huge range of factors that affect metrics, from video-specific issues like duration, style, creativity and production quality (budget!) to audience-specific issues and marketplace competition. Some things like engagement are fairly easy to measure, and a quick online search will give you a good starting point for the ballpark metrics a film is likely to get. Other things, such as CTR, brand uplift and sales increases are far harder to predict. The answer is to set your own standards as best you can at the start of the process, then run tests and update the KPIs to specifics as soon as you can.

Look at previous campaigns to try to extrapolate as much data as you can, making sure that you don't just stop at views but that you dig down into the analytics. Look at engagement, view time and every other metric that you might want to improve with your new campaign. If you have no track record to refer to, you might want to consider making two versions of your film and testing a couple of messaging options so that you can at least see which one works best, to give yourself a direction of travel. If you are running paid placements such as in-stream (skippable) or programmatic adverts, it's possible to measure a video's success with no reference to other films or industry standards. Most of the major social platforms run an A/B testing service, and you can speak to your account manager or media agency to set this up. A/B testing is fairly standard in its approach. Once you choose an audience and activate a campaign, most of the audience is served the video ad and a small part of the audience is not. At a given time during or after the campaign a sample of the audience is surveyed with a proportion of those surveyed having been served the ad, and a proportion having not been served the ad. The difference in brand awareness between the two groups is the brand awareness uplift that you've gained. If there is no difference in awareness between those that were served the ad and those that were not it is time to get a new approach or new agency!

If you want to go beyond those tools and poll consumers on more specific questions you can run a survey of the film before launch. Google Consumer Surveys offers this service and if you have no other metrics to compare to (and indeed even if you do) it can be a very useful exercise.

Finally, if you feel that you want to know exactly what impact your film is going to have on people you can have it focus-grouped or tested in a lab situation. There are many companies that do this, such as System 1 in the UK (formerly known as Brain Juicer). This agency has a highly detailed system that uses interviews and reactions from either live or online audiences to access video content. It gives a simple mark out of five that reflects how much the audience was engaged.

Summary

Planning for video can seem like an epic and uphill task, but at its core it is simply the following:

- Understand the journey you are on – where you are right now, where you want to go and how you intend to get there.

- To maximize benefits, plan videos that focus on both short-term sales uplift and long-term brand awareness.

- Use emotional motivators to drive behaviour change.

- Remember that different audiences will react to emotional stimuli in different ways.

- Set KPIs that are relevant to the specific business challenge that you have, and make sure everyone on the team knows what these are in advance.

- Track your success against industry standards, your own previous films or external testing.

- You can build a solid video marketing plan by answering seven questions:

    1 What are your campaign objectives?

    2 Who are you talking to?

    3 When are you talking to viewers?

    4 Where is your audience?

    5 What are you saying?

    6 How will you activate?

    7 What are your campaign KPIs and metrics?

References

1 Les Binet and Peter Field
   2013
   The Long and the Short of It: Balancing short and long-term marketing
   IPA
2 Marie Oldham
   5 January 2017
   Challenge Byron Sharp and grow your brand
   Campaign Live
   www.campaignlive.co.uk/article/challenge-byron-sharp-grow-brand/1419995
   (archived at https://perma.cc/75XH-XCPJ)

3 Jane Cunningham and Philippa Roberts
2012
Inside Her Pretty Little Head: A new theory of female motivation and what it means for marketing
Marshall Cavendish International Asia Pte Ltd
4 Ezra Fishman
5 July 2016
How long should your next video be?
Wistia,
https://wistia.com/blog/optimal-video-length (archived at https://perma.cc/S6LP-XPZK)

07

Step 2: production

Good work: you've made it through the heavy crunch of planning and you now step into the bright light of creativity. This is where we take the big plans, goals, KPIs (and very often the expectations of the entire management board) and come up with a plan for a film that is so wonderful that it changes the future of your brand! From there we actually have to make the thing. That might mean bringing in an external agency or creating our own magic in house (which I cover in more depth in Section Three). In this chapter we consider first how to develop ideas, then we look at practical ways to structure your brand story in video and finally we get into the nitty gritty of video production, and the things you need to think about. These three things are interconnected and are not a linear decision making process, so be aware that as you change one you will need to consider how you change the others.

Visual storytelling/getting better creative

Thousands of videos are uploaded every hour, so how do you ensure that yours stand out? In this opening section we look at how story and creative work hand-in-hand to deliver powerful video. Before we move on, though, let's allow ourselves a moment to be inspired by some truly creative work; work that takes a simple brand idea (the plan!) and turns it into something truly wonderful.

'The power of X', made for TEDx Summit, is a film that will stand the test of time. As you watch it, bear in mind that it features no computer trickery whatsoever. It is a beautiful and simple idea executed immaculately. The truly epic thing about this film is how they did it; having the confidence to take a simple child's toy and grow the idea to a massive scale is remarkable. The behind the scenes film shows just how epic and brave this creative vision was.

TEDx Summit intro: the power of x
15 April 2012, TED Blog Video YouTube channel
▶ **Video 45**

How to make a human arabesque: the making of the TEDx Summit video
19 April 2012, TED Blog Video YouTube channel
▶ **Video 46**

Now we are all fired up, how do we make our video creative? How do we get to a point where we are thinking about winning those Cannes Lions and other top awards? If you have a great agency on board this is where you need to give a clear brief and allow them the space to do their best work, or if you are working at a smaller level you can start to guide the process yourself and input thoughts and ideas through the process. Before going further there is one thing that will lead to great creative more than anything else. It is more significant than people and more significant than budget.

It is time.

If you rush creative work it simply will not be as good as it can be. This point is brought to life in no uncertain terms in the following illustration of the effect time pressure has on creativity. Children are given 10 seconds to draw a clock; unsurprisingly all the clocks are basic, and essentially the same. They are literally the first idea that the children had. Yet when the same group is given 10 minutes to complete the task the results are wonderful. Flowers, cats, kites and hugging people are emblazoned on the pages, none of which would have been possible without time. It's a simple thing but whether you are briefing an agency, leading an internal team or burning the midnight oil yourself, time is what you need.

Creativity requires time
4 December 2013, rodgerwerkhoven YouTube channel
▶ **Video 47**

Differentiation vs distinctiveness

Almost all marketing teams focus on what makes them different, hoping that persuading consumers the product is different will increase sales. But small differences won't drive brand growth. In a busy marketing world where opposing brands are also pushing into your prospect's space it is more important to be distinctive. When planning the content in our videos we should be looking to be distinctive in our category. This is covered at length by Byron Sharp in *How Brands Grow*, so it really should be on your reading list.[1]

Just for a moment imagine that you are marketing director of a blender manufacturer, and your product works in a brand new way that is 'different' in the market. You choose to make some mid-funnel 'how to make cakes' content to draw attention to your blender. In this you explain that the blender moves in a particular way, and believe this should make a difference in the market. Is this enough to stand out? Well not really; although the offering is different it is in no way distinctive, and neither is the content you are making. A much more effective approach is to decide to stand out from all the other the blenders in the market space. Can you see where this is leading... yes, you guess it – 'Will it blend?' – the most distinctive blender campaign ever. It's an oldie but a goodie, and there are very few marketing campaigns with their own Wikipedia page.[2] There's a lot to be learned from this creative approach to a product that is in essence just like everyone else's. The videos revolutionized brand exposure for Blendtec and have been driving sales since 2006.

FIGURE 7.1   Blendtec

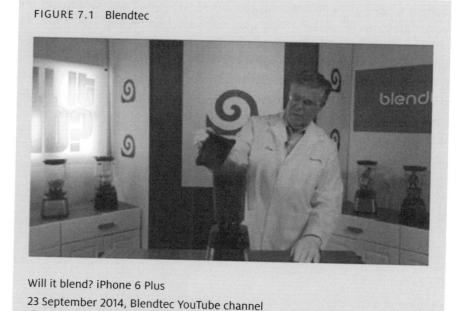

Will it blend? iPhone 6 Plus
23 September 2014, Blendtec YouTube channel
▶ **Video 48**

Let's now look at a more recent example. Bodyform have always had a distinctive voice in the market (literally, as no one cannot forget the 'Whoah, Bodyform… Bodyform for you' that blasted out of every TV). In their 'Wombstories' campaign they revolutionized how periods are discussed in marketing and did a clear sweep of just about every creative awards ceremony there is.

> Bodyform: Wombstories
> 1 July 2020, Bodyform UKYouTube channel
> ▶ **Video 49**

If you want to see a perfect lesson in how a brand's tone of voice develops over the years it's worth watching some of the earlier campaigns that are a reflection not only of marketing, but also of society as a whole.

> Bodyform – whoooa Bodyform for you – UK advert
> 31 December 2007, Nina Perez YouTube channel
> ▶ **Video 50**

Finally, let's take a look at what can happen when you simply make content that is just like everyone else's. It's a trap that many brands fall into, especially when they are using archive to tell their story. Now, it is possible to tell very distinctive brand stories with archive, but you can easily end up with something very bland. When I have a client that is in danger of doing just that I show them the video below, which typifies every generic corporate video ever!

> This is a generic brand video, by Dissolve
> 21 March 2014, Dissolve YouTube channel
> ▶ **Video 51**

So, take from this that great content is distinctive and does more than just offer an explanation of why you have a slightly different product.

Helping your external agency deliver more creative content

Developing a great relationship with your external agency can be massively rewarding for everyone involved and will lead to far better creative output. Here are a few things that will help you get the ball rolling:

- Give them time. When you do settle on an agency, try to give them as much time as you can.

- Be focused. If you are not sure of your exact goals or how to reach them, a more strategic agency will be able to guide you through the process.

- Give a clear brief. The brief is the most important thing in the handover from planning to creativity. If you don't have one, you can work with a good agency to develop one together; just remember to build in time to do that.

- Be brave. If you are going to the time and expense of making a video it needs to stand out. I can understand that within brands there is a fear of taking too many risks with marketing materials; often, a great first idea will be watered down by a general consensus across the business to go for something that will not cause offence. But if the creative vision of a film is mediocre it will deliver mediocre results, so this is a time to let your agency stand up for their ideas. There is one film that I show in meetings to underline the need to be brave – the Dissolve film mentioned above. This is a film that reminds us what happens if we stick to the standard corporate line and reach creative by consensus rather than around a brave vision.

- Be open about your budgets. There is always a tendency not to tell prospective agencies what budget is available. There is a thought that agencies will spend up to what's available and not give best value. My position on this is the opposite. Yes, they will offer you a creative solution that goes up to your budget, but they will squeeze every penny they can from it to be competitive. If you don't say what budget you have the agencies have to make loads of assumptions and spend their time coming up with ideas across a huge range of budgets, rather than focusing on the best idea for what you have. Further to this, if you give three agencies the same brief and the same budget you can compare like for like, whereas if they all guess at what budget you might have you will have to compare totally different starting points.

Evaluating creativity

If you're making videos in-house, it is likely that they are creative with a small c; however, those with bigger budgets or at multinationals will be embracing the big C. Whatever your ambitions for the creative side of your output it's useful to be able to critically evaluate the creativity of the work. Here is the process of how to evaluate creative work:

- *Is it competitive, relevant and true?* This is a good question to form a quick sense-check of a proposition. Is the idea unique and does it differentiate you from the competition? Is it something that the target audience want or care about? Is it something true to the brand or product, something that can be substantiated?

- *Does it create impact, communication and persuasion?* This question is good to check the creative execution of the proposition. Will this piece of work stand out and get noticed? Does it get across the message we want to land? Does it say what we want to say in a way that will engage the audience and endear the brand to them?

Creative storytelling

A core part of the creative process is how we will tell the story of your brand, product or service. The more creatively we tell the story, the more distinctive, memorable and powerful it will be. In this section we will explore structures for stories that help you map out what you need to say. We will look at a structure that I developed at Hurricane that's the perfect way to build a brand narrative in film (EFA!) and another structure that's used everywhere, from documentaries to brand films (three-act structure). To show how these work in practice we will be choosing one type of video to talk about as an example. There are hundreds of types of videos to choose from but the one I am going to talk about first is the brand film, as understanding how to make one will give you useful insights across the range of videos you might create. A brand film might be a paid commercial, it might sit on a homepage like a brochure, or it might be the basis of a consumer campaign. It's a video that communicates who you are and what you do rather than a fame-building viral or a social shareable. If you're new to video and are making one film, this is the type that you are most likely to go for. If you're a brand that uses lots of video it's the type that you most certainly have somewhere in the plan.

A structure for brand films: Emotion, Fact, Action!

As we covered earlier in the book, our minds try to make as many decisions as possible with System 1, primarily as it takes the least energy and is quicker than having to consciously think about everything. If a decision is a bit harder, or requires more conscious thought, it gets flagged up to System 2. The easiest course of action at this stage is for System 2 to agree with what its more rudimentary relative has decided. Challenging something, finding out more info, thinking things through and reaching a measured conclusion take mental effort – something our brains like to reserve for the 'big decisions'. This all means that we tend to stick with decisions that have already been made, to avoid the greater effort required to change our mind.

Neuroanatomist Jill Bolte Taylor wrote: 'We live in a world where we are taught from the start that we are thinking creatures that feel. The truth is, we are feeling creatures that think.'[3] This can be illustrated at a personal level by how we choose a new home. If we are honest with ourselves, house purchase boils down to how we feel about the building itself. There are many logical things to consider but somehow these things are more flexible than the like/don't like decision. When I find a house that I love, one that my System 1 brain for whatever reason decides is the one for me, my System 2 brain starts to worry. Is it near enough to the right school? Does the roof need fixing? Is the gas bill too high? To help address these concerns I open up Excel and make a thorough list of pros and cons. But it's all too easy to adjust the weighting I give to issues, so that all I am doing is using the facts to back up a decision that is already made. 'Well, it's OK that it's a long way from the station as I need to walk more', or 'Now we are closer to the shops' are easy ways to adjust weightings. It takes a radical thing, such as a really bad surveyor's report, to put me off a house I really love. A classic case of System 2 sticking to a decision made by System 1.

The same principles apply when creating brand films and marketing campaigns. Once an emotional connection is made and people feel connected to your product, they will look to back this up with facts. That is why the first thing a brand story must do is make an emotional connection with audiences. Then it can move to factual discussions. Finally, an effective film needs to change behaviour; we need the audience to go somewhere or do something. This set of requirements takes us neatly into the first way that we can structure films for brands: Emotion, Fact, Action! (EFA!). Later sections deal with other structures, but for me this is the one that all brand managers should understand. Once you recognize it you will see it everywhere. EFA!

is an awesome structure for many pieces of content, from brand films to corporates, but there are many ways to skin a cat; I wouldn't position this as the only option, just an excellent starting point. It is especially useful for B2B communications or B2C where messages have to be more than simply 'Drink this, it will make you happy.'

Emotion

Effective videos open with an emotional message that is directly linked to the emotional driver of our audience. You planned this out in the previous chapters so you know what messages will resonate. All you have to do now is put that really punchy, emotional message at the start of your film. If you can do it in 10 seconds or less and include people (or something tangible) in the footage, even better.

If it's been a while since you read the section earlier about emotion in video (you may be like me and read books like this in doses over several weeks!) you should start by reminding yourself of the System 1 theory and how emotion affects behaviours with brain chemistry (covered in Chapter 2). You should also look at the planning around personas that you did in Chapter 6. If you want to see how I've written emotion into the opening of a script take a look at the Airbus case study on page 119. When you're up to speed you can crack on, as you've nailed how to grab people's attention at the start of your film!

Fact

If you get the emotional opener of the film right, people will be engaged, will have already bought into your brand, and you're ready to tick off the final System 2 boxes with some facts. When putting any facts or detail into a video you have to be absolutely certain they really need to be there. The 'So what?' test is vital here. If the facts don't directly align to the emotional driver at the start, they have no place in the film.

People living in cities see around 5,000 ads a day, up from 2,000 in the 1990s,[4] and it's getting to the point where people are actively pushing back against messages. Decision fatigue is a well-documented blight of the modern world that causes consumers to make bad decisions and shut out irrelevant messages. People will appreciate a succinct message – without being prescriptive on the duration and quantity of what you say, just remember that doing less will achieve more.

The other thing to bear in mind is at what level you should explain facts. There is always a temptation to fully explain, but is that really necessary? This question really boils down to what type of content it is and where you are in the funnel. At the top of the funnel (when looking to attract attention and grow fame), facts can be merely the acknowledgement that something exists. In the consideration phase, Hub or Help content can go into more detail as people are engaged and actively searching for more information.

DECISION FATIGUE AND THE CONTENT SOUP

Can the modern consumer deal with more content? Can they make more decisions about things? Not really, no. The speed of our decision making rises steadily each year. We make over 200 decisions a day about food alone[5] and our heads are getting tired. Decision fatigue is a psychological term referring to the cognitive implications of having too many choices. This well-documented condition sees a deterioration in decision making when people are faced with an increased number of decisions, or if they have to make decisions for a longer period. Measurable effects of decision fatigue include:

- **Decision paralysis:** This occurs when people have too many choices so they simply avoid making any decisions. For example, a financial brand offering 50 investment and pension funds rather than just five will see a 10 per cent lower participation rate.[6] It's too hard to choose, so we don't.

- **Impulse purchasing:** After a prolonged period of shopping with multiple decisions (for example the weekly supermarket challenge), consumers are more likely to make impulse purchases at the checkout when nudged in the right direction. This is a good or a bad thing, depending on which side of the till you are standing on.

- **Reduced ability to trade off:** Binary choices take less energy than calculating a balance of positive and negative effects. The more factors involved in decision making, the poorer the decisions.

- **Regret and anticipated regret:** Even if we make a choice, we're less satisfied with it than if we had fewer options to choose from. We worry that we've not made the right choice, which means we don't feel as good about the thing we have. We can now have one of thousands of pairs of jeans but we're not satisfied we have the perfect pair, so do we really like these jeans after all?

There is an excellent TED Talk on 'the paradox of choice' by psychologist Barry Schwarz, in which he says:

> Findings from three experimental studies challenge the implicit assumption that having more choices is necessarily more intrinsically motivating than having fewer… people are more likely to purchase gourmet jams or chocolates or to undertake optional class essay assignments when offered a limited array of six choices rather than 24 or 30 choices.[6]

The ways for brands to combat decision fatigue include:

- Keep messages simple, have single goals and stick to them.
- Say one thing at time and stick to the principal message.
- Focus on timings, as you need to talk to your audience when they have a willingness to engage.
- Say less to achieve more.

Action!

So, we've made an emotional connection and given the viewer some (although not too many) facts. Now it's time to get our audience to do something, because if your video doesn't change behaviour and attitudes or drive action it's just a futile exercise. The final part of the EFA! structure is Action! and it will be very closely tied to the KPIs of the campaign. An Awareness film at the top of the funnel might have KPIs about driving traffic to the site, in which case the Action! should be a measurable link (eg Bitly) to a homepage or inner page. If it's a piece of Hub content designed to aid Consideration goals, the Action! driver could be to ask people to subscribe. Finally, if it's a piece of content at the end phase of the funnel, when you are looking to deliver cold hard sales, the Action! will be a simple 'click to buy now' type message.

With your KPIs clearly in mind it's time to think about how we drive viewers to Action! and get them to take action.

ACTION! WITH EMOTION

The first and most obvious method of driving Action! is to revisit the emotional message from the start of the film. If it got people hooked, then it should be strong enough to get people to do things. For example, a film based on 'Make your life simpler' would revisit this with a straightforward message of 'Start making your life simpler today – click here'.

ACTION! WITH TECHNOLOGY

Technology can give the end of a film a little bit more bite; an interactive link, a hyperlink to somewhere else or a second film that auto-plays are all ways that technology can drive people to take action at the end of your films. These techniques are especially good at converting people to sales or keeping them within the media player environment to engage further. For me, the most exciting technologies ask viewers to click for more, click to buy, or click to register interest. To really work, these platforms should be overlaid onto the video itself. I cover this further in Chapter 8 when we discuss activation.

ACTION! WITH A QUESTION

An excellent way to encourage further actions is to pose a question to the viewer. This immediately drives them to think more and engage.

At this point it's also worth noticing how Chipotle motivates people to take further action with a direct link to download a game featuring the same characters – thus building engagement and consideration by using the Action! principle from EFA!.

> The scarecrow
> 20 March 2017, Sampics Animation YouTube channel
> **Video 53**

Practical steps to building your EFA! structure

With your new understanding of the EFA! structure in single pieces of content it's time to give you the practical tools you need to start building your award-winning epic. I've been writing narratives for TV and video for many years and over that time I've honed down the 'messaging session' where we plan out the structure of a film. In this section I'm going to take you through the process step-by-step.

The things you'll need to build an EFA! structure with your team (or yourself) are:

- the biggest Post-It notes you can find (don't use the cheap ones as they never stick);
- all the information that you came up with in the planning stages, such as key points of difference, emotional reasons that people use, how you want to differentiate yourselves, etc;

- as many stakeholders as you can persuade to give up an hour of their time – this is key, as if you can get people to agree as you go along it will save an awful lot of time;
- one marker pen;
- one wall!

The first thing I do when starting a messaging session is to go over what we already know. There is no point getting halfway through the session and having a debate break out over what the actual point of the film is. This is a position I've been in many times with large corporates, so I now proactively get it all sorted at the start.

This first summary should cover:

- goals of the film;
- audience of the film;
- strategic approach to the campaign;
- how success will be measured.

Normally this is where things get interesting early on. It's likely that in a room of stakeholders there will be many different agendas. The sales team will want to bang on about big-ticket items, the CEO might want to drive future vision of what might be, and individual department heads will probably want their own messages to be bigger than anyone else's. Your job as the head of the session is to help everyone get to the key goal. I normally do this with a simple idea – let's say one thing, say it really well and get a successful film. If you can write the goal of the film up on a wall it's even better, as later on in the session you can just point at it to bring people back to focus.

With everyone on the same page it's time to open those Post-Its. I always put three up along the top of the wall with big lettering saying Emotion, Fact, Action! These will form the overarching structure of the film and we will run through how to fill in all the bits you need right now.

The next thing is to go around the room and ask all the stakeholders what emotional motivators customers might choose for your brand or this particular service. You're looking for the genuine reason that customers will care about your brand. This is in effect 'The Big Idea'. Do you represent freedom? Are you the brand of happiness? Will you make the world a better place? If you need guidance on this, you can look again at the planning part of this section. Be as creative here as you can be, digging down under the skin of the ideas until you get to the real nub of what the motivators might

FIGURE 7.2   Post-It planning

be. Keep asking 'So what?' until someone comes up with an insight that is fresh and accurate. At this point you are in full-on creative brainstorming mode, and getting it right is a skill that has taken up many books on its own. In essence, though, no ideas are a bad idea, and everyone is encouraged to put things forward. I would normally start the session by laying down ground rules that no one should close any ideas down and even the wildest ideas are open to discussion.

All the answers you get go onto a sticky note and are added underneath the 'Emotion' label. This creates a huddle of possible key messages to open with. You may find that people naturally start throwing features and benefits of the product into the mix. These can also go on a sticky note but keep them to one side for now. You will need them at the next stage.

When you've drained all the possible reasons why people may emotionally engage with you it's time to move on to the second topic. Ask people in the room (or just yourself if you're a solo creative ninja) what facts you have to make people buy. This might be customer services, particular features, customer testimonials and so on. These all go on the wall under Facts, and to this are added any features that popped up earlier in the session that you were keeping to one side.

FIGURE 7.3   Post-It planning: Emotion

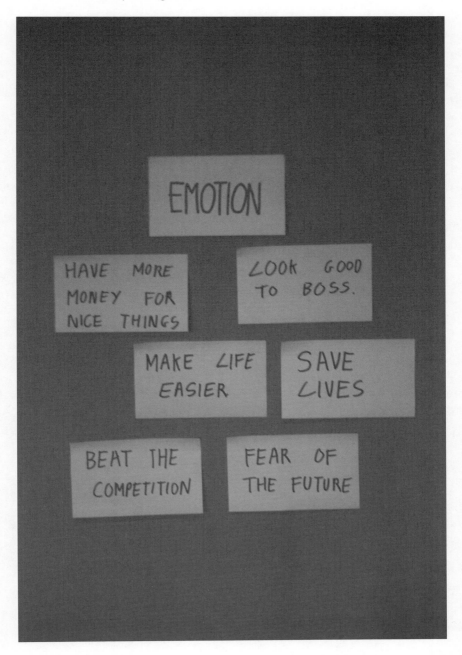

The final part in this data collection phase is to ask what you want to viewers to do next (the Action! message). Think carefully about this. Where are they watching the video? Do you want them to find out more or to get in touch?

FIGURE 7.4 Post-It planning: Fact

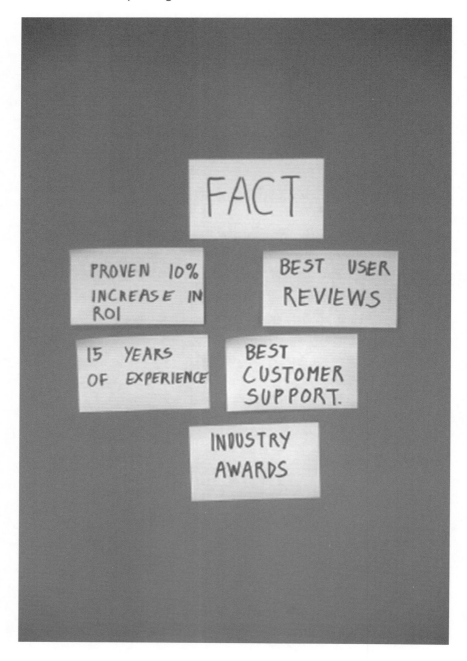

These things should directly link to the KPIs you set in the planning stages and will directly relate to what part of the funnel you are in. For example, if this is an awareness-raising campaign it might only be a short ad and you

FIGURE 7.5   Post-It planning: Action!

want to drive traffic to your content hub. If this is Hub content already you may want to drive subscriptions. Finally, if it is the Action! phase you may be looking for a direct link to a purchase page.

By this point you will have a very messy wall covered in Post-Its. Before doing anything else, take some photos of it for posterity. The illustration I've used in Figure 7.6 is a simple version, but you could easily end up with 20 messages under each section.

This is the point where the job really begins, and you face the uphill task of reducing your board to a 30- or 60-second film. You do, however, have one very easy and powerful tool at your disposal. I was first taught this simple technique on a TV director's course at the BBC's London Elstree studios. It is the power of 'So what?' and it's the best narrative advice I've ever had.

When I run messaging sessions, I read out each Post-It in turn and ask the room... 'So what?' If the answer doesn't stack up or isn't related to the central focus of the film (that you wrote on the board earlier for all to see), it gets binned. Within a short amount of time, you will be down to core messages. As the number of notes gets smaller you can start combining some thoughts or becoming increasingly challenging with your 'So what?' until

FIGURE 7.6   Collated messages for EFA!

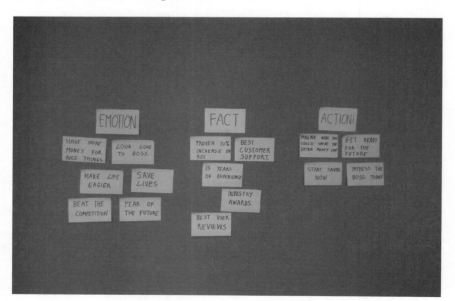

FIGURE 7.7   Final EFA!

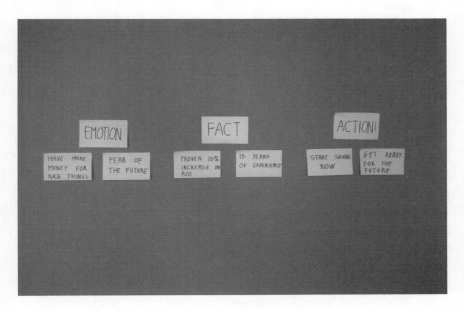

you have a core set of themes. You will probably get to a single emotional reason to engage pretty quickly, but typically brand and marketing teams have more issues stripping back the number of facts in the middle section. I believe that you should have as few facts in a video as possible to tell the story. Your website, white papers, brochures and Help content are the places for detail – not brand films, adverts or big Hub content. The simple rule here is 'Say less, do more.' If the idea cannot be defended well enough, it comes off the wall.

At this point you can start putting the sticky notes into the order in which they will run. Play around with this and move the order around until you have something that flows. That is where the real joy of working in this way comes to life as you can restructure the narrative order with ease.

And there you have it, your brand story condensed into the EFA! structure using a highly effective messaging session... now you can start getting creative.

CASE STUDY
EFA! Airbus Defence and Space

I've made countless films using the EFA! structure and I've been thinking about which one to share. I've plumped for this campaign created for Airbus Defence and Space. The main reason for using this one is that it is so closely tied to the process above.

The project started when we were approached by Astrium Services (who then went on to become part of Airbus Defence and Space), who had a challenge for us. The company operated multiple satellites flying around the globe providing ultra-high-definition pictures of the Earth from space. This imagery was sold to a massive range of markets, from civil construction to farming and defence. The industry was tech heavy, and all marketing typically focused on how many pixels the pictures would be and how up-to-date the images were. The marketing team wanted us to help them connect with audiences in a new way and change the conversation from pixels, specifications and images of satellites to emotions. They wanted to move from product messaging to brand messaging.

The messaging session we ran with them worked exactly as we outlined earlier. First, we discussed emotional motivators that people could relate to and during this conversation the creative director here at Hurricane, John Lanyon, came to the insight that people did not buy the technology – they did not even buy the data. What they really bought was the amazing things they could do with the data when it was in their hands. With the data they could feed people, protect the environment and keep countries safe. This was the governing idea of the film and it would inform the opening narrative of the Emotion section as well as graphical elements throughout.

The next part of the process was to work with the team to go through all the key facts that had to be put forward in the Fact section. During the messaging session dozens of key differentiators were put on sticky notes and discussed. In the end these were whittled down to the track record of the company, the experience of the people that worked there and how many people used the service. This proved credibility but didn't get into product-level specifics.

Finally, we moved to planning the Action! section. The goal for the project was brand awareness and to get coverage in the print and online press. Therefore, we wanted to end on an emotional high that was bold and clear in the marketplace and we revisited the theme of looking to a brighter future that was used in the opening sections.

The film was activated through traditional and online PR, as well as with paid placements. You can see the whole film at this link:

Airbus defence and space
Hurricane Media
 Video 54

Three-act structure: an alternative to EFA!

The EFA! structure is well suited to brand films of all types, but it is not the only way to do things. Those with a keen interest in storytelling will know that there is a universal story structure that's been with us since the dawn of humanity. It has been honed over millions of years of stories told around campfires and is central to how we understand the world. Gustav Freytag developed a model 150 years ago known as the dramatic arc, and identified the constituent parts of drama as exposition, rising action, climax, falling action and dénouement (resolution).

Freytag's arc is perfect for the structures of plays or dramas but is slight overkill for a short-form film; however, his governing principles of a set-up, followed by change, leading to a resolution are sound for every story. If we simplify things a little, we get a great way to tell compelling brand narrative and it can be seen in a wide range of marketing videos. At its simplest, the three-act structure that leads the viewer from one place to another is best illustrated by the idea of 'Into the woods':

Act 1: Our characters have a happy life, and they don't change what they do. They certainly don't go 'into the woods' as the woods are dangerous.

Act 2: Something in the dynamic changes; the characters find out something or a new person arrives. Things have to change for the character to survive/win/be happy. Thus, the characters do in fact go 'into the woods'.

Act 3: Having taken the leap, things are different. They might be better for some people and worse for others, but they are different.

This idea is expanded incredibly well by the British TV writer John Yorke in his book *Into the Woods: How stories work and why we tell them*.[7] And the three-part structure can be adapted very simply to work for brands like this:

Act 1: There is a way of doing things and it's not great.

Act 2: There is a new way of doing things and you should do it (ie you need to go into the woods).

Act 3: When you take the leap and do it the new way your life will be better.

This narrative was used really well by Dollar Shave Club in their now infamous launch video:

Act 1: You currently use razors that are expensive and unnecessary.

Act 2: Our blades are better, and we give people jobs, so take a trip into the woods and give it a try.

Act 3: When you go for it your life will be better.

DollarShaveClub.com – our blades are f***ing great
6 March 2012, Dollar Shave Club YouTube channel
▶ **Video 55**

Another brand film that uses this three-act structure is a wonderful animation for Chipotle Mexican Grill:

Act 1: A young man looks around him and sees that food is being produced wrongly; it's not fresh and it's falsely advertised. This is a sad place to live.

Act 2: He finds a healthy natural red pepper in a field and realizes that he can do food better – so he 'heads into the woods' and sets up on his own food store.

Act 3: His food is wonderful, it's hugely popular and it makes everyone's life better. The animation even goes as far as giving his shop the name 'Cultivate a better world'.

The scarecrow
20 March 2017, Sampics Animation YouTube channel
▶ **Video 56**

The nitty gritty of video production

You've got a totally cool creative vision, and you know how you are going to tell your story. Now you need to make the actual video. Now we get into the detail of video production, so here's the top line of what you need to know.

I've put the flow of video production into three sections reflecting the three overarching disciplines and briefly described each step. If you work with an agency, they will do much of this for you, but if you are building an in-house team it's a good place to start. I've had 20 years to hone this process and have made plenty of mistakes along the way that you can learn from.

Stage 1: pre-production workflow

1 *Creative briefing.* It all starts with a good brief. Articulate the plans you have and give goals and parameters. Then the team coming up with ideas for the film can do their best work. If you can include what total budget you have for this then all the better. A bad brief is a bad film.

2 *Initial creative concepts.* Think of as many ideas as you can that hit the brief, give it time and be open to new thinking. At this point you should stick to 'What if we interviewed a key opinion leader?' or 'What about an animation that explains how it works?' rather than exact details.

3 *Review of concepts.* From a selection of creative directions, choose the one that you think will hit the brief best.

4 *Creative planning.* At this point you know the brief and what the overall idea is. Now it can be worked up into scripts, interview questions, storyboards – really any collateral that you need to get the idea signed off by the relevant people before production.

5 *Review of creative and amends.* Cast a supportive but critical eye over the final creative and make amends to get it to a place you are happy with. Keep it to one or two rounds of amends or else you will never get the project off the ground.

6 *Sign off.* This is a key part of the process if you want to be efficient. Get the idea signed off by all stakeholders before you make it. Reshooting something because the CEO didn't know what it was going to be is embarrassing and expensive for everyone. With everyone on the same page you can move into production

Stage 2: production workflow

1 *Filming.* Rushes creation (unedited footage in the same format as it was created in is called 'rushes').

2 *Graphics*/design work.

Stage 3: post-production workflow

1 *Edit.* Film and graphics assembly.

2 *First cut.* A rough assembly of the narrative with covering shots, not overly polished, as it is likely to be changed in the upcoming review process. This should be made for the primary activation channel of your campaign. This is normally YouTube, as it is going to be a longer version than the edits for other channels and it is easier to make films shorter later than it is to make them longer.

3 *Review.* Does the first cut answer the brief? How can it be improved? Start to think about how it will be recut for other platforms. A key thing to do at

this stage is to ensure that all featured people, music and footage have the correct release forms, and permissions in place. If an interviewee has not signed a release form it is easiest to drop them now, or to approach them for a retrospectively filled-in form, than to find out when the film is finalized.

4 *Amends.* Structural amends to bring the film in line with previous review. At this stage the film is polished further – the edit team should be happy that the version that moves on to the next round is good enough to be the final one.

5 *Review.* This time focusing on polish rather than structure. For example, are all nametags correct? This is the version that would normally be shared with less direct stakeholders who need to sign off. But brief them beforehand on what to expect so they don't start pulling things apart.

6 *Amends final and play-out.* Any final amends are done at this point and the film is exported to the format of choice.

7 *Final check and upload to the OVP of choice.* Make sure the file is watched carefully for glitches or inaccuracies before it is uploaded.

8 *Optimize descriptions, tags and titles.* See page 126 for tips on this.

Stage 4: delivery

1 *Recut film* for other versions and platforms based on the final signed-off version.

2 *Prepare final films* to move into the activation and testing phase, described in Chapter 8.

3 *Paperwork* (release forms, archive notes and contracts).

4 *Project review.* Did the creative answer the brief, and what lessons can be used on the next production?

5 *Feedback.* Give feedback insights to teams on review and next steps... and don't forget the praise!

Summary

You're all done, the film is made! Good work. Let's just look back at the key points we're learned:

- Allow yourself time to be creative.
- Focus on developing something distinctive.

- Story is the vehicle through which we emotionally engage with an audience, communicate our message and excite them to change their behaviour.

- Stories come in many different forms but the most common for brands can be divided into 'Emotion, Fact, Action!' and 'three-part structure'.

- Video production runs in four stages: pre production, production, post-production and delivery.

References

1   Byron Sharp
    How Brands Grow: What marketers don't know
    11 March 2010
    Oxford
2   Wikipedia
    Will it blend?
    https://en.wikipedia.org/wiki/Will_It_Blend%3F (archived at https://perma.cc/
    EJ8U-VCYM)
3   Jill Bolte Taylor
    October 2006
    My Stroke of Insight: A brain scientist's personal journey
    Penguin Books
4   Louise Story
    15 January 2015
    Anywhere the eye can see, it's likely to see an ad
    New York Times
    www.nytimes.com/2007/01/15/business/media/15everywhere.
    html?pagewanted=all&_r=0 (archived at https://perma.cc/8H7A-T6B2)
5   Brian Wansink and Jeffery Sobal
    1 January 2007
    Mindless eating: the 200 daily food decisions we overlook
    Environment and Behaviour
    http://journals.sagepub.com/doi/abs/10.1177/0013916506295573 (archived at
    https://perma.cc/W5C3-MREG)
6   Barry Schwarz
    July 2005
    The paradox of choice
    Ted Talks
    ▶ **Video 52** (archived at https://perma.cc/5H6Q-W9Q8)

7 John Yorke
2014
Into the Woods: How stories work and why we tell them?
Penguin

Further reading

Sheena S Iyengar and Mark R Lepper
2000
When choice is demotivating: can one desire too much of a good thing?
Journal of Personal and Social Psychology
www.researchgate.net/publication/12189991_When_Choice_is_Demotivating_
Can_One_Desire_Too_Much_of_a_Good_Thing (archived at https://perma.cc/
JXW9-E625)
Statisticbrain
Attention span statistics
Statistics Brain Research Institute
www.statisticbrain.com/attention-span-statistics (archived at https://perma.cc/
QU83-ESJW)
Unbounce
Decision fatigue: definition
https://unbounce.com/conversion-glossary/definition/decision-fatigue/ (archived at
https://perma.cc/5C66-7V5S)

08

Step 3: activation

We've planned our campaign, made a great story and positioned it to reflect the identity of both the brand and its audience. The key final step to a successful video is to ensure people actually see it, through a broad-ranging activity known as 'activation'.

What is activation in terms of video marketing? Quite simply it's the activities undertaken to ensure the video is seen, talked about and shared; and it can be done in many ways. Your approach to activation will change depending on which part of the sales funnel the film is looking to affect, as differences in how the video is activated will impact different areas of the funnel in different ways. If you're looking to raise awareness with a 'fame' campaign, activation will be heavily focused on pushing into the social feeds of new people. If the video is designed to keep in touch with people and ensure they maintain a connection to the brand, activation will be more focused on existing social channels. Having a clear idea of goals and KPIs will give better results (refer back to Chapter 6 on planning if you need a refresher). Key to successful activation is measurement, as with no solid markers of progress you cannot effectively test and grow. There are many brands that have wasted considerable budgets on things that haven't worked, and without the metrics to notice. In this chapter we will look at how to activate and measure the success of a single film. In Section Four we build on these principles and relate them to multi-video campaigns and testing.

Video activation can be grouped into four types (owned, earned, paid and viral), which we will look at further later. However, before choosing one of these approaches and spending the entire year's marketing budget buying paid ads on Google Display Network there is something that needs to get done. It's something really easy that many brands don't get right, and indeed if you don't do it, it is tantamount to throwing your money down the drain. Before unleashing your video on the world, it must be optimized for search.

Stop! Optimize

Before you go any further with launching your video there are a few steps to make sure it gets the best start in life. A well-optimized film has a greater chance of picking up organic traffic, will be watched by more people, will have a lower bounce rate and will drive more traffic to where you want it! However, as anyone who works in SEO will tell you, organic search success doesn't happen without effort, so let's look at the steps you will need to take before campaign launch.

Titles and keywords

Having titles and keywords that are as attractive and searchable as possible seems like an obvious goal. However, a huge number of brands miss out on this simple opportunity to improve ROI. Very often, someone in the marketing team uploads a video made by an external production company or internal team and jumps straight to the activation phase. If this same person followed the simple steps below, the brand would be a little closer to its end goals.

Titles should do two things: attract viewers to watch and provide searchable words that will appear on search engine results pages (SERPs). The basic principle here is to go for the shortest title you can that is descriptive, engaging and directly relevant to the video. 'Gardening tips: growing roses in cold gardens' is going to be a lot more successful than 'rose food brand_ edit 1'. I'm purposely keeping my tips platform agnostic so they will work across the board, but as YouTube is such a substantial player it's good to note one thing: every YouTube video gets its own page and unique URL with meta tags that are drawn from the descriptions added when it's uploaded. The title of the video is used as the title tag, the description is used as the meta description, and the YouTube tags are used as the meta keywords. It's because of this that what you add at the uploading stage can vastly affect your video's performance.

The permitted length for titles varies across video platforms but I'd recommend keeping it under 70 characters (including spaces). YouTube will offer the chance to put in up to 100 characters and Facebook will offer even more but these will be truncated in most search results so it's best to avoid this. Shorter still is even better; data suggest that titles perform best on YouTube if they are between 41 and 70 characters and on Facebook if they are under 40. This data is underlined by the fact that videos with titles over 70 characters perform 37 per cent worse than their shorter-titled cousins.[1]

When looking for keywords to include I'd recommend Google's keyword planner. Although not specifically for video it adds lots of insights: ▶ **Video 57**.

It's also worth looking at titles that might deliver results with videos at the top rather than webpages. Some phrases are more likely to suggest a video would be helpful and so search results will reflect that. Action words along with phrases that suggest needing to see something moving are more likely to have video results listed above text results. The phrase 'dancing shoes' comes up with webpages, but 'dancing moves' comes up with videos.

If you're working on help content, look at Storybase.com, which takes keywords and finds the long-form questions around them that people are searching for. For example, when inputting 'alloy wheel', the tool shows 59 questions that are often searched for on the topic. Number one is 'What is an alloy wheel?' and number two is 'Fix alloy wheel curb rash'. Both of these can help you come up with a useful title.

When constructing titles, don't feel afraid to use colons or dashes. These will help you get more keywords in and help people to see instantly what the video is about – for example 'Car maintenance: fixing alloy wheel curb rash'. It's worth noting that most search engines prioritize content that will help their users to find answers so it would seem logical to use the actual questions they are looking for, but viewers themselves are not keen on videos that open with questions in their title. On average, Facebook videos perform 22 per cent worse when they began with a question word and YouTube videos perform around 24 per cent worse.[1] The key, therefore, is to answer questions without using opening phrases like 'What is' and 'How to'. The example above should not read 'How to fix wheel curb rash' as the more simple 'Fixing wheel curb rash' will give better view rates anyway. Words that are likely to push you up the SERPs are things like 'fix', 'tutorial', 'review' and 'testimonial'. It's also worth noting that if you are looking to pick up traffic from non-video-based search engines it can be beneficial to put 'video' in the title. For example, 'Video on how to fix alloy wheel rash'.

Descriptions

The description of your video is just as significant in search as the title, although you have more space to play with. Most search engine spiders can trawl descriptions, and snippets of it will often appear in SERP results, giving an opportunity to encourage people to watch. Descriptions should be as engaging as possible and directly allude to the content of the film. Descriptions that go off topic are not going to do you any favours and are more of an irritation to viewers than anything else. A common crime is text copied and pasted from websites that are 'brand general', not 'content specific'. Include the keywords that you have targeted in the title within the description; once is OK but if you can make it work linguistically then a second time wouldn't hurt. As your description will be seen in many places, but you have no control over how much of the text will be displayed, you should write a description in a similar manner to how a journalist writes an article. Make the opening section tell the whole story and build on this with detail later on. In journalism this is done so that when a pressured editor has to lop the bottom off a story to fill a specific space, it will still convey the key information. In the same way, YouTube gives you 5,000 characters to play with but it's best to get the story told in the first 150 as these are the ones that appear as snippets in search. With that done you can go into greater detail.

There is always a debate about whether or not to include links to a brand URL near the top of a description. For me it boils down to the objective of the film. If you're looking to drive Action parts of the sales funnel you will want to include a direct link to a product right at the top as that is the point of the film. If, however, the film is designed to drive engagement and keep people watching more, a link can actually distract from the point of the exercise. In these cases, the link itself just wastes a vast chunk of your 150 characters and chases away traffic.

Video thumbnails

Thumbnails are the main visual hook for your content showing up in search results, across platforms and in related content collections. They're an easy opportunity to attract more viewers and an even easier opportunity to put them off. 90 per cent of the best-performing videos on YouTube have custom thumbnails.[2] Most video platforms will automatically choose a thumbnail for you but the best thing to do is to upload one of your own that is either a screen grab of the video itself or something bespoke made for the purpose.

Here's a rundown of top thumbnail tips:

1 *Faces get more clicks.* People react to people and thumbnails with faces (and, even better, ones that make eye contact) can deliver great click-through rates.

2 *Backgrounds matter.* Bright and primary-coloured images stand out against the white background of YouTube and other platforms. It's a technique being used heavily by YouTubers and other vloggers so you

will want to make sure you don't end up associated with the wrong people, but bright is better.

3 *Text on thumbnails can increase clicks.* You will already have a strong title so you can avoid text-heavy thumbnails, but if you are really trying to up click-ability you can try a three- to four-word phrase. This is really useful in a series where people can choose multiple options. Make sure you use a heavy outline or contrasting colour to stand out from the image behind it.

4 *Put watermarks on thumbnails.* A watermark or consistent logo will identify a series of content. Look at *Vice* magazine on YouTube to see how they use watermarks and faces to draw attention: (▶) **Video 58**.

5 *Let the picture tell the story.* If you're selecting an image from the video or making one from scratch, it's worth using an image that tells the story of the video. A thumbnail that visually shows the audience what the video is about (eg a woman holding a cake) will work better than a thumbnail that just shows the audience what happens in the video (eg a hand pouring sugar into a pan).

6 *Avoid the bottom right corner on thumbnails.* Many video platforms will put player controls, viewing figures and function buttons in a corner, and that's normally the bottom right. It's also the corner where a western language viewer will look last, due to reading top left to bottom right. So, it's best to avoid it as a place to put anything important. On this note it's best to avoid any substantial text along the bottom as pop-up players will cover it. Eye tracking has shown that people scan websites and videos in an F-pattern and thumbnails are no different.[3]

7 *Deliver the image in the correct format.* An easy win, this one. Make sure you upload the right image type. You can always find the correct specs with a quick online search.

Get a style. Reflect your brand and keep style consistent across each video on that platform. You can push the brand guidelines on this one as you have a lot of considerations. Yes, keep it on brand, but try not to lose sight of the tips above. One channel that has got this right on YouTube is Kurzgesagt: (▶) **Video 59**.

8 *Don't get sucked into a strategy of 'bait and switch'* (the action of advertising goods of a certain standard with the intention of substituting inferior or more expensive goods). It might not be as illegal in the realms of video as it is in real advertising, but not being served the content that's alluded to is massively annoying for viewers and will ruin a good reputation.

With the imagery of the page nailed, it's time to move onto text elements of the video and the digital home it lives in. An easy win in this area is to add closed captions (CC), which are the subtitles that appear on videos. These are sometimes for different languages but increasingly they are for access to those who are hard of hearing and for viewers who cannot, or do not want to, have the audio on. Closed captions are not like open captions as they can be turned on and off as required by the viewers. The bonus of closed captions is that they are searchable by search engines. This doesn't happen automatically as the auto-capturing software tends to come up with gibberish. But with a little legwork you can submit a script manually that will be indexed and therefore searched. A study, this time by Facebook, showed that captioning video ads increased total video view time by an average of 12 per cent.[3]

TEST AND REPEAT

When working with thumbnails, it's really worth conducting tests. Currently in YouTube there is no direct thumbnail analytics data available, but you can piece together results from other metrics. In Google's TrueView advertising platform, it's possible to see the relative click-through rate for all the videos that are uploaded. If you have time to upload the same video twice with different thumbnails you can compare them, or you can look at a number of similar videos that you have uploaded to see what works best. If you're not using AdWords or are on non-Google platforms keep your eyes on 'views per unique visit' and 'views from subscribers' as indicators of how clickable thumbnails are. You can always switch out thumbnails after a short while and see what effect it has on click rates. Video marketing platforms like TwentyThree and Vidyard actually have built-in functionality that allows you to test which thumbnails are performing best.

The main places you will be adding closed captions will be YouTube and Facebook, so below are some links for the most up-to-date advice on how to do it on those platforms:

YouTube best practice: ▶ **Video 60**

Facebook best practice: ▶ **Video 61**

Interactivity

Interactivity is a key technique for driving behaviour during and after a video. Levels of possible interactivity vary across online video platforms but almost all platforms now offer something, from the call to action screens on Vimeo, through YouTube annotations, to the advanced functions of paid players like Wirewax, but for now it's worth noting that when looking to optimize videos, adding this extra layer can deliver real and measurable results. If your KPIs are hard metrics such as email addresses for lead generation, this can be a vital tool for keeping the numbers people happy.

Media types: owned, paid, earned and viral

With your video nicely optimized, we can start to activate it into the world, and we can introduce the four methods of activation:

- *Owned views:* any views that occur on marketing or social media channels that your brand created and that you have direct control over.
- *Earned views:* views that come about because you have encouraged people to speak about and share your video.
- *Paid views:* any views on media that are external to your brand that you have paid to drive traffic and awareness.
- *Viral views:* views that come from the sharing of your brand's content. These views theoretically cost you nothing, although you will probably have paid for other types of views to get them shared or paid a bit more in production costs to create content that is intrinsically shareable in the first place.

Owned channels

Owned channels are great for building engagement with your followers, although they won't build your brand's sales long term (as mentioned earlier, you need to look to new audiences for that). For now, let's look at how you maximize the effectiveness of owned channels.

OWNED CHANNEL: EMAIL

Email is still relevant as an owned channel and it is very often the best channel for B2B messaging. If you have a good email platform like Dotmailer or

Hubspot you can think about personalizing emails that send videos to specific recipients. You can serve different content to different sections of your database, but even with a single piece of content it is worth only sending to the right people, as too many emails will put anyone off a brand. If using email, it's vital that you track opens and click-through. If your email system is a bit basic and its tracking metrics are not that rigorous, it is worth using a link shortener like Bitly and giving each targeting group a specific link – that way you can see what is working and who has clicked to watched what.

Emails can have videos attached but I cannot counsel against this strongly enough. You are suddenly at the mercy of firewalls and you will get a load more bounce-backs, especially from corporates. Instead, send embedded links that point through to your player of choice. If you are doing a lot of emails, ask some of your target clients what links they can see most easily. For example, very often YouTube is blocked by corporate firewalls, but Vimeo is not.

Emails should be visually engaging and make it very clear that video is the key point. Don't mix your messages or weaken the focus of the mail by throwing in too many ideas. A big visual play button in an image at the top is the way to go, as viewers will then be looking to engage with more content. And don't forget to make it a title worth clicking in the first place.

Emails will be much more effective if they are personalized. You will have vast amounts of data on your email insights about who has watched and shared topics. Aim to talk on a personal level with email targets using deep user profiling and shared events. This boils down to personalizing your engagement campaign based on user behaviour and attributes and it will massively increase the success of your content.

When viewers do click through from an email, consider where they are going to go. A landing page on your owned channels is a good idea, but if you have a well-stocked media hub that will encourage further viewing it's good to send them there. Whatever you do it should be a smooth process where viewers don't have to figure out what to do; they should get to the content they are expecting in as few clicks as possible. Set the destination video to autoplay if you can.

If you have very sales orientated KPIs then specific calls to action like 'Buy now' or 'Let me find out more' should be surrounding the video when they land on the splash page.

Finally, if you are into email activation and want to hugely increase your performance, I would recommend 'personalized' videos as they are a really powerful tool when talking to people about whom you already have data. I go into more detail on this on page 237.

FIGURE 8.1   Owned, paid, earned and viral views

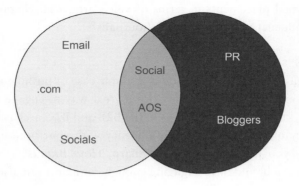

LINKEDIN, FACEBOOK, YOUTUBE AND OTHER SOCIAL PLATFORMS

Social channels will appear again later in this section under paid placements, as they are great at growing audiences with media spend. However, we should consider them in owned as well, simply because you will already have a substantial audience willing to engage in conversation with you. The key to activating an existing network is to tell them about your content in a way that reflects who they are and what you are launching. Keeping things conversational is normally the right way to go.

Consider the time and day when activating channels; a quick dig through your analytics and past campaigns will show when people are most receptive, which will stop you disappearing down their feed without being seen. This is especially true of fluid platforms where you can disappear from view after a few hours, so getting the peak time right is essential.

Once the campaign is in people's feeds make sure you are engaging with comments, re-tweets, likes, etc. Obviously if you have engaged an agency to handle this, they should have this work covered, but if you are doing it yourself make sure that someone is allocated to this task. And whether you do it in-house or externally, make sure that you consider working hours, as launching on a Friday afternoon when everyone in your office goes home will just mean stale interactions on Monday morning.

Earned

Earned activation can be an effective way of delivering KPIs and is similar in many ways to old-school PR. It gets its name as brands put effort into persuading others to talk about your content. By opening conversations with others, you earn mentions, good words and coverage. The three main areas of earned placements in terms of video are social channels, blogger outreach (influencers) and digital PR (journalists).

EARNED ADS: SOCIAL CHANNELS

This is the easiest one to action and is a simple case of pushing new content out to your existing social channels. It's a great way to engage with people that already know you and it works in the B2B and B2C arenas. It will push up frequency of contact and people's fluency with your brand; however, it won't make you famous (see Byron Sharp, *How Brands Grow*[4]). If you phrase things right and have engaging enough content it can also lead to the activation of secondary influencers, which is the best way to grow attention exponentially (read more on this later in this chapter).

ACTIVATE YOUR SHARERS

In the distant Wild West of 2010, we all talked about the 90:9:1 ratio. This posited that only 1 per cent of an audience would actively get involved by sharing a brand's posts. 9 per cent would comment and 90 per cent would do nothing. 2010 is a lifetime ago in the world of digital marketing, and technology (including reaction buttons and easy share options) has increased the ratio. But we can still only expect a maximum of 10 per cent of followers at best to get involved[5] and we can call them Super Sharers. If you can find your 10 per cent and motivate them with specific deals or attention you can make a big difference to the speed that a campaign can spread. If you have run a previous campaign, it's worth looking at who shared it and approaching them directly. This is a simple process and there are lots of social listening tools to help you find your super sharers and key influencers. At Hurricane we use Hootsuite but Followerwonk, BuzzSumo, Topsy and Cred are all widely used.

Once you've found eager sharers, approach them with offers, or even better some unique insights or information that makes them feel special. I wouldn't go as far as offering things specifically in return for a mention as this is a grey area and merges with paid advertising. It's best for the authenticity of your brand that they simply know about what you are up to and choose to share it.

I cannot say it enough but put a system in place to track all of this activity so you can see what works and then get it even better next time.

EARNED ADS: INFLUENCER OUTREACH

Enlisting a connected audience to share your content is fine, but what about getting in front of new people? Clearly the best form of new business is that which comes through recommendations. A thumbs-up from the right blogger or publication can make a huge impact to KPIs. If you have sufficient budget, you will probably be bringing in a PR agency or specialist video marketing company at this stage. They will work with you to identify targets and run the outreach work. However, if budgets are tight or you want to be actively involved in the process there are a number of things you can do.

Let's first look at how we can harness the power of influencers in a target market to push viewing figures. Not to be confused with straight influencer marketing, we are talking here simply about harnessing relationships with influencers to directly promote your video. For me there are three types of influencers: profile influencers, working influencers and micro influencers.

Profile influencers are effectively celebrity endorsement machines, and the stars behind them are making big money.[6] A quick search for 'YouTube star earnings' brings up some huge earning figures. In 2016 the top earner on YouTube was PewDiePie, who earned over $15 million by talking to his 50 million fans about gaming. He is the first person to ever reach 10 billion YouTube views and was named one of *Time* magazine's most influential people that year. If your video is designed to be broadcast to a mass audience and you need a heavyweight influencer, you're unlikely to avoid a substantial investment. However, if influencers are the way you want to go, you don't need the massive celebrities to make an impact. It is often better to look at working influencers, who allow a more targeted spend.

Working influencers are people who are experts in their field, carry great authority but possibly don't consider themselves to even be an influencer. They would certainly see themselves as being a long way from a vlogger star. If you're broadcasting to a niche or micro-niche audience, it's very possible that working influencers will promote content to their audience simply because it's relevant. This is especially true if working with specific health-care issues, hobbies or skills. If you're looking to leverage the credentials and connections of these people, it has to be genuinely useful content, though; it is highly unlikely that a straight commercial piece will gain much traction. Use social media listening tools as mentioned earlier or the influencer tools in this chapter to identify the right people for your brand.

At the opposite end of the scale to profile influencers are micro influencers. These are well worth considering if you have tight budgets and/or products that work to very niche audiences. How you define a micro influencer depends on the size of your target market, but somewhere between 10,000 and 100,000 followers is a good measure. If you find the right person that has a small number of highly engaged fans, and you can offer really relevant content, you stand a good chance of getting support for your video.

Think back to the identity part of your planning and it will give you a good insight into the kind of people that might be helpful.

THE SECOND-WAVE INFLUENCER

To add a further level of complexity to this landscape we can add the phenomenon of second-wave influencers. These are viewers who share content received from other influencers and once activated they are a key motivator of videos going viral. I like to illustrate this principle in terms of cults. The most important person in launching a cult is not the founder but the second person to get involved. Until the first person has a follower, they are just a crackpot with an idea. It is the validation conveyed by a follower that elevates the cult leader to the status of someone worth watching.

In tests conducted by Ogilvy for Twitter,[7] it was found that only 20 per cent of videos motivated a second wave influencer but of these, 90 per cent were successful (with success being top percentile for engagement and sharing). So, how do we get this powerful person on our side? The same study showed that second wavers are driven by the desire to be part of the discussion, to be seen to be topical and to initialize discussion. Secondary influencers want to add their own point of view, with 60 per cent agreeing that this is a reason to share content – a percentage that jumps to 77 per cent among the most influential users. The key to activate this group is to encourage comments and discussions that give them a space in which to get involved.

If you fancy a break and want to see the second-wave influencer principle in action (albeit not with a cult) take a look at this lovely, but somewhat shaky, video from the Sasquatch music festival. The video follows a would-be influencer dancing on the side of a hill. To begin with he is just an oddity to be laughed at, but as soon as someone joins him (at 21 seconds in) it snowballs into a full party. Although everyone can watch the influencer dancing, it's the secondary influencer that drives mainstream acceptance. Just skip ahead to halfway through the video to see what they can do.

Sasquatch music festival 2009 – guy starts dance party
27 May 2009, dkellerm YouTube channel
 Video 62

TACTICS FOR DRIVING ENGAGEMENT OF SECOND-WAVE
INFLUENCERS

Research by Ogilvy and Twitter has highlighted some useful points when
looking to activate second-wave influencers:[8]

- Encourage active involvement in a conversation; think beyond a view and a
  share.
- Understand the network potential of influencers and their ability to drive a
  second wave.
- Appeal to the motivations of influential people with large audiences who are
  likely to become secondary sharers.
- Utilize relatable moments with time-specific content that make second
  wavers feel part of the conversation.
- Make content easy to discover and don't underestimate the power of social
  news feeds.

TOOLS TO IDENTIFY PRIMARY AND SECONDARY INFLUENCERS

There are a number of online tools to help you find influencers, and although
they do tend to be heavy on the profile influencers you can still use many of
them to find working and micro influencers. The tools break down into a
variety of types: influencer networks that bring a preselected choice together
(much like a talent agency), platform-specific search tools, marketplaces
that connect both sides of the market, and databases that have extensive
lists of influencers.

Before listing out some of the major online tools that are available to
mine influencers, note that an important tip is to build relationships with
influencers well in advance of your campaign. The reason for this is two-
fold: first, it avoids the panic of having to find someone quickly and second,
they can help you to focus your content into areas that are actually useful
for their audiences. A thoughtful campaign will be a better campaign.

- *BuzzSumo:* buzzsumo.com A subscription-based tool used by a significant
  number of large agencies and brands, BuzzSumo provides insights into
  popular content and the influencers sharing it. A simple search bar at the top
  allows quick input of keywords to search by topic or a specific website to
  find the most popular content. A mass of results will be delivered, and it can
  be heavy on press articles, but a simple sort button on the left allows for

filtering by type including article, infographic, guest posts and interviews. This helps you dig down to find influencers who may be useful. It has a good Facebook Analyser to see what content is trending there.

- *Followerwonk:* followerwonk.com A platform with a specific focus on Twitter analytics, allowing useful insights from its data. The system aims to help brands find and connect with new influencers in their niche.
- *HYPR:* hyprbrands.com Claims to have over 30 per cent of the world's largest brands, agencies and influencer marketing platforms using its data and access to 10 million influencers. It's a large player that is well worth a look.
- *Scrunch:* scrunch.com A single platform that allows brands to search over 20 million profiles and 10 billion posts as well as run outreach campaigns.
- *Kred:* www.go.kred Platform with 300,000 members that aims to help marketers identify, prioritize, and engage influencers, based around their Kred Score system.
- *Brandwatch:* www.brandwatch.com This paid social media analytics service is a major player and offers a wide range of interconnected services.
- *Traackr:* www.traackr.com This is another major player in the content marketing arena, used by PR and marketing professionals around the world. The platform offers an influencer search engine, profiles, share of voice reporting, sentiment analysis, trending content and more.
- *Tribe:* www.tribegroup.co An Australia-based self-serve marketplace that connects social media influencers with brands. They classify an influencer as someone with 3,000+ real followers and specialize in Facebook, Instagram and Twitter.

As mentioned earlier, it's likely that larger brands will have a PR agency on board to help activate with earned views. It might not be for all campaigns though, and even marketing teams with agencies in place, alongside those with smaller budgets, may find themselves needing a little self-sourced PR activity. Below are some good tools to help get things activated through PR by sending out a press release (wire) and through content marketing platforms.

- *inPowered:* www.inpwrd.com A content amplification platform good for sending releases across a variety of topics. It has an interesting payment model as you only pay for users who spend at least 15 seconds with your content, and you are not charged for bounces. It also offers audience insight, alerts, influencer research, tracking, social analytics and reporting so it can be a useful tool in one box.

- *Prowly:* www.prowly.com Good for sending out multimedia press releases and used by agencies including Grey and Dentsu. A heavyweight bit of kit but worth looking at if you are serious about committing to PR as a way of activating content.

Paid activations

Paid activations are by far the best of way of growing an audience and in turn driving brand growth. It is also the costliest of the activation methods, as you will be competing for attention on the open market and the winner will have deep pockets. All major social platforms offer paid ads, and the best approach is to figure out where to find your audience, how best to talk to them and then use the relevant platforms accordingly. For guidance on this have a look at Chapter 6 for insights around planning.

If you're not lucky enough to have the budget for an agency you can use the following as the basis of your own campaign. If you do have a media or full-service agency working for you, an understanding of what is available and the possible pitfalls is still useful. Here I'm covering entry-level approaches as well as more advanced techniques. If you're skimming this book for useful information on video advertising, I'd say make sure to look at Chapter 9 where I help you avoid getting defrauded of your hard-won budget.

PAID ADS: SOCIAL ADS IN WALLED GARDENS

Platforms like Facebook and YouTube have created self-contained ecosystems; visitors consume content on a single platform and share, comment and engage in the same space. This creates a walled garden community that is fairly well regulated and measurable, although clearly when you give media budget to these platforms it only reaches their network (I will be going into the exceptions of this later).

PAID ADS: YOUTUBE PRE-ROLLS

YouTube pre-rolls (also known as skippables) are a type of in-stream advertising that plays your advert in front of videos that viewers are about to watch. It is a cornerstone of a successful video campaign and an effective tool for getting view counts up. An excellent choice at the start of a campaign, they drive viewer numbers up quickly so later visitors see a decent total. You might not find this very important but a view count of sub-1,000 (or whatever minimum is relevant to your brand) isn't the best look and pre-rolls will quickly get you over that. The other good thing about pre-rolls is that they are highly targetable. You can create targeting groups by keyword or interest group and as it all plugs into Google Analytics you will have tons of data to work with as you move forward. You can get going with a pre-roll campaign for very little cost, but really anything less than $6,000 of media spend is not going to make a difference, and you won't have that much data to work with.

When running these in-stream ads, consider using a different cut of the ad for different groups and running A/B testing on what gets the best results against your specific KPIs. If you're looking for some inspiration on the biggest online ads around, there is always an entertaining 10 minutes to be had going through the YouTube ads leader board: ▶ **Video 63**.

A big benefit that can't be overlooked, especially if you are running a 'fame' campaign to drive brand awareness, is that the first five seconds of video are served free of charge. You only pay for the media if viewers stay beyond the five-second mark. A typical campaign that pays for 1,000 views will be served to between 10,000 and 50,000 people (impressions). This means that you get five seconds of free advertising. To be most effective a YouTube pre-roll should be highly engaging in the first five seconds so that people stay and watch, but it should also include a brand logo or key message to cash in on free awareness if they choose to skip. The number of brands that miss out on what is essentially free media from YouTube is staggering, especially as it is really easy to fix with a simple re-edit. The ratio of impressions to views will be directly affected by how attractive the video looks; a better-looking video will get fewer free 'five-second views' as people will stay and watch it... but that's a good position to be in.

While we're on the subject of skippables, let's talk about the art of making ads that are not skipped. I've given a brief summary of the three main approaches below.

1   *Use audience-specific data to customize a targeted pre-roll ad.* A single type of pre-roll ad can be successful, but if it is targeted at a specific audience using search data it will perform much better. At a simple level this is targeting your ad groups properly, but there is room to push it so much further. The agency Colenso BBDO worked with Burger King to create a video campaign with 64 different versions of a video, which were served to viewers searching on specific terms. The adverts name-checked the search term, giving the viewer an experience that was directly connected to what they were watching.

Burger King anti-preroll case study 2
12 December 2013, Victoria Young YouTube channel
(▶) **Video 64**

2   *Play with the format.* Everyone watching and advertising on YouTube
    (▶) **Video 65**. knows about the skip function, so why not have fun with
    it? Openly asking people not to skip can be a very direct approach. Nail
    Communications in the United States played with this idea and created
    a 'Don't electrocute the puppy' concept that massively reduced skip
    rates. Another agency that had fun with the format was Almap BBDO,
    who created a video for Volkswagen that clicked on its own skip button
    on your behalf, to underline the automatic gearbox of a new car.

Why are we all doing YouTube pre-roll wrong?
15 July 2014, NAIL Communications YouTube channel
(▶) **Video 66**

Automatic skip ad Volkswagen AlmapBBDO
16 April 2013, AlmapBBDO YouTube channel
(▶) **Video 67**

3   *Turn off skip function.* The nuclear option in the war to stop people
    skipping is to completely turn off the function, forcing people to sit
    through your ad before getting to the content they want to watch. If you
    want viewers to swear at the screen as your video is forced into their face
    while they make a mental note never to touch your brand again, go
    ahead and turn it off. If that's not the result that you want, then I'd stay
    away from this option.

PAID ADS: IN-DISPLAY ADVERTISING

The next form of YouTube activation is in-display ads. These sit in YouTube
searches and alongside content results. As with pre-rolls, you will need a
decent media spend to make an impact, but it's an easy way to get going
with paid placements. As with all advertising methods, make sure someone
on the team is drilling down into the analytics to build a proof of ROI.

Facebook has its own version of in-display ads that also work in a highly
targetable manner; in Chapter 5 on OVPs I compared the two platforms. At
this point it's worth noting that Facebook ads will get you into people's feeds
quickly and deliver high volumes of traffic in a short amount of time. However,

this will be short-lived as the ads move down the stream and the only way to get them back up again is more spend. YouTube ads will not deliver such immediate impact but will have a longer tail and grow engagement over time. If you want 'fame' over 'engagement' I would favour spend towards Facebook and vice versa. This is simply because if you are going for engagement you will be using other pieces of content that you want people to watch, so delivering viewers to a YouTube channel is ideal. If, however, you are only using one piece of content in a campaign there is not much point driving viewers to a channel that has nothing else on it, so a Facebook ad could be more successful.

PAID ADS: PROGRAMMATIC

Outside the walled gardens of social platforms there is a whole internet ready to carry your ads. Brands reach these by using an automated process of buying advert impressions across millions of sites, called 'programmatic advertising'. In this process, videos are placed on sites that have allowed their space to be placed out for open bid auctions, with the highest bidder getting seen by the viewer. It's highly targetable and you normally get metrics on where the adverts were served, CTRs, engagement and more.

Here is a note of caution on programmatic: once you step outside the walled gardens of the large social players you are in the Wild West of internet advertising and it's very much a case of 'buyer beware'. A worrying number of brands have seen budgets sucked up by fraudsters who offer little or no genuine return on budget – see Chapter 9 for more on video ad fraud so that you don't end up getting caught out. In the same chapter I also cover brand security and discuss how programmatic ads face the same issue as social sites in that ads can be placed next to inappropriate or offensive content.

One of the biggest players in the programmatic arena is Google, which breaks your video out of its walled garden and onto other sites using two systems: Google Display Network (GDN) and Double Click. At the other extreme of scale from GDN are smaller technology sites such as Brandzooka that offer self-serve advertising placements. These sites are typically easy to use and they can give good results in terms of views. One downside of simpler sites is that metrics and analytics can be very limited if you are looking to prove ROI.

Aside from which platform to use, when considering programmatic there are a few things that should be considered:

- *To autoplay or not?* The debate on whether videos should autoplay has been going on for a long time and is gradually gaining clarity. To summarize the current thinking, autoplay ads are great if you are looking to drive brand awareness as you are pushing your message into people's lives. However, greater and deeper engagement will come when people have a choice. Facial recognition studies by IPG Media Labs have shown that people are more engaged with videos that they choose to watch, as opposed to those on autoplay. In fact, click-to-play ads result in emotional reaction levels that are nearly four times higher than those of autoplay.[11] Autoplay drives awareness but at the expense of viewer satisfaction. However, this can be offset by the better results from bigger players, as outlined in the following section. On some platforms, though, you simply won't have a choice over the matter and will have to do what it deems best.

- *Bigger video players are better:* If you're paying to place ads on websites you should be looking for them to be on the biggest player you can get. Large players drive higher levels of awareness than smaller players and this has been supported both by consumer interviews and facial expression analysis. Large video players deliver significantly better emotional impact than small video players during autoplay ads, somewhat offsetting the lower engagement that autoplay will deliver.[9]

FIGURE 8.2   Player placement will affect performance

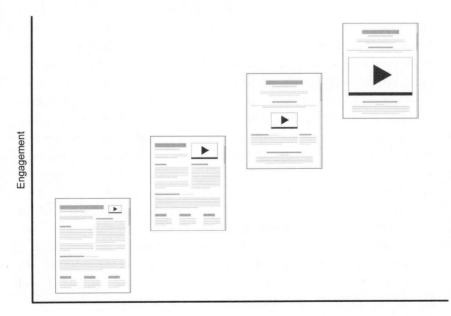

- *Website quality:* The perceived qualities of sites on which videos are placed will directly impact on how people perceive the brand. On the positive side, this means that you can get a 'halo effect' (by placing your content alongside other great work). On the negative side, however, a bad site can drag your content down with it and waste your ad spend. With this in mind a detailed list of where your videos are being placed is essential so you can keep an eye on their quality. The study by IPG Media Lab that I mentioned earlier also looked at what people thought was important about video adverts that they watched. The results showed that the success of a video on a third-party site is in many ways outside of your control. When a panel of 1,261 people were interviewed about why they were satisfied with a video ad they gave these results:[10]

  o   I trust the website: 90 per cent.

  o   The ads were relevant: 66 per cent.

  o   The ads were engaging: 64 per cent.

  So, brands that spend a significant budget on producing relevant, engaging content should really pay attention to placing it on sites that people trust, as it can be a significant driver of success.

- *Ad blocking:* End users blocking ads, both to their feeds and to the sites that they visit, are becoming an increasing challenge for advertisers. Juniper research estimates that in 2020 ad blocking cost publishers US $27 billion in lost revenues, accounting for a decrease of almost 10 per cent of the total digital advertising market.[11] Users can now choose to upgrade to advert-free subscription services or use paid blockers to prevent messages getting into the content they read. This is an interesting phenomenon as it means that people that have the money to block ads are going to see less than people who cannot afford to block them. This poses a particular problem for brands that are trying to reach wealthy markets, and in some ways it is a form of 'tax' on poorer users who have to make their way through more commercial messages to get to content.

  So how do ad blockers work? It's a fairly simple process, really. Advertising media doesn't sit on the same servers or infrastructure as the content around it (they are pulled in from third-party storage areas). So, it is a straightforward technical task to create software that identifies the origins of content, recognizes it as different from the code of a page itself and blocks what the user does not want to see.

There are a number of solutions to ad blocking, and which one you choose will depend on whether or not you are tied to traditional advertising models and approaches. The first set of solutions tries to break through the firewall of ad blockers and comes from the angle that it is a technical battle to be won. There are a variety of software solutions that work to beat the blockers, usually working to hide or disguise the origins of the ads so that ad blockers cannot identify their origins and flag them to be blocked. The issue here is that if people are actively trying to block ads, are they actually going to be happy when one gets through due to technical backend wizardry? Yes, this approach is good for publishers and media buyers as they can keep their valuable (revenue generating) statistics up... but it is not good for brands that want to reach people in a positive conversation.

The second set of solutions to ad blockers is for advertisers to adjust their mindset, to move away from a reliance on paid space and towards engaging content that is flagged as something users want to consume. This is at the heart of the difference between a publisher and a broadcaster, and it is the approach that makes most sense to a content creator like me.

Buying your own social media ad space

When it comes to buying ad space on social platforms, it can all get a little overwhelming. There are lots of moving parts, and it's very easy to waste money. I really recommend getting an agency on board to do the media buying unless you have an expert in house as, although it might appear cheaper to buy your own media, if it's less effective it can actually just be a false economy. However, for those that have some experience with ad words or other types or buying already, or that simply want to learn, there is no reason to not start buying media on a small scale and build from there. In this section I will run through the steps that you need to take in order to activate your videos with social media ads.

Step 1: set your budgets

First things first. How much to you want to spend on paid ads? To begin with this may be hard to answer, as you simply won't know what's needed. Ads on most social networks are sold in an auction format. You set a maximum bid for a target result (such as a click), or a maximum budget per day.

As a rule of thumb, I would budget for campaigns to cost between 30 per cent and 60 per cent of the budget you have spent on production. As an example, if you are making a $20,000 video, expect to spend a further $6,000 to $12,000 on ads. If you are starting out, or have a low budget video, think of a minimum spend of $5,000 on your campaign. Any less than this and you will struggle to see useful patterns in the data to help improve. Although, even if you can't afford this much, every little will help.

When you advertise with paid social, you'll typically set a total budget for each ad you run, and the platform will try to spend your budget evenly throughout the time that they run your ads. You won't be charged more than the budget you set. Remember that you're always in control of how much you spend. A word of caution from me is to be careful with loading large quantities of credit onto an ad account before you know how it works. It's easy to make a mistake in a setting and spend the whole budget on the wrong campaign... I know this because I've done it!

You will hear two terms 'budget' and 'spend'. It's useful to know the difference:

- *Budget:* The maximum amount of money that you are willing to spend for the placements of your ad. This also breaks down further into daily budget (the average amount you're willing to spend on an ad every day) and lifetime budget (how much you're willing to spend over the entire runtime of your ad).
- *Spend:* The amount you actually pay (ie how much money was used from the budget).

The pricing of social media ads is normally based on an auction system in which your ads compete for impressions based on bid and performance. More popular audiences will receive higher bids and will cost you more to reach. When you run your ad, you'll only be charged for the number of clicks or the number of impressions that your ad received.

You will generally pay for social ads using one of the following methods, which one will depend on your campaign goal:

- cost per click (CPC);
- cost per 1,000 impressions (CPM);
- cost per conversion (CPConv);
- cost per video view (CPV).

Several factors impact how much social media ads cost (beyond what your competitors are bidding). These include campaign objective, audience type, geography, time of year and even time of day. For example, research by AdEspresso shows that the average Facebook CPC is $0.40 on Sundays, but nearly $0.50 on Tuesdays and Thursdays.[12]

One thing to do as you allocate budget is to decide if you want to focus on impressions (how many people see it) or engagement (how many people take an action during or after the content). Both can be valuable for your business but it's impossible to do both at the same time, so choose the one that aligns with your business goals. If you're looking for direct actions after the ad, focus on engagement; if you want to be seen by a wide audience, focus on impressions.

Step 2: define target platforms and ads types

There is a dizzying array of social media ad formats out there, with each platform creating their own variants and approaches, from carousels to collections and stories. Each will work in a different way and offer you different results so expect some trial and error. Your first tasks are to decide on which social channel your audiences spend their time on, and which ads will reach them best. Pew Research[13] have collated a great resource that will help you decide which social platform is best for your ads. It breaks down the usage of 11 major social media platforms by factors such as age, gender, salary bracket and educational attainment. I'd recommended starting with one platform first and taking any learning from that into other places. Don't forget that any insights you have from previous (non-video) paid campaigns will be super-useful as you start your first video ads.

If you want to get up to speed on the various types of paid social media adverts on each platform, take a look at this blog post from Hootsuite that covers everything from Facebook Carousels to Instagram Collections: ▶ **Video 68**.

With the choice of platform and ads made, you can start to create your campaign. Every platform will have a slightly different process, but they all allow you to target the interests and needs of your audience and customers. Use your buyer personas to define targeting groups by demographics, keywords, interests, geography and more.

Once you have run a campaign you will have created a list of people that have interacted with your content. These people can be served further ads in a new campaign (or in a later phase of this one) in a process called 'retargeting'.

SUPERCHARGING YOUR TARGETING

Here are some tips to supercharge your targeting

1 **Target your competitors' audiences**

   Almost all social platforms have audience insights tools that will help you target your ads effectively. What's more, they will enable you to see (or figure out) what your competitors are up to. Facebook Audience Insights, for example, is an amazing resource that not only gives data on your FB campaigns, but that you can use to make educated guesses about what your competition is doing elsewhere. Using your competitors' research as a starting point is not the perfect way to begin a campaign but also not a bad idea if you want to get going quickly. Here's a link to a great article on Hootsuite that tells you exactly how to do it: https://blog.hootsuite.com/social-media-advertising/.

2 **Use custom audiences for remarketing**

   Remarketing is a powerful targeting strategy to connect with potential customers who have already expressed interest in your products. Use your social platform's insights panel to show your ads to people who have recently viewed your website, content or social posts. Most platforms will call this list a custom audience and almost all of them will require you to install some form of pixel tracker on your site (for example Facebook Pixel).

3 **Life events targeting**

   It feels a bit 'stalkery', but you can target ads at people going through major life events from birth, through to graduation, weddings, illness and death. It's worth going through your customer personas and seeing if you can connect life events to each one.

4 **Target people similar to existing customers**

   Lookalike targeting allows you to build lists of potential customers who share characteristics with people who already buy from you. This is especially powerful on Instagram and Facebook. The good thing about this is that you don't even have to build a library of data, as the social platform will use its knowledge and do it for you.

5 **Let your organic posts inform your ads**

   You are probably already posting content to social every day. Some of these posts will work and others won't. Dig out the data on clicks, likes, shares and comments, then cherry-pick the high-performing messages for inclusion in your social ads. To this point, if you are about to advertise on a network that's new to you, put out some organic posts first to gather data on what works and what doesn't as lessons from one platform may not translate to another.

Step 3: write strong copy

The copy that accompanies your ad will have a big impact on its effectiveness. To ensure your copy converts, ensure that it is straightforward and compelling, and be prepared to test multiple options. There are many services that will automate this for you using AI including copy.ai, copysmith.ai and the one I would recommend, the wonderful phrasee.co.

Step 4: measure your ad's success and react

Social media advertising comes with a multitude of metrics to monitor the success of your work. It's easy to get swamped in data, so be sure to focus on the metrics that matter most to your business. Here are three of the most commonly monitored metrics that you should keep an eye on:

- *Click-through rate:* The number of clicks your ad has, divided by the number of impressions it received (clicks/impressions). This will show you the relevance of your content and how well it converts interest to action. A high average CTR shows that your ad is drawing traffic to your website. So, what is a good CTR? Well, according to AccuraCast, top-ranking ads can expect a CTR of 7.11 per cent while an ad ranked at position 9 only has a 0.55 per cent CTR. Google's Rich Media Gallery offers a benchmarking tool that shows you the average CTR for various types of display ads and has loads of other resources to get you all the latest insights about paid ads: (▶) **Video 69**.
- *Cost per conversion (CPC):* Every campaign should have one core conversion goal (signups, app install, downloads, visits to blog posts). To calculate CPC, divide the amount of money you have spent by the number of conversions that resulted. This gives insight into whether your ads are profitable and helps you project your future ad spending.
- *Conversion rate:* The conversion rate of the number of visits to your landing page that result from your social media ads provides a good idea of the quality of the clicks you're receiving, as well as the performance of your landing page. You can also benchmark your social ad traffic against the conversion rate of traffic from other sources.

One you know what is working and what's not, you can optimize an ad's performance. One of the great benefits of social ads is instant feedback. You can gauge the effectiveness of a sponsored post in minutes and follow up with advanced analytics reports. The best practice is to test several ads with small audiences to determine what works best, then use the winning ad in the primary campaign. Testing one ad against another to determine what works best and refining your strategy is known as A/B testing. It's a critical part of your social media advertising efforts.

There are plenty of free resources to support and enhance your social media advertising. Here are some of the essentials:

Google Analytics: Web analytics service that tracks and reports website traffic.
(▶) **Video 70**

Unsplash: Free, high-quality images and photos. No attribution required. Download and use for any project. (▶) **Video 71**

Facebook: Successful Facebook ads case studies. See how other businesses are using Facebook advertising. (▶) **Video 72**

Headline Analyzer: Helps you to write more effective ad headings and copy.
(▶) **Video 73**

Social Media Examiner: A huge social media marketing resource. (▶) **Video 74**

Jon Loomer: Advanced resource for Facebook marketers. (▶) **Video 75**

Core DNA: Exhaustive list of further resources. (▶) **Video 76**

Summary

So that was an epic chapter, which is what we should expect when talking about activation. It is after all the basis of how we get people to watch content and therefore how we influence their behaviour. In Chapters 14 to 18 we take all these principles and apply them to multi-video campaigns, introducing the all-important subject of testing and adapting. However, for now let's take a moment to review the key takeaways of activating a single piece of video content:

- Spend time setting KPIs that are relevant to your objectives and share and agree them with all stakeholders before the launch. Whenever possible make them measurable and specific – such as '10 per cent more click-throughs from contact form' rather than 'Sell more'.

- Optimize the content that you create for organic search.
- Plan to use a good spread of owned, earned and paid placements, with a focus on where you know your audience will be.
- Harness influencers and secondary influencers to get the word out.
- You may not need to pay big money for a profile influencer; sometimes working influencers and micro influencers will have a better and more direct link to your audience.
- Test what works before committing to a huge media spend, and keep a close eye on metrics throughout the campaign.
- Autoplay, player size and ad blockers are all things to consider when you embark on big paid placement campaigns.
- Don't forget that the best way to get cost-effective activation is to have creative, shareable content that people actually want to watch.

References

1 Andy Smith
29 October 2015
BuzzFeed video titles deep-dive: Facebook vs YouTube
Buzzfeed
http://tubularinsights.com/buzzfeed-video-titles/#ixzz4dqtaasxD (archived at https://perma.cc/D9C2-NKVL)

2 YouTube
Lesson: make clickable thumbnails
YouTube Creator Academy
https://creatoracademy.youtube.com/page/lesson/thumbnails?hl=en-GB (archived at https://perma.cc/UQ94-AFJM)

3 Facebook for Business
10 February 2016
Capture attention with updated features for video ads
www.facebook.com/business/news/updated-features-for-video-ads (archived at https://perma.cc/CC4M-CCBH)

4 Byron Sharp
2010
How Brands Grow: What marketers don't know
Oxford University Press

5 Holly Goodier
   4 May 2012
   BBC online briefing spring 2012: the participation choice
   BBC
   www.bbc.co.uk/blogs/bbcinternet/2012/05/bbc_online_briefing_spring_201_1.
   html (archived at https://perma.cc/8F8S-UW9E)

6 Anneta Konstantinides
   7 December 2016
   Nice work if you can get it: the world's highest-earning YouTube stars who
   make up to $15m a year from their online shows
   Mail Online
   www.dailymail.co.uk/news/article-4007938/The-10-Highest-Paid-YouTube-
   stars.html (archived at https://perma.cc/62ZB-K69R)

7 Ogilvy Consulting
   14 November 2016
   The power of second-wave influencers
   Slideshare
   www.slideshare.net/socialogilvy/the-power-of-second-wave-influencers-
   68906611 (archived at https://perma.cc/G7YE-F8C2)

8 Twitter, Ogilvy & Mather and TNS
   May 2016
   Video discovery and sharing: behavioural analytics and quant survey, US & UK
   Slideshare
   www.slideshare.net/socialogilvy/the-power-of-second-wave-
   influencers-68906611 (archived at https://perma.cc/G7YE-F8C2)

9 IAB and Advertiser Perceptions
   April 2016
   2016 IAB video ad spend study
   www.iab.com/wp-content/uploads/2016/04/2016-IAB-Video-Ad-Spend-Study.
   pdf (archived at https://perma.cc/N7LP-JRS7)

10 Jared Skolnick and Shawn Baron
   2016
   Understanding the drivers of standout video experiences
   IPG Media Lab
   www.stoneward.com/wp-content/uploads/2013/01/Undertone_white-paper.pdf
   (archived at https://perma.cc/9QRS-Z5FX)

11 Sam Barker
   5 November 2016
   Future digital advertising: AI, ad fraud and ad blocking 2017–2022
   Juniper Research
   www.juniperresearch.com/researchstore/content-digital-media/future-digital-
   advertising-strategy-report/subscription/artificial-intelligence-advertising-fraud
   (archived at https://perma.cc/FXL5-H298)

12 Madis Birk
17 November 2020
Understanding Facebook ads cost: 2019 & 2020 benchmarks,
AdEspresso,
https://adespresso.com/blog/facebook-ads-cost/ (archived at https://perma.cc/
C67V-GFYR)

13 Pew Research
12 June 2019
Social Media Fact Sheet
www.pewresearch.org/internet/fact-sheet/social-media/ (archived at https://
perma.cc/W2VC-GAH2)

Further reading

Tobi Elkin
8 June 2016
Survey finds 90 per cent of people skip pre-roll video ads
MediaPost
www.mediapost.com/publications/article/277564/survey-finds-90-of-people-skip-
pre-roll-video-ads.html (archived at https://perma.cc/BA94-P6ML)
Kavi Guppta
12 March 2015
3 ways YouTube pre-roll ads forces marketers to rethink video advertising
Contently
https://contently.com/strategist/2015/03/12/3-ways-youtube-pre-roll-is-forcing-
marketers-to-rethink-video-advertising/ (archived at https://perma.cc/4X4R-QN8P)
Kissmetrics
7 marketing lessons from eye-tracking studies
https://blog.kissmetrics.com/eye-tracking-studies/ (archived at https://perma.cc/
V368-8X88)
YouTube Insights Team
June 2015
The first 5 seconds: creating YouTube ads that break through in a skippable world
Think with Google
www.thinkwithgoogle.com/intl/en-gb/marketing-strategies/video/the-first-5-sec-
onds-creating-youtube-ads-that-break-through/ (archived at https://perma.
cc/9R3F-4TVQ)

09

The dark underbelly of video advertising: how to avoid losing money

Throughout this book we are talking up the benefits of video in brand marketing, but nothing is perfect and video is just as open to failings as anything else. Often, if things go wrong it's down to user error or bad planning, but sometimes it's caused by operators with loose moral compasses, or even crooks looking to defraud the unaware. This chapter shines a light into the darker corners of online video so you can see the traps that can lie in wait. At one extreme this will help you pick up on an agency that's not sticking to best practice and at the other it might stop you losing money to fraudsters. So, let's make our way through the darkness, rising in severity from some difficult practicalities of life, to some questionable practices, through to the pretty immoral and finally to the downright criminal.

Poor viewability

When is a video view really a view? This is a hot topic for all online advertisers; after all, what is the point of paying to get your ad on a page if people can scroll right past it? This is an everyday topic so why is in this chapter? Well, very simply, if you pay for a video to be viewed you are probably getting less for your money than you think. The Media Rating Council and IAB standard put forward that a viewable video impression is counted when at least 50 per cent of an advert's pixels are visible on screen for at least two consecutive seconds.[1] It's worth reading that again, because it tells only half the story – for only two seconds. To me that doesn't really seem like a view, but you will be paying for the space.

Now we know what a 'view' is, we can look at the term 'viewability', which is something different. Viewability is a metric that tracks only impressions that can actually be seen by users. For example, if an ad is loaded at the bottom of a webpage but a user doesn't scroll down far enough to see it, that impression would not be deemed viewable.[2] The average viewability of video ads across the web (not including YouTube) is 54 per cent (on YouTube it's 91 per cent).[3] When videos are not viewable, it is normally because they load in a background tab, they are not watched for over two seconds, or they are below the fold. If you would like to see this in action there is a useful tool from Google with 'live view' technology that gives a real-time demonstration of when an ad is (and is not) counted as a view: (▶) **Video 77**.

This really does demonstrate why video ads must be highly attractive in the first two seconds and encourage people to stay on until the message has been conveyed through the creative. Viewability has improved over the past decade, and will continue to do so. Mobile video viewability showed significant improvement from 2016 to 2017, increasing from 40 per cent overall to 58.2 per cent, this being the first time that mobile outperformed desktop display viewability.[4] Now videos on mobile devices have much higher viewability than desktop.

So how does viewability plug into how brands pay for ads? Cost per impressions for internet ads was originally based on a simple formula: the amount of times that an advert was served to a site was how many times an ad was seen. This metric, normally bundled into units of a thousand, was applied to video ads just like everything else. However, the basic metric didn't take into account that many ads fell either side of a fold and might be only partially visible; it also didn't account for the fact that a video might be played only part of the way through. This is why the most contemporary thinking is based on cost per thousands viewable (CPMV – M represents 'mille', Latin for a thousand). Every platform and advertiser has a different set of rules, so it's a good idea to ask about viewability before giving them your money.

Here are a few points to maximize the viewability of your campaign:

- choose ads that are in larger players, avoiding 300 x 250 ads or smaller;
- use publishers that measure every impression, not just samples;

- choose players that are at the top and centre of pages, as these are more viewed;
- compare publishers' own guidelines on viewability and choose to run with the best ones.

Brand safety

The next thing in our look into the dark side is brand safety, and how easy it is for a brand to be positioned alongside totally inappropriate content. All the major social media platforms have found themselves in hot water with this issue, and in truth it is a very hard one to fix. At one end of the spectrum, having adverts and content placed alongside hateful and extremist content seems an obvious thing to avoid, albeit something that is hard to enforce. But at the other end, where content is only mildly inappropriate, where does one person's 'not worried' meet someone else's 'offended'?

A study by Integral Ad Science showed that brand safety infractions in their study group decreased from 9.5 per cent of impressions in 2016 to 8.6 per cent in 2017.[4] However, with the advent of fake news and the increase in violent and extremist content, brand safety is still a hot topic and one that is not going away. This study also listed the things brands find most likely to cause them issues, which unsurprisingly covered adult images, offensive language and violence.

In March 2017 brand safety was pushed into the spotlight when Google was heavily criticized for not policing the content that it placed video adverts next to. Stories hit the news that not only were adverts for brands like the BBC, McDonald's and L'Oréal appearing on extremist pages, but the publishers were actually earning large sums of money from them. Around the 2017 Super Bowl, Hyundai created an advert hailing US troops which ended up as a pre-roll to a video supporting Hezbollah.

An article in the *Guardian* newspaper listed a number of YouTube publishers with extreme views that had profited from adverts placed by well-known brands.[5] This was clearly a moral and PR disaster for the brands concerned, and a flurry of brands and large media agencies left the platform until something was done. The head of Google Europe publicly apologized and outlined steps to curb the issue, and although these fell short of actively seeking out negative content, they did bolster the flagging process for users and came with a promise to keep looking into the issue.

The issue is not one confined to YouTube; all platforms that don't or can't screen every individual publisher are vulnerable to the problem. It is especially an issue in programmatic advertising, where brands have less visibility of exact context and are one step removed from publishers. If you're sending the campaign out to a media buyer, you should be asking them what steps they are taking to avoid brand exposure to negative content. If the campaign is being run in-house you should explore how the platforms you are using can be used to enable blocking technology, preventing negative brand alignment before ads are played. An online search for 'online brand ad protection' will throw up a number of technology solutions.

Fake views

'Fake view' is the term used for the black hat technique of artificially building the view counts of videos, and it's a really interesting topic. At its simplest it is fooling a video player that a video has been viewed, so the counter counts it. It's something that's very easy to do; it's done for a vast array of reasons, and there are many brands and publishers that have been tempted by it. Any video hosted online can be made to appear far more popular than it really is. Fake views are the rarely spoken about dark secret of mobile and online video. Facebook, Google and countless other OVPs can be manipulated by those who want to, and unfortunately you can see tell-tale signs of this happening on many brands' videos.

There are two main reasons that videos get fake views. First, the owner of the video can buy what they believe to be genuine views but end up being fraudulently sold cheap fake ones. This has a massive impact on the marketing strategy, as a brand will suddenly discover that they are not getting engagement from their creative and their campaign will appear to be a failure. Second, someone who is not popular can buy fake views to appear well loved, which is something that many music artists have been accused of.

Agencies that sell fake views are of course engaging in something immoral and sometimes criminal. But some brands make themselves targets for it; if a brand sets unrealistic view expectations and has view count as the only metric of success, there is a temptation for weak-willed agencies to turn to the technique. At my agency Hurricane we have never engaged in this but we have seen the dynamic of how it can work. On several occasions we've been approached by a prospective client who wants to do a video where total views is the only objective. These clients have had no budget for 'true' activation through proper channels. A small retail brand expecting a million views for a product launch film without a significant ad spend or existing social support is always going to be a massive stretch, so where are they expecting views to come from? When we've had this situation our team has diplomatically backed away from the project, but it is often clear that other agencies have been willing to step in and offer the impossible. In all instances where this has happened, a short while after the project went live it was clear that they had massively inflated figures with fake views. When the view numbers being demanded are unrealistic for the product or marketplace, bad practice can start to creep in.

The temptation to knowingly buy fake views can be great. Imagine you're in a rock band starting out and trying to impress a label, or maybe even a larger act trying to attract impressionable individuals as fans. What kind of PR would millions of views in a month generate for you? You could prove that you were the hot ticket. In 2012 the technique hit the headlines when a number of large music labels had videos taken down from YouTube. The take-down affected Sony Music and Universal substantially, and immediately afterwards they were left with only eight videos between them. At the time, a Google statement said: 'This was not a bug or a security breach. This was an enforcement of our view count policy.'[6] The music industry countered that this had not been a deliberate manipulation of views, but an error that had crept in when migrating videos across different channels. It is also possible that some of the view discrepancy was due to de-spamming, where YouTube removes counts from videos that automatically play without intervention from the viewer or pop-under videos that viewers may not actually see.[7] Although the big headlines have dropped off on the subject, fake views are still very much with us. A quick web search for 'buy YouTube views' will throw up dozens of companies offering the service.

From my perspective as a marketer it's obvious that fake views are fundamentally fraud. Brands that build their views in this way are lying to their customers, and if it gets found out it will have a massive negative impact on their image. Brands that do it on purpose take their chances and may well get away with it. However, what I find especially worrying is that there are production companies and agencies that sell fake views to clients without flagging the reality of what they are buying. This is fraud on a much bigger scale.

But how can we tell if views are fake? Well, there are a few very clear signs to look out for. I've conducted an experiment on YouTube to demonstrate how it works. I posted two similar videos: one I left to do its own thing, and for the other I paid a fake view supplier based in Eastern Europe to do their work.

The first thing I needed to do was to make two videos, so I looked around for a topic. Watching my boy Spencer using an Xbox controller on Minecraft, with his fingers moving at incredible speeds gave me a suitable starting point for a video. I decided to make a short film about how many times a player clicks their controller playing Minecraft. I chose this for a number of reasons: it could form a searchable question, 'MINECRAFT CONTROLLER CLICK SPEEDS – how fast do you click?'; Minecraft is one of the most searched and viewed topics online so it actually had a chance of picking up some organic traffic; and, finally, I could do the filming while I sat on the sofa.

I made two versions of the video and put them both on YouTube. One was edited and optimized to be as searchable as possible, and the other video was edited with less rich text content and not optimized at all. I went even further than that, minimizing the chance for organic views by giving the second video a title that was in no way connected to the content and that was incredibly unlikely to be searched for. The only way that someone would search '@!$%^@!$%^@!$%^@!$%^' would be if their cat sat on the keyboard.

I put both videos live on YouTube and was ready to start the experiment. The first film, with an actual title and description, was left to pick up what views it could, and while it was doing that I found a fake view service. This is incredibly easy to do and an online search for 'buy YouTube views' bought up a number of options. In the end I chose my service and paid $17 for 15,000 views, which is 0.00046 cents per view (which seemed pretty reasonable compared to the 5 to 12 cents for a legitimate view).

From a conversation with the 'service' provider I got a good idea of how they do it. Basically they embed the video on a website multiple times along with a number of other videos that they are also working on. This site is opened on multiple devices at the same time and they scroll from top to bottom to activate the videos. I never managed to find out if they were auto-playing the videos or if they clicked play on each one. However, the basic outcome was that they could register thousands of views in a day or so. One can only imagine the reality of this process on the ground, as this must have been done in a click farm with a substantial number of people involved. This is an area that constantly gets highly negative coverage; workers in Bangladesh were found in a click farm working on a three-shift system and being paid as little as $120 a year.[8] When I looked for a service I tried to get one that seemed to offer better conditions to its staff and I avoided the insanely low fees offered by some (one service offered me 15,000 views for $3).

The interesting thing was that I was offered the chance of buying views from any country, which I hadn't expected to be so easy; the click farm uses IP redirects to the country a customer wants the views to come from. I chose to have all the views from the UK to see what would happen. I was also offered likes and subscribers but I didn't need to go down that route to make my point.

I've put together a table of some key points and stats from the experiment (Table 9.1).

TABLE 9.1   Fake views: Minecraft video comparison

Title	MINECRAFT CONTROLLER CLICK SPEEDS – how fast do you click?	@!$%^@!$%^@!$%^@!$%^
Description	How fast do you click when playing Minecraft? How fast can your finger go? This 30-second text looks at how many clicks you do – and gives a scary result for every hour that you play!	Left blank
Comments	1: 'Great video! I like it.' (*I was quite pleased to get any comment at all to be honest.*)	0
Views after four days	0	16,524
Views after four months	7 – typically around three weeks apart for each view.	16,524 – no views at all after paid period.
Devices	Tablet 43% Mobile phone 37% Computer 20%	Android on mobile – 100%
Audience	63%	99% !!

As you can see, the fake views did their job. My video with no title looks on paper to have been very successful, and if I were looking to convince people of my fame as an online filmmaker this would be an excellent value-for-money solution. So what does the way the views happened tell us? Well, first the spike in views on the fake video is immediate and very short-lived; the organic video has low views but they are spread out. This is how you can have a good idea that a video is using the technique, as the fake view services just get it done as quickly as possible. If you were trying to get a smooth curve you would have to run multiple campaigns at the same time and it would all get very messy. Real ads are similar but not as extreme; a well-run campaign will be on a high number of sites and run for a while, not just 24 hours. You can be even more suspicious if the quality of the video content doesn't seem to justify a big ad spend.

Another tell-tale sign that the views have been faked is that they are all from the same type of device, compared with the real video which has views from a number of sources.

So, now you can get an idea if a suddenly popular competitor has used this black hat technique, but more importantly you can look at your analytics and determine whether an agency you have asked to deliver views is taking a few major shortcuts to success.

Ad fraud

In our rundown of online video's darker side we now move into an area of all-out criminality. Advertising fraud is a big money maker for those with fewer morals that you or me. In 2016 ad fraud cost brands $16.4 billion, meaning that nearly 20 per cent of total digital ad spend was wasted.[9] The level of fraud outside the walled gardens of social platforms is even higher than within them, with programmatic ads suffering the most. An investigation by White Ops has identified that a group of Russia-based cybercriminals is stealing up to $5 million daily from premium-video-focused advertisers using a network called Methbot.[10]

For any online advertiser these are truly worrying figures. But how does it work? Well, the answer is that it works in many different ways, and it's always changing, but Adweek has an excellent summary of the processes if you are that way inclined: ▶ **Video 78**.

The only way to avoid fraud is to remain vigilant, ask a lot of questions of your suppliers and invest in specialist third-party software (third party being the operative phrase here as you don't want it to be supplied by the same people that are selling the ads!). Research by Integral Ad Science showed:

> significant performance variation between campaigns using ad fraud prevention and those that did not. There was a significant reduction in ad fraud for

advertisers that proactively defended against ad fraud using technology... This reinforces the importance of utilizing optimization tools to protect the entire buy.[11]

References

1 Think with Google
May 2015
Are your video ads making an impression?
https://think.storage.googleapis.com/docs/are-your-videos-making-an-impression.pdf (archived at https://perma.cc/A4TH-KFHS)

2 Jack Marshall
27 February 2014
WTF is viewability?
Digiday
https://digiday.com/media/wtf-viewability/ (archived at https://perma.cc/2X8K-MCSP)

3 Google
May 2015
Are your video ads making an impression?
https://think.storage.googleapis.com/docs/are-your-videos-making-an-impression.pdf (archived at https://perma.cc/5Y65-KSNH)

4 Integral Ad Science
H1 2020 media quality report
https://insider.integralads.com/h1-2020-media-quality-report/ (archived at https://perma.cc/C7BK-FR6L)

5 Olivia Solon
25 March 2017
Google's bad week: YouTube loses millions as advertising row reaches US
Guardian
www.theguardian.com/technology/2017/mar/25/google-youtube-advertising-extremist-content-att-verizon (archived at https://perma.cc/UFT9-TZS5)

6 Damien
Gayle 28 December 2012
YouTube cancels billions of music industry video views after finding they were fake or 'dead'
Mail Online
www.dailymail.co.uk/sciencetech/article-2254181/YouTube-wipes-billions-video-views-finding-faked-music-industry.html#ixzz4ch1G0nia (archived at https://perma.cc/CHL7-45DS)

7 Billboard
21 December 2012

What really happened to Sony and Universal's 2 billion missing YouTube views
www.billboard.com/articles/business/1483721/what-really-happened-to-sony-and-universals-2-billion-missing-youtube (archived at https://perma.cc/22XJ-YHXC)

8 Charles Arthur
2 August 2013
How low-paid workers at 'click farms' create appearance of online popularity
Guardian
www.theguardian.com/technology/2013/aug/02/click-farms-appearance-online-popularity (archived at https://perma.cc/V55R-EP2W)

9 Financial IT,
16 March 2017
What happens next: how to reverse the rising tide of ad fraud
https://financialit.net/news/infrastructure/what-happens-next-how-reverse-rising-tide-ad-fraud (archived at https://perma.cc/AKP3-8CNU)

10 Wikipedia
Methbot
https://en.wikipedia.org/wiki/Methbot (archived at https://perma.cc/UZ28-FLK9)

11 Integral Ad Science
H1 2020 media quality report
https://insider.integralads.com/h1-2020-media-quality-report/ (archived at https://perma.cc/B38M-3W2J)

Further reading

Internet Advertising Bureau
IAB measurement guidelines
www.iab.com/guidelines/iab-measurement-guidelines/#dvad (archived at https://perma.cc/S28J-C8TR)

DIY video projects

10

DIY video production:
so, it's up to you now?

It's the moment every marketing manager dreads. It's just another ordinary day and just another ordinary meeting, then someone casually drops a bombshell: 'The new CEO wants to do a really good video of her talking about the new release... but there's no real budget and we thought we'd do it ourselves...'. At this point the room goes quiet and all faces turn to you, each one clearly relieved that it's not going to be them that has to do it. Suddenly you find yourself thinking about dusting off the creative skills you've not used since university and panic starts to set in.

The number one thing to do in this situation is to enquire as to why it's being done. As content marketers we are not here to fill the world with more stuff, we are here to add value to what people know and to stand out in the marketplace. It's worth checking that there is a clear business need for making the video in the first place. One of three things will come of this:

- Everyone will realize that there's no clear plan for what to do with the content and it will get gently shelved so you can breathe easy.
- There is in fact a clear plan and you are going to make content that is an effort but worth it.
- There isn't really a clear plan but the CEO still wants it done and you're the one doing it, now hurry up and get started.

The first thing many people do when they find out they have to undertake a project like this is phone their trusted video supplier. Do they fancy sending a film crew to the company HQ that afternoon in return for a cup of machine coffee and either a free parking space or a one-way bus fare? In some instances, this can actually work; I've dug people out of similar holes before and will certainly do it again. If you're nice to work with, it's only a one-off and you give the agency lots of other work you might be surprised at how much you can ask for.

If, however, you don't have that kind of emergency backup or this is going to be a regular event and you're truly on your own, this is the section for you. In a former life I was a camera and edit trainer for the BBC, and I've taught many people to make great-looking video. We're going to go over the basics of making DIY video, from the kit you'll need to filming and editing skills.

What camera, and using a smart phone

I've been into photography and cameras since I was about 13 when I scraped together what money I had and bought a Minolta stills SLR (an x300s if you're as big a nerd as me). Thinking about it, I'm pretty sure one of the reasons that I started an agency was so that I'd be able to buy any camera kit that I wanted, and today I film on the best that money can buy. But with cameras it's easy to get carried away and sometimes a simple set-up will do. So, let's start this DIY section with the very cheapest option: the video camera that's already in your pocket. Most modern smartphones will shoot HD video; the newest models shoot pretty good 4K footage so you're off to a good start. That said, if you pull your phone out of a pocket, dust off the lint and start recording it's going to look and sound rubbish. We will talk about technique shortly, but in terms of kit you should look to add a few bits.

Smart phones

Later in this section I will be looking at general camera skills, but here are a couple of tips specific to mobile devices. First, don't get tempted into using the pinch function to activate your device's digital zoom. It's not actually zooming in optically, it just spreads the pixels that are there over a wider area. Although it looks like you are getting closer you're just reducing quality and causing unsightly pixelation. You can always get the same effect by cropping the image during the edit further down the line, so you may as well just get the best picture that you can to start with. You can buy adapters that clip onto the front of your device to change the focal length optically, and some devices have dual lenses (set at different focal lengths) so you can switch between the two without losing quality.

A key thing to remember when shooting on a phone is that they are designed to run in fully automatic mode unless you tell them not to. This means they make decisions on focus and exposure on your behalf. This sounds like a great idea, but it leaves all the decisions to a computer that doesn't really know what a good shot looks like. In automatic you'll find the device keeps adjusting focus, exposure and colour, all of which is very off-putting for a viewer. The easiest thing to do is to use the exposure and focus lock mode. On an iPhone this is as easy as tapping the screen and swiping up and down the screen to change the exposure of a shot. One day I'll find out how Android phones work but I'm sure it's probably about the same.

Finally, make sure there is actually enough memory on your phone to record the interview onto. Running out halfway through is going to be a pain. A one-minute video captured at 720p HD will use about 60 MB of space on your phone; at 1080p HD it's more like 130 MB of space. So make sure you have plenty spare or can plug in a new storage card if needed.

Smartphones have their place, but if you're looking to add a bit more gloss you can easily take a step up in production values. Someone in your office will be a keen photographer and will have a still camera that also shoots video; even better, they used to be keen but now their camera sits in the cupboard gathering dust and they won't mind how long you keep it.

Almost all modern DSLRs shoot 1080 or 4K video and will have come with decent zoom or prime lenses (see 'nerd jargon' box on page 179). Again, with these cameras it's normally the sound that lets them down. You can plug in a microphone to the audio input but you will get the best quality if you use an external audio recorder and microphone. Something like the Samson QL5 CL lavalier microphone with a Tascam DR-60DMKII four-channel portable recorder is a perfect set-up for most occasions. If you wanted to go extra professional a Sennheiser radio microphone (made up of receiver and transmitter) is the way to go.

Sound recording on your phone

The single biggest thing that lets smartphone footage down is sound. Microphones need to be as close as possible to the mouth of the interviewee so standing four metres away is going to sound awful. A general rule for clear audio is to get your microphone as close to your subject as possible. For interviews I would suggest getting a wired, clip-on lapel microphone (or lavalier) that goes into the phone's headphone socket. Make sure you get a long enough cable to reach your interviewee. If you have to film more than one person talking at once the best you will be able to do is get a directional mic that plugs into your phone. If you can't get a microphone, borrow another phone and get it as close to the interviewee as you can to record sound. Once you've done that you cut the new audio over the other camera's footage in the editing stage. It will help if you get them to do a loud clap at the start of recording, so you have a clear reference point of how to match them together.

My recommendations:

- iRig Lav clip-on lavalier/lapel microphone for iOS and Android;
- Shure Motiv MV88 microphone for iPhone or Android;
- Rode IXY microphone for iPhone or Android.

Keeping it still

Ask a professional camera operator to film a talking head and they will put the camera on a tripod every time, without fail. That's because nothing lets footage down more than the shakes. You can buy a simple table-top tripod or a larger floor-standing one to meet this project's needs. The best you can afford is the best guide for this. If you get a larger tripod rather than one made for phones make sure you also buy the correct holder for your device or you won't be able to connect the two together and will have to strap it on with duct tape. We've all done that, but it doesn't give the professional image that you're after!

Apps for smart phones

There are loads of apps our there for harnessing the power of your phone. I recommend these:

- FiLMiC Pro (paid) (▶) **Video 79**
  - o   the one I use!
  - o   manual control over your photos and video recordings;
  - o   HD and 4K video recording;
  - o   hardware accessories available.
- Cinema FV-5 (paid) (▶) **Video 80**

- o 'pro' level controls;
- o good sound options;
- o HD and 4K video recording.
- Open camera (free)
  ▶ **Video 81**

Shed some light on the matter

You can now hold the camera steady and actually hear the interview; the final thing that will make a difference is lighting. It seems a bit hardcore for DIY shoots, but buying a panel light that gives off soft, flat lighting will make a massive difference. Make sure it's a 'bi-colour' model so that you can use it in daylight or electric light. Also, get one with a stand and a diffuser to make the light nice and soft. If you buy a V-lock battery and charger to go with it you won't be rummaging around under your colleagues' desks for a power socket. As always, the more you spend, the better the kit will be. Take a look at something like the Ledgo 600BCLK lighting kit.

Practical skills: a mnemonic for success

Now you've got your camera, sound and lights it's time to get cracking with production. While running countless training courses I've developed a simple mnemonic to remind people what to do: CoFFES. As in a nice cup of coffee (but missing an E… I didn't say it was perfect). This stands for colour, focus, framing, exposure, and sound.

Co: colour

No video camera is as clever as the human eye, and when they are used in different lighting conditions they can get confused. That's why you can adjust colour temperature to match your surroundings. Get it wrong and your picture can be too blue or too orange. On mobile devices and basic cameras this can be as simple as matching an icon to where you are: a sun for outside or a light bulb for inside. On more advanced cameras you may find the reading is in degrees Kelvin: 5200 for daylight, 3200 for tungsten bulbs. If you are able to dial in the Kelvin you want, just keep changing the settings until the faces are the right colour. If in doubt go a little more on the orange side, as then your interviewee will look more tanned than sick.

F: focus

The most important thing to focus on in any scene are the eyes of your subject. Get this wrong and no matter what else you get right the shot will be a failure. First make sure you turn the camera's autofocus off, or it will keep trying to focus on the thing that's right in the middle of the frame. Then, just before recording, zoom right in to the eyes, check the focus and zoom back out again. On some cameras this might not work, as they don't hold focus through the zooming range, in which case you might be able to find a button to make the camera's LCD screen do a little zoom in for you to check what's going on. If you do zoom in the screen don't forget to un-zoom again or your framing will be wrong.

F: framing

The composition of a shot is a massive area of theory that takes up many books on its own. To get going, the only theory you need to know about is the rule of thirds. Imagine putting two equally divided lines across the screen horizontally and another two vertically, slicing the picture into nine areas. The most interesting place to put the main subject of the picture is where the lines intersect; this means that when interviewing someone don't whack them in the middle, instead put them to one side. The empty space in the

FIGURE 10.1 The rule of thirds

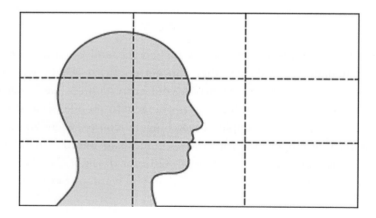

frame is called 'looking room'. Once you understand this basic principle you will never take a dull picture again.

Framing also includes something called eye-line. If your interviewee is talking to an interviewer off-camera, you should try to get the person they are talking to as close to the lens as possible. This gives a natural feel. If the interviewer is too far to the right or left the shot will feature too much profile and feel very odd. If the person being filmed is talking to camera (like a presenter or vlogger) they must unerringly look down the barrel of the lens. If their eyes flick around they will look like a shifty politician.

Also take a moment to have a look and check that there are no unexpected additions to the shot. A yucca plant coming out of the CEO's head and an empty coffee cup are typical suspects for this kind of thing.

E: exposure

The next part of CoFFES to think about is E for the exposure of the shot. Key to a shot looking natural is for the skin of your subject to look natural. Too bright or too dark and it's going to be a bad shot. Just adjust the exposure settings until the skin tones look right, and don't worry too much about other areas. Advanced cameras will have features such as zebra'ing to show when skin tone is just right. Make your life easier by avoiding a large exposure range in the shot (the difference between the darkest and brightest bits). Although your eyes can see dark and bright at the same time, only the most expensive cameras are able to deal with it well. Practically, this means not sitting people beside or in front of windows, and maybe pointing a lamp into a dark corner of the shot if you don't want them to appear too dark.

S: sound

Once you have everything framed well, exposed correctly and the right colour you can get the sound right. Is the microphone close enough to the subject? Is there rustle on the microphone as it's rubbing on a shirt? Has everyone in the office next door stopped talking? This last one is really key as background noise doesn't seem that bad when you hear it in real life, but when filmed it can be much more obtrusive and make spoken word hard to understand.

So, that's CoFEES. A simple, straightforward way to get the most useable footage. Simply follow all the steps methodically and you will get footage that does you proud.

11

DIY video: advanced tips

Once you're up and running making videos you will quickly find that, despite being a lot of work, it's all worth it because the impact they can have on your business is immense. You'll quickly be putting out multiple productions, and at that point there are more things you need to know. It's time to move up a gear with some professional production, editorial and technical tips.

Production tips

Release forms

In 25 years of making content, I've only ever had one contributor pull out of a project once filming has taken place. Although the odds are low, someone changing their mind and withdrawing from a production can have major implications for your business. So, asking them to sign a release form is a sensible idea. At the simplest level you can draw up an agreement yourself that includes personal details, a description of the contribution and that they hand over all copyright to you for all uses. This is often enough to help people understand the commitment they are making. However, if you want to get something legally binding you will need to ask your legal department or an external specialist lawyer to draft a document that fits your needs. Remember that contracts have more standing if a fee is exchanged, no matter how small. Consider paying contributors £50 towards a nice meal, even if they are offering their services voluntarily. This is not only a nice gesture as a way of saying thanks, but it underlines to them that a contractual arrangement is in place.

Copyright and usage

Copyright is a massive area, and one that I can't explore fully here. However, the main thing to remember is that you cannot use anyone else's music, illustrations, clips or videos without their permission. There is no exception to this rule. If you put someone else's work in your video you may get away with it if no one finds out, you may have it taken down from YouTube if they spot it, or you may get involved in legal issues and have to pay fines. The risk is yours to take, but for me it's simply not worth it.

If you do purchase the rights to use music on footage, ensure that you buy rights for the correct usage. There are dozens of different licencing options in every library. Things to watch out for are that fees for using content in paid placements are often higher than for unpaid placements, and some libraries only sell usage for a limited amount of time (if you are still using the video outside of this period you will probably get a bill). The people you are buying from know that it's easy to tick the wrong box on checkout (deliberately or accidentally!) and they are good at checking how their content is used. Once again, the risk simply isn't worth it.

Copyright works both ways, of course, and you need to protect your films from being used by others. For those in the UK I would recommend the inclusion of a copyright notice at the end of the film which both acts as a deterrent against infringement and names you as the copyright owner. You can also use an online platform such as the UK Copyright Service (https://copyrightservice.co.uk/) to register your work for around £50. This may not stop others from using elements of your film, but registration like this means that there is a dated, independently verifiable record of your prior claim, which will speed up or even avoid legal claims.

Under US copyright law, simply by being the creator of something in a 'tangible' form means that you own the copyright. Legal documentation is not needed; however, it is always best to add a copyright logo and disclaimer to your content for due diligence. Putting this disclaimer below at the start or end of the video is useful (although in and of itself it is not complete legal protection):

Copyright (or ©) [year released] by [name of owner]. All rights reserved.

If you are in the USA you can also register your video content with the US Copyright Office (https://copyright.gov/registration/). This way, should any issues arise you have solid proof for your case. Simply go to the Electronic Copyright Office webpage, register with the service by creating a username and password, fill out an e-form, and attach your original video with it.

Editorial tips

Listen with your eyes

When we converse it's polite to let the other person know you're actually paying attention. So, when your interviewee is talking, it's natural to make noises of encouragement; 'U-huh', 'Of course' and 'I see' are all things we say when listening to others. But when this is playing in the background of someone talking on camera, it's just odd. Where are these strange noises coming from? Who else is in this room anyway?

It will seem very rude at first, but learn to agree with your eyes and nod instead of talk. If you find it odd looking straight into someone's eyes as they talk, ask the contributor to look at the side of your head and you can just look down at your notes.

My name is...

A key interviewing skill is getting contributors to repeat your question in their answer. A clip of someone saying 'hat' is not much use to you. What you really want is for them to incorporate your question into their answer: 'The thing I like to wear outside is my hat.' If you correct your interviewee a couple of times at the start of the proceedings, they will soon get the hang of it. I normally explain this to interviewees by stating, 'If I ask you your name please reply "My name is Pete", not just "Pete".'

Ears open

If you can, keep the headphones on all the time. Monitoring the sound as you record will deliver much better end results. Rustles on the microphone, background noise and air conditioning hum all stand out when you listen using headphones and you will find out in time to fix it.

In and out

As you conduct your interview, pay attention to where you will start and stop the clip in your final edit. These 'in' and 'out' points are central to making a good film that flows. If you can't hear any suitable ins and outs when you're recording, it's unlikely that they will suddenly appear once you start editing. I often let contributors do the take once, saying as much as they like, then work with them to get clear 'ins' and 'outs'. Repeating the question is a good way to start, and ending on a clear point rather than tailing off is the best way to finish.

Don't be too practised

It's not advisable to let your interviewee practise too much. The temptation is for contributors to plan their answers to the word, which sounds like a good idea until they come to record, when suddenly you can see them trying to remember their lines rather than just talking. It comes across as wooden and never natural. It's for this reason that I never share exact questions before the shoot; at most I share bullet points of what I want to cover.

B-roll

For those at an advanced level (or if you don't have long enough with the contributor to do things in two shot sizes) you can shoot additional footage called covering shots (also known as B-roll or cutaways). These clips can be laid over edit points to mask the joins and avoid jump cuts. It is best to shoot these after the interview so that if there is anything relevant to what was discussed you know about it. As a beginner I would avoid any handheld shots, pans or tilts, as they can make the film look cheap. Instead concentrate on non-moving, well-framed shots.

Relax

If you're relaxed and calm, your contributor will be relaxed and calm. Even if you are new to the game, exuding an air of professionalism will make for much better results. Get your contributor to take a few calming breaths, do the same yourself and you're good to go.

Technical tips

Data safety

If your data is only in one place it is nowhere. *Back it up!!* In this industry we can spend days (and vast sums of money) getting a shot to look good, and in the end it is recorded to a glorified SD card. I've driven homes from shoots with £100,000 worth of effort sat on three very small cards in my glove box. All it takes is for these very small things to be misplaced or for disaster to strike. As soon as you record something, copy it to two places and also make sure you back up the project. If you are flying or travelling a long way, it's best to have two people carry a copy each, so that at least if one set of bags goes missing you still have a copy.

Shot sizes

If you're doing an interview it's a good discipline to get it recorded in two sizes – once as a wide shot and another time as a close-up. This means that when you come to edit you have choices and you can edit out the mistakes, 'ums' and 'ers' without having to use a jump cut or covering footage. With 4K (UHD) video footage this is really easy. Simply frame a wide shot of the person you are interviewing, then when editing on a 1080 (HD) timeline you can zoom in and out between a cropped shot and the wide whenever you want to.

FIGURE 11.1 Framing for two shots with 4K

Timeline

Record wild track

In a noisy environment such as a conference hall or office, take a minute to record the background noise without the interviewee talking. It's odd to see a whole film crew standing in silence looking at a microphone, but it's a common thing on a shoot. The great benefit of having this audio is that if you make an edit where the background noise changes you can edit in your own sound effects.

Master the key light

If you are using battery or mains lights, don't fire your main light straight at your contributor's face. If you do you'll flatten out their features and they will probably squint a lot. Instead, position your main (key) light on the same side as the person asking the questions. If the interviewee is sitting left of frame and looking into the right of the frame, position the key light right of frame and vice versa. This means their facial features will then cast a nice shadow onto the side of the face that is towards the camera. You're not

FIGURE 11.2 Key-light placement

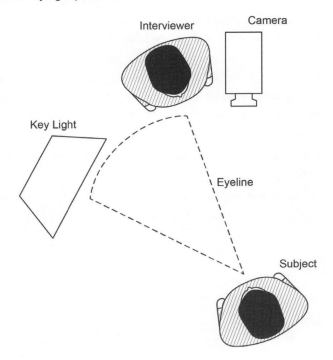

looking for anything drastic but it makes faces feel more alive. If you really want to get advanced just search online for 'three-point lighting' and fill your boots with how to make interviews look gorgeous.

In the next chapter we'll get our masterpiece edited and onto the web, then it's back to the boardroom for pats on the back and the inevitable issuing of more video projects.

NERD JARGON

Learn to speak camera jargon like a true nerd:

- *1080:* a shorthand for HD video. It refers to height of the picture in pixels. Usually referred to as 'Full HD' it is actually 1920 x 1080.

- *4K:* a similar measurement to 1080 but many more pixels. It has become a catch-all term for ultra-high-definition pictures ranging from just under 4000 pixels high to around 5000 pixels high. Some TVs call it UHD.

- *File type:* there are thousands of file types around; the term refers to the computer code wrapper that goes around the video code to make it play on different machines. Mp4, .mov and Mpeg are all really common file types.

- *Codec:* this is the actual data within the file type (wrapper). It's pretty nerdy but sometimes your player will ask you to download codecs if it can't read a file.

- *Compression:* if you want to make video files smaller you compress them. Making files smaller is useful for sending things to people, but the more compressed they are the worse they look. That's why getting a 3MB video file by email is never going to be great.

- *Zoom lens:* lenses that have a variable focal length. They are useful as they are so flexible.

- *Prime lens:* lenses that only have one focal length. These tend to be better quality as they are only designed to work well at the one thing they have to do.

12

DIY video: editing your work

You've got the interview in the can perfectly and it's time to edit it into shape as a film. I'm avoiding a deep dive into technicalities here, as that's what online tutorials are for. However, this chapter covers a quick run-down of the actual editorial process of editing, which is often the bit that technical types forget to talk about.

The number one thing here is to keep sight of your original goal. It's likely that during the interview you covered a fair few more things than planned. That's OK, but before letting them into the final version think back to the 'So what?' question. If a clip can't justify itself against the goals, it doesn't go in.

When editing a talking head, you are really looking to make it say what needs to be said as quickly as possible. When people talk, we naturally add words, 'ums' and pauses, or even head off on slightly irrelevant tangents. The editing process removes extraneous information and reorders clips of the interview for maximum effect. Get an interview as short as possible and it will be much more effective. When you get really good at editing, you can take five rambling paragraphs and turn them into one punchy and effective sentence.

Anytime you can 'see' how the audio relates to a picture, it's something known as sync. In other words, if you can see the source of sound and can hear the sound it is making, it's sync. Interviews and actuality are perfect examples; cutaways, close-ups, etc are non-sync. The first part of editing is to do a sync pull from the interview where you take all the relevant bits that you might want to use and put them in a row on one timeline.

Once you've done the first sync pull, save the timeline as a different version to the one you will be editing from now on before you do anything else! Soon you will be deleting things and you don't want to have to go back to the source files to get something back if you change your mind.

When I've done the 'sync pull' I quickly go through and delete any large chunks that are clearly not relevant. This shouldn't take too long, as it's just an initial clear-out of the non-relevant footage. With your sync pull done and thinned out, you can start grabbing clips and putting them into the order that makes the most sense. You might place a clip from the end at the start or move things around completely. I always start this process by putting similar answers right beside each other; then I can choose the best option and delete what I don't want.

At this point you will have something starting to look like the structure you want, but way over length. Assuming that you filmed the interview in two shot sizes (wide and close-up) you can use these to edit the clips more closely. Simply start your edit with a bit you want from the wide shot. When the contributor says something unwanted or you want to change topic, delete the stuff you don't want. Then move to the close-up version for the following bit of the interview. The changing of shot size makes the edit feel acceptable to the viewer and the shot doesn't jump. Continue this back and forth from the wide shot to the close-up until it's all done.

In terms of what technology to use for editing, there is plenty to choose from. Free software includes Windows Movie Maker, VirtualDub, Zs4 video editor and many more. For those on Mac, iMovie is probably the most accessible for beginners. At Hurricane we use Premiere Pro as it plugs into all other Adobe applications, making the insertion of graphics and audio really efficient. If your marketing department already has a subscription to Adobe Creative Cloud you will have access to this with no further fees.

Extra tips on editing

- The main idea of the film should be made clear as early on in your film as possible. No need to keep people waiting. Get to the point and avoid unnecessary detail.
- Keep the edit as short as possible by asking the question 'So what?' about each clip. If you can't justify why it's there, take the clip out.
- Although you want a short film, avoid really tight cuts or chopped-up dialogue that sounds fake by maintaining a natural flow of dialogue.

The last stage of editing is getting the final version of the film out of the edit suite and into the world. This export process involves compressing your original footage into a file type and size that the web can deal with. Compression is very much a dark art and you will have to experiment to find a file that is neither huge nor that looks terrible. To get you started, here's what I would export for use on YouTube or other platforms. If you do this you really won't go far wrong.

- File type: Mp4
- Codec: H264
- Size: 1920 x 1080
- Bit rate: 20 mbs
- Key frames: automatic
- Audio: AAC stereo

ONLINE EDITING AND VIDEO TOOLS FOR CONTENT CREATION ON A BUDGET

For me, nothing currently beats the value for money of a subscription to Adobe Creative Cloud. With one licence you get access to video editing, motion graphics, Photoshop, Acrobat and more. However, it is still a monthly fee. For those on a tighter budget I've pulled together a few resources to look at.

- Rev: get transcriptions and subtitles for your videos cheaply, accurately and fast. ▶ **Video 82**
- Lumen5: a video creation software that helps marketers, publishers, and brands create video content in a breeze, without any technical expertise. ▶ **Video 83**
- Typito: create stunning text videos online. ▶ **Video 84**
- Narakeet: create narrated videos quickly. ▶ **Video 85**
- Kapwing: great for simple video editing, or getting a screengrab from a video. A collaborative platform for creating images, videos and GIFs. ▶ **Video 86**
- Kapwing Convert: convert video files to other (more useful) video files. ▶ **Video 87**
- FilmoraGo: easy to use mobile app with basic editing functions and effects. ▶ **Video 88**

Creating effective video campaigns

13

Multi-video campaigns: an introduction

In Section Two we looked at how the three steps of planning, production and activation can guide you to make great video content. You took this model, did some thorough planning, made an emotional film that reflects your identity, and then you used some effective activation to get it watched. So now you're sitting pretty on the success of a job well done! Excellent, but I'm afraid this is where the hard work really begins.

One great piece of content isn't going to move the market for you. Bearing in mind that the highest levels of brand growth will come by balancing long-term uplift and short-term sales, individual pieces of content won't really deliver the well-rounded and highly successful campaign you're looking for. Content becomes truly powerful when it drives long-term engagement, so to make a mark you're going to need to repeat your success many times over.

This section takes the principles of effective content and helps you scale them. We will learn how to build and activate a video plan that delivers to goals and works in synergy with your broader branded content plan. It's aimed at brands who are attempting to build successful video marketing campaigns and looking to either do as much as possible in-house or to understand the entire process when working with external agencies.

Planning and activating campaigns is a complex topic, with many entry points and lines of discussion. I've simplified the process into a six-step plan, allowing us to follow a logical flow of ideas. Before we go further into specific steps and case studies, it's worth reflecting on what actually makes a great campaign and how we can try to maximize our chances of success. The first part of this, what makes a great campaign, is really rather subjective. If you're creatively minded, you might want a campaign that looks great and is totally new; if you're a numbers person you might choose something that delivers measurable profit for the brand. Pragmatic marketers might like campaigns that have longevity and that grow the brand over time. However, we should probably be looking for campaigns that do all three.

Thinking like a publisher

Before getting into brand video and strategies I had another life as a film-maker at the BBC. I spent my 20s and 30s travelling the world making documentaries for BBC1, BBC2 and the Discovery Channel. My days were filled with crafting films that looked into the heart of all sorts of topics covering poverty, drug addiction, the Gulf War, cheetahs, military history and even a married couple that lived with wolves… you name it and I probably did it. During this period my focus was always on storytelling, how to make it better and how to keep people watching, with a laser-like focus on editorial integrity and quality. Since leaving broadcast I've done 15 years in the brand world, and although I still use many of the same skills I've found the mindset of the brand industry to be totally different. Reflecting on it now, I can summarize that in the traditional model, publishers look to attract and retain attention, relying on advertisers (or public taxation) to fund them. Advertisers have typically paid to inject their message into the viewer's attention and rely on consumers to fund them. Think of the classic TV ad in the middle of a wonderful documentary about tiger sharks; the publisher gets your attention and is funded by washing powder shoving its way into your attention. It is no wonder that people push back against this kind of intrusion. The symbiotic relationship between advertiser and publisher is still there, but consumer demand and changing technologies are dramatically changing the model. Now the mindset of brands that want to engage audiences is shifting to be more like that of a publisher.

I've put a few ideas down to help differentiate publishers and advertisers, and then we can talk about how the modern market requires us to think in a hybrid manner.

Traditional publishers think about *pull*:

- Who is my audience and what do they want to watch?
- What does my channel (eg BBC1, Discovery) stand for and is that what the audience wants?
- How do I get people to come back and watch more?

- How do I make my programme exciting for my audience?
- How do I stop people switching over to a different channel? (The lengths we went through to do this were epic.)
- How do I get people back next week?
- Does my channel have a good editorial mix so people come back?

Traditional brand advertisers think about *push*:

- Where can I place my messages to get the most attention?
- Who can I pay to take my ad and will it reach my audience?
- How can I change the behaviour of my target market?
- Is my message emotional and engaging?
- How do I raise awareness of my brand?

These questions are simplified, of course, but they draw attention to my central point, that brands traditionally *push* messages while publishers *pull* audiences.

The hybrid advertiser/publisher model

This model of marketing is changing. In the contemporary landscape the gaps between content creators, publishers and brands have never been narrower. Just take a moment to look at Little Things (www.littlethings.com), a publisher-owned site that has grown a solid audience with regular content on home, cooking and food. Now compare it to P&G Good Everyday (www.pggoodeveryday.com) a brand-owned site that has grown a solid audience with regular content on home, cooking and food. This also builds in a reward system to keep people coming back. They are very, very similar in approach; both covering the same topics and both with similar content. One is a publisher, the other an advertiser. Where does one stop and the other begin?

PG Everyday
 Video 89

As brands make their way in this marketplace, they need to adapt the old methods of *push* by adding the publishers' methods of *pull*. Not doing both misses the returns available through the higher engagement rates and long-term brand growth that comes from an engaged audience.

There are some practical ways that you can take the road to thinking and acting like a publisher:

- View the world through the eyes of your audience and think about what they would watch.

- Constantly challenge your team with the question – 'Is this actually worth people's time?'

- Don't waste effort making content that isn't for the right audience.

- Put someone in charge of editorial – preferably someone from a content creation, not marketing, background and empower them to challenge all the content you make.

- Focus on the system by which content is made; it might be an external agency or an in-house team but it needs to run like clockwork.

- Have a proper content review system in place – like an editorial meeting.

- Schedule in release dates but also dates of first draft, review and amends, which helps avoid missing the release dates (in the publishers' world, missing deadlines is simply not an option – TV shows and newspapers do not just skip a release). As we will see later, a regular release schedule can help build audiences.

This discussion could keep going but the point is made; now we can start to look at some other considerations of great video campaigns.

Video as a conversation

Brand growth is increasingly based on a conversation with customers; indeed, the idea of 'conversation marketing' has been around for a good few years. Video is a great tool for being a part of the ongoing conversation process. It might simply be that you release a video, then release more when people are engaged, and you have metrics on who is talking about it. Or you might go as far as providing a forum for people to discuss the topic. At least you should be listening to what the audience say and adapting accordingly.

Let's go back to the Clean & Clear example that opened the book. The brand moved from a push-focused, TV-heavy mindset, which wasn't working, to one based around conversations with young girls about skincare. They drove this with influencers and a solid video campaign, resulting in higher engagement and sales. As you move through the planning of your campaign, be on the lookout for opportunities to listen to the audience and adapt accordingly.

Bodyform nailed this approach when a member of the public called Richard trolled their Facebook page with a tongue-in-cheek rant about how periods were portrayed in advertising. Bodyform's media agency Carat spotted a golden opportunity to respond and brought in the outstanding shareable video experts Rubber Republic to create a video response within 48 hours of the post going online. This became 'Bodyform responds: the truth', a video to set men straight on the reality of periods. The film was an instant hit with over six million views, and won several international awards including a Cannes Gold Lion, a Mashie and a Webby nomination. It's not a bad result from listening to the conversation and taking part.

FIGURE 13.1   Bodyform responds: the truth

SOURCE Courtesy of Bodyform

Bodyform responds: the truth
16 October 2012, Bodyform YouTube channel
▶ **Video 90**

One video platform is not enough: the need for a multi-platform approach

People live their digital lives in many different places. At different times of the day and for different things people will have a variety of stop-offs in the digital landscape. These differences are amplified by variations in age, demographics and interests:

- YouTube's audience is spread over 88 countries that speak in 76 languages. The audience is skewed towards the older millennial generation (25–34 years old) and the most popular videos amongst consumers are instructional or how-to videos. YouTube is a good fit for longer-form content and uses playlists to group similar content so viewers can explore around a topic.[1]

- Facebook has a heavier skew towards female viewers and reaches millennials less well than YouTube. It is increasingly seen as the network for older people, especially as the people that adopted it in their early 20s move well into adulthood.

- Twitter is slightly different again, skewing slightly towards male users in the 18–49 year old bracket. The platform is very well suited to driving surges of awareness and engagement.[1]

- TikTok is the place to be to reach Gen Z and Gen Y, but anything shouting about brand too much that doesn't leverage fresh comedy or influencers is going to struggle.

But demographics are not the only drivers of the need to use a variety of platforms. Free online video platforms have a few quirks that you may not have considered. A key one is that they want to keep viewers on their platform, rather than on your brand, so they drive viewers from the end of one video to another one on the same platform. This can cause unexpected issues and actually lose you engagement. As an example, at the end of a YouTube video embedded on your site it will direct viewers to another video on the actual YouTube site (unless you add interactions, which we talk about later). I was recently working with a brand and on digging into analytics we discovered the videos sitting on their product pages (embedded from YouTube) were driving hundreds of hours of engagement time away from their site. They had paid good money to get people to the .com only to have a free player lure them away again.

ARE YOU ACCIDENTALLY DRIVING TRAFFIC AWAY FROM YOUR
WEBSITE?

If you have YouTube videos embedded on your site it's possible you are unwittingly
opening the door for people and tempting them to leave. Unless you put
something else in place, YouTube videos offer up other videos on your channel – or
related channels – when they finish. If viewers click this, they leave your site.

To find out if you are affected, open YouTube Analytics and go to 'traffic sources'.
If you see your own website listed as a source of traffic to your YouTube channel it
means people have watched an embedded video on your site and then left to come
to YouTube. If this is your strategy and there is lots to watch on your video channel
that's fine, but normally you would hope for it to be the other way around!

The best way to avoid this is to use non-referring players like Vimeo and JW player,
or to go for higher-spec OVPs like TwentyThree, Ooyala, Vidyard or Brightcove.

Six steps to an effective video campaign: an introduction

I've outlined the need to run videos across multiple platforms in enough
detail. Now we can put that topic to one side and get in deep on how to start
putting a multi-platform campaign together. I've split this into six steps,
which we will explore in the next three chapters:

1 Review: where are your brand and its content now?

2 Set goals: where are your brand and its content going?

3 Plan: content planning and programming strategy.

4 Set up: building the perfect content hub.

5 Create: creating high-volume video content – and making it easy.

6 Programme and activate: multi-video campaign activation and testing.
   How to grow ROI.

Reference

1 Greg Jarboe
   18 January 2017
   Branded social video: 46 per cent of consumers confirm they made a purchase
   after watching
   Tubular Insights
   http://tubularinsights.com/branded-social-video-impact-
   consumers/#ixzz4iY34iXN5 (archived at https://perma.cc/U3JH-TGKK)

14

Steps 1 and 2: reviewing brand content and setting goals

As marketers and brand professionals, you will have a clear direction in which you want to take the brand. Hundreds of articles and books exist on how organizations create this sense of direction; this book builds on these to see how video strategy can get you where you want to get to. This chapter helps define where your brand's content is now and where you are going. It may be that many of the upcoming steps you have already done, which is excellent, but even if that's the case you should skim over things to make sure you have everything in place.

First of all, we will look at where you are now. Very few brands have no video content at all, so the first thing to do in a campaign is an audit of what you have already. You will be surprised at how much out-of-date, off-brand and old content you have lurking around. With that done we will look at a crucial step in reaching a destination, which is to know exactly where that destination is. To be successful you need to be able to coherently vocalize a vision of what success looks like, which everyone can work towards and have a sense of mission on how to get there. This applies equally whether you are doing all the work yourself, have an internal team, or are working with an external agency.

Where are you now? Video content audits

If you don't have any content at the moment you can easily skip ahead to the next section, but if you have more than a few videos it's worth doing a content audit. This might be at a brand-wide level or a project-specific level, depending on what you are looking to achieve. It takes a while, but it will almost certainly throw up points that you had never thought about. A good content audit is a mix of empirical and subjective measurements that interrogate how good your content is and what lessons you can take from that.

Start an audit by getting all the videos that you have visible on your channels onto a spreadsheet. I normally do a different sheet for each channel as otherwise it can get pretty epic, pretty quickly. When doing a YouTube audit, it's easiest to make a group of videos in 'video manager' and export them as a CSV file. List in your sheet all useful data about your current content including upload date, likes, shares, comments, subscriptions, views, click-through rate, etc.

There are many more insights to be had about your content, and a good SEO or video marketing agency will be able to add a lot to the conversation. But if you are a details person (or don't have the budget for an agency) you may want to drill down further into each film yourself; it will give interesting insights if you do. Crack open the video metrics on the relevant platform and lift the lid on view times, engagement rates, shares and more. While you're there, look at traffic sources to your site and which videos are driving traffic.

With all this done, you will quickly be able to assess what has worked and what hasn't, and it is time to move on to less subjective data.

Vital things to know about your content are:

- Is it on-brand?
- Did it achieve its goals?
- Did it deliver ROI?
- Was it correctly optimized (see page 126)?
- How effective were the thumbnails?
- What kind of content was it? Hero, Hub, Help or Go!
- What part of the digital sales funnel does it cater for – Awareness, Consideration, Conversion or Retention?
- How creative/distinctive is it?

What you notice from this list is that the questions are rather subjective; for example, there is no easy definable metric on how 'on-brand' a film is. But what we can do is score content for comparison. I normally score things out of 4, based on the model below, or assign a value to each content type.

0 = The content very poorly correlates to the desired metric.

1 = The content mildly correlates to the desired metric.

2 = The content correlates strongly to the desired metric.

3 = The content correlates very strongly to the desired metric.

This gives each film a mark out of four that can be compared, and that over time can be improved. Put this in the spreadsheet and you will start to build up a good picture of where you are. When all the above is done the leg-work is finished and you can quickly run off charts that will show where things have worked and where money has been wasted.

Setting goals

So, we've looked at evaluating the current content that your brand has and now we can look to the future. When starting on the road of integrating video into a marketing plan it's worth taking the time to create a vision statement (where you are going) and a mission statement (how you will get there). Statements like these can initially seem a bit like overkill, especially if you already have well-formed brand visions. But it only has to be two paragraphs put together in 20 minutes of thinking, and it will form a powerful reference point as you move through the process. Remember that we are not starting from scratch and creating a vision for your brand here, it's something you already know. We are simply focusing people's mind on what we need video to do. The clarity of thought that you get from it will really come into its own when you start to prioritize content and budgets further down the line.

A vision statement for a great campaign

The first thing to do when looking at a vision statement is to jump to the end. A good vision statement is an expression of the end destination, one that will inspire and energize a team around a shared idea of success. At this point we're not looking for a mission statement (an expression of what we will do). Very often these two things get mixed together, which reduces the effectiveness of the process. There is plenty of time to talk about the journey later; for now, let's focus on the destination (vision).

Research by Forbes of 50,000 employees has shown that those who find their organization's vision meaningful have engagement levels 18 per cent higher than average.[1] That's engagement that can be put to good use in reaching your goals so it's worth getting the statement right.

Create a vision statement based on the points below and you won't go far wrong:

- Create an expression of the best outcome possible for your video campaign.
- Write in the current tense as though you have arrived.
- Use real words, not business nonsense.
- Speak to all team members, not just senior management.
- Avoid getting into the detail of how you will get there.
- Don't keep the vision to yourself; share it with everyone at every level. It gives you an opportunity to present leadership and avoids misunderstandings further down the line. It also gives you a sense of satisfaction when you look back in six months' time and realize you've nailed it.
- Keep it to video goals and try not to wander into wider brand issues (easier said than done but just keep specific).
- Remember this is the 'where to', not the 'how'.

As inspiration, you can see some of the world's best vision and mission statements in ▶ **Video 91**.

With a clear vision of what you want to do in place, it's time to vocalize how you will get there. In planning terms this is where it starts to get exciting as we can dig down into the real solutions you need. It's time to put together a mission statement where we define how we will get to our destination and form action-oriented goals. Again, this is only a short piece of work, but it is super helpful as you move through the process.

A mission statement for a great campaign

The first step in creating a mission statement for your video strategy is a clear understanding of the problem. It might be that you are looking to create a mission that's for a very broad goal, such as becoming a 'go to' site for content. Or it might be that you're looking for a video campaign to solve a specific issue in your sales funnel… maybe there's a fame and awareness issue or a problem that people do not engage or fully understand what you do? It doesn't really matter what it is, you just need to be able to state what it is.

Here are some crucial points to consider when building a mission statement:

- Consider a problem or challenge and put in a broad idea of how you will tackle it.
- Keep it short and sweet, avoiding the temptation to elaborate. A sentence is best, two is not bad and a paragraph is OK.
- Keep the mission statement outcome-orientated.
- Keep the language and goals inclusive of all stakeholders.
- Remember this is the 'how' not the 'where to'.

When constructing the statement, it's worth remembering the work of Byron Sharp[2] and the IPA Binet and Field.[3] The most effective campaigns motivate both short-term sales activations and long-term brand engagement, so a vision of a future that encompasses both of these is a good starting point. As we move through the process of defining where we want video to take a brand, it is worth bearing this dual focus in mind. If we find our mission is becoming too focused purely either on the short-term or the long-term goals it might be worth taking stock. As always, though, the real world is a more complex place and if the campaign is purely to do one thing it may not necessarily have to be as broad in scope – it is just worth making sure you are aware of the decisions you are taking.

As we reach the end of this chapter we have vocalized where your brand content is and where you want it to go. This will allow you to work with internal and external teams in a coherent and focused manner. Now it's time to start on the next step in the six-step process: building a campaign plan.

References

1 Joseph Folkman
22 April 2014
8 ways to ensure your vision is valued
Forbes
www.forbes.com/sites/joefolkman/2014/04/22/8-ways-to-ensure-your-vision-is-valued/#322143964524 (archived at https://perma.cc/C5EY-FFCH)
2 Byron Sharp
2010
How Brands Grow: What marketers don't know
Oxford University Press
3 Les Binet and Peter Field
2016
The Long and the Short of It: Balancing short and long-term marketing strategies
IPA

15

Step 3: content planning and programming strategy

In the previous chapter we looked at where the brand is now and where it is headed. With that done our campaign is nearly under way. The next step is to plan what types of content are needed and when they should to be released. With that in mind, look again at the digital sales funnel and its four stages, outlined in Section Two (page 71). Identify which part of the funnel you are looking to address. Is it Awareness, Consideration, Action or Retention?

At the narrow top end of the funnel, you may be looking to increase your brand's fame levels. This would involve creating a body of content that can be pushed out through paid activations or found via organic search. Further through the funnel you may be looking to keep people close to the brand until they are ready to buy. This would lead to entertaining or learning-based content. Finally, at the bottom end of the funnel you might be looking to convert engagement into sales. It's likely that successful campaigns will be looking to deliver across these three phases but specific problems such as e-commerce conversions or short-term sales boosts may focus on only one.

A potential customer of your brand is on a journey from initial awareness to purchase. This is a linear journey, but it's certainly not a straight line. There is a time when they are unaware of you, a time when they are interested in finding out more, a time when they have questions, a time when they are comparing you with others and, finally, a time when they have the debit card ready to go. Each one of these stops on the journey is an opportunity for content to drive the customer towards purchase.

Now consider how the four video content types (Hero, Hub, Help, Go!) work at stages of the sales funnel. With insights into the funnel stage that you want to affect, and the content types available, we can start mapping out

FIGURE 15.1   The consumer journey

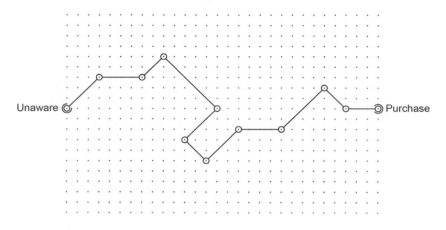

FIGURE 15.2   The stages of the funnel

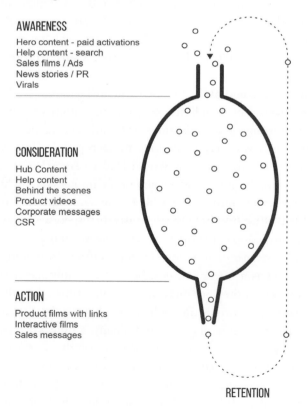

what content to use, when. Figure 15.2 outlines typical solutions to problems at each stage of the funnel. Note that the bulge in the middle of the chart represents how long people are likely to stay around as they consider their purchase, rather than being a reflection on how much content there is at the point, or indeed the budget that has been spent on it. You may have far more content at the awareness stage; it really depends on your business needs.

The content tree

Doing this exercise quickly generates a lot of content requirements and it is hard to keep track. What's more, you won't be using all four content types on all channels, and you will have more of some types than you do of others. But there is a simple framework that will help you see how it all works towards your goals. The way that I explain this to people is by using a content tree. It's a simple and visual way to discuss how different pieces of content sit in relation to each other. I will be looking at this more in the next chapter when we discuss content hubs and how multiple pieces of content are hosted online and presented to viewers. I'm aware that I've already got you thinking about two models: the digital sales funnel and the consumer journey. But now I'm going to throw another in here. I appreciate it's another thing to get your head around, but you may find one model more suitable to your content or indeed that one resonates more with the way you think, so it's worth understanding them all.

The content tree is a useful approach to considering all your content, but it is especially helpful for video as there will be such a disparity in costs between different production methods. It will help consider content platforms but it is really a tool to help you consider the campaign in its entirety. Figure 15.3 shows how a content tree can be laid out. The top of the tree is typically (although not always) the content through which people will encounter your brand for the first time. It is also the content used to redirect a brand image or positioning. In old-school marketing this was the world of TV ads, print and other above-the-line activities. Now it is dominated by large-scale virals, paid brand work, celebrity endorsements and Hero content. You might not have much of this type of film, but it has got to look great, be distinctive yet totally on-brand, and have a substantial weight of paid activation behind it (as it is less likely to pick up organic search). The top of the tree is also where we typically see emotionally driven work, due to its nature of being so brand focused. It has the widest possible audience, as it is looking to raise fame levels over all other goals.

FIGURE 15.3   The content tree

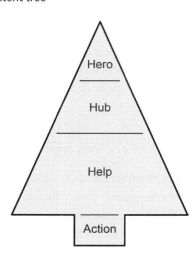

As we move towards the base of the tree there is more content, reflecting how audiences moving through the funnel are looking for more specific answers to their questions. This is still brand-level emotional content, although it is likely that you will want to consider segmenting this content into multiple audiences.

CASE STUDY
A multiple video campaign: adidas Football

A brand that excels at creating an effective tree of content that answers potential and existing customers' needs is adidas Football. This is a brand that, through the agency We Are Social, has nailed video strategy. Take a moment to look at four of their media platforms: YouTube, Facebook, Instagram and Twitter. Along with noting that they use each platform very differently, you can see that they have a strong mix of content for people at any stage of the consumer journey.

YouTube: ▶ **Video 92**

Facebook: ▶ **Video 93**

Instagram: ▶ **Video 94**

Twitter: ▶ **Video 95**

Each of the adidas channels approaches things in a different way. YouTube (a 'fixed' platform) is used in a similar way to a classic TV channel, with live broadcasts, catch-up series and trailers. More fluid channels like Facebook are used as vehicles to activate content into people's feeds. Although they treat all platforms very differently, let's just consider the output as a total body of work.

Awareness-raising videos that are activated with sizeable media spend can be considered to be positioned at the top of the tree. These films are big, attention-grabbing thumb stoppers. Style- and attitude-driven films featuring the world's biggest players like Paul Pogba dominate this level of content. It's all-out Hero content, focused on attracting attention and being distinctive.

Below this in the hypothetical tree of content there is a large body of work that is still brand and emotion focused, but that is not so heavily activated. It listens to and reacts to the audience, mixing all the most powerful elements of social from instant feedback to a sense of real engagement.

Never follow feat Paul Pogba – adidas Football
22 November 2016, adidas Football YouTube channel
▶ **Video 96**

The channel feeds the viewer with regular, topical and engaging films. The content is there to build engagement with the brand and mostly sits on fixed channels (most notably YouTube).

This approach was most evident in the 2014 World Cup campaign, which saw adidas Football move from traditional advertiser to all-out publisher. The link below is for a case study created by YouTube that shows how they worked with adidas during the campaign.

Go behind the scenes with adidas – YouTube advertisers
27 January 2015, YouTube Advertisers YouTube channel
▶ **Video 97**

Adidas Football also creates a high volume of content designed to answer questions and add detail for those looking for it. We can consider this as the base of their tree. Again mostly sitting on YouTube, this content pushes up organic search as well as retaining people in the world of adidas Football's content.

Taken as a whole, this body of video content:

- answers the opportunities raised by people's needs and interests through the buying cycle;
- listens to and reacts to the audience's feedback and engagement;
- uses different platforms in different ways;
- contains a great number of films that answer interests and questions, keeping viewers engaged and keeping them on the channel;
- has fewer Hero-level films than other content but those is does have are highly distinctive and pushed on channels where paid activations can raise awareness well.

Although adidas Football doesn't talk of its content in terms of the tree we discussed above, it does reflect the framework. I'm indebted to Joe Weston, adidas Football's Group Account Director at We Are Social, for his reflections on how video campaigns deliver at the sharp end.

At the very base of the content tree is a small amount of highly tactical Go! content that is designed to drive people to convert. It might be that you have a piece of this content for each campaign or that you simply have a brand wide film that is used across the board to encourage people to take action.

Having looked at content in the widest sense, we may feel ready to delve into the planning of when to release it and activation techniques, discussed in the next chapter.

Create better video campaign structures with content mapping

Anyone in content marketing will be familiar with content mapping, the exercise of aligning the persona types of your customers with their stage in the marketing funnel. Let's put this into the context of your video strategy. Here is a simple yet effective exercise to help you think about maximizing the opportunities that occur through the customer journey and it can form a starting point for planning how to most effectively activate each piece of video.

Create a simple table in your software of choice and list in the left-hand column all the buying personas that are applicable to the brand. Then consider what stages there are for them in the buying journey and map this along the top. It's then a simple case of thinking about what content might help at each of these touchpoints. Refer back to the digital sales funnel on page 71 and video types on page 73 for some pointers. At this point, don't worry about budgets or practicalities, just get an outline of what you think the dream scenario would be. Later on we will look at how to prioritize how you get this done.

Programming

The timing of when you release videos and start their activation (known as programming) will tie directly back to the objectives of your campaign. A well-planned-out video campaign will run to a few basic principles. In Chapter 4 I referred to the theory of 'always-on' marketing, and as we plan multi-video campaigns this can be put into practice. Brands should look to be creating short-term buzz with awareness campaigns, building engagement with regular hub content and giving viewers a reason to come back with regular help (or hygiene) videos. The rest of this chapter looks at a few key points to consider when writing your programming strategy.

Timings: what day should you release content?

Timings of when you release content will boil down into one of two types: either it will be built around a specific event that cannot be moved, or it won't. We can consider this as being either tent-pole or campaign marketing.

Tent-pole marketing is the process of using big events around which you launch your marketing activity. The term originally came out of Hollywood and was used to describe the hype surrounding popular movies; in an effort to secure people's attendance at the cinema, studios would increase activity up to the release date, creating a graph of engagement that resembled a pole with a tent hanging off it. The term really is now usually applied to any event that is used as a focus for marketing activity. This might be an event that you set up, but more usually it is one that is already a firm fixture in the calendar. Fathers' Day, Easter, Halloween, Wimbledon and the Super Bowl are all obvious choices on the list. The key to video in tent-pole based campaigns is to add constructively to the conversation, not just add to the noise.

But when should you release videos that are focused on a tent-pole event? The answer is to be as clever as you can about it. A really popular event will have hundreds of brands creating content on the theme, so consider how to make something that doesn't get lost in the noise. A film for April Fools will have to go out on the morning of 1 April, but something around Halloween can be launched anything up to a week before. Invariably, though, once the event has passed, your video will become stale quickly, so a post-event launch is best avoided. There is one exception to this and that is if the film is created during the event itself. In this case consider live streaming or super-fast turnaround edits. At Hurricane we have a system of working overnight to create edits for launch at 8 am the morning after an event, which means the content fits in with the news narrative of the day. This is especially key if the event runs over multiple days (such as a golf championship) where content from the previous day is still part of the ongoing conversation.

When there is no large-scale event to build hype around, brands must construct their own campaign tempo. The best approach is to use wider campaign timings as the hook around which you can build a video schedule. Consider launch dates of products as a good starting point. If they don't exist you can use the video itself as the tent-pole around which to make the noise.

Both tent-pole and campaign approaches will work best if you can build hype around the launch with other video content. Your social media team or agency will have some insight on what they can best work with, but this will no doubt include teasers (maybe two weeks, one week and one day before launch), behind-the-scenes clips and 'making ofs'.

Moving away from events, let's look at release dates at a more micro level. The worst months of the year to post are May and September as these are months when a lot of YouTube and other social media users are either finishing or starting school, away on sports seasons, or on vacation.[1] The best days for videos are typically Thursday or Friday. Consider the weekend for longer-form content. One way to combine both of these is with teaser or shorter content during the week and longer-form content on the weekend. It is advisable to conduct A/B testing across the campaign to see what works best for your audience.

Timings: what time of day is best?

Time of day matters, and it's not just because of when people can actually spare the time for a video. Throughout the day, people become more or less open to messaging and they change their decisions based on how many they have already made. In a study of 1,100 decisions made by Israeli parole boards (judges, criminologists and social workers), it was found that prisoners who had

FIGURE 15.4   Best days to post videos for consumers

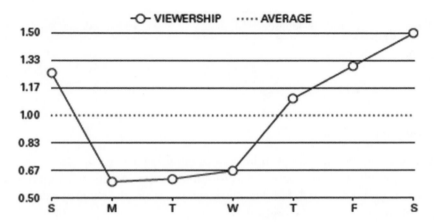

their parole hearing early in the morning received parole around 70 per cent of the time. However, only 10 per cent of those who appeared late in the day were likely to receive parole.[2] It would seem even judges get tired and grumpy.

So, when should you post? A quick answer to this question (albeit an annoying one) is to release videos when your audience is watching. The long answer is in fact constantly changing and depends on the channels you use and the audience you have. We will go into a few rules of thumb now, but before we do, note that there are online tools (such as Coschedule) that will help add insight and automation to your release schedule.

The best times to upload a video broadly depend on the day of the week; your wider marketing schedule and audience type will affect which day you choose but it is worth knowing which hours typically work best.[3]

Long-tail and short-tail activations

When planning release schedules, consider that the best results will come from rapid awareness building, but also from conversations. Campaigns will of course need to be 'front-loaded' with content that makes a splash, but then there should be a steady release schedule of related, engagement-building content. This will also use a mixture of platforms, making the most of Facebook's high awareness rates at the start of a campaign and YouTube's long-tail retention and organic search benefits (see page 55 on OVPs).

TABLE 15.1   The best days to post videos (rough averages across all channels)

Monday	Tuesday	Wednesday	Thursday	Friday	Saturday	Sunday
14:00–16:00	14:00–16:00	14:00–16:00	12:00–15:00	12:00–15:00	09.00–11.00	09.00–11.00

Publish regularly and build a series

Thinking of content ideas can be a substantial barrier to content creation. One way to make ideation easier is to build a series. An episodic approach built around themes will build engagement and make the channel a destination through the week. An episode a week is a good starting point but if you want to go all-out consider having a number of series stripped across the week. It's a substantial time investment so may be more appropriate for pro YouTubers than brands, but it's worth considering if you have a super-keen team with plenty to say. By covering the same topics on the same days, viewers will know when to tune in, and search engines will reward your commitment by bumping you up the rankings.

Don't overdo it

We all love content, and are sure that our followers want to hear everything we have to say, but when looking at release schedules heed this warning... don't overdo it! 57 per cent of UK consumers actively take steps to avoid brands that send too many messages. An even higher percentage un-follow brands on social, close accounts and cancel subscriptions to cut down on brand messages.[4] Great content is going to increase your chance of engagement but remember that consumers have limited patience for excessive contact. The best way to get around this is to ensure that your content is self-discovered by viewers rather than being forced into their lives; they are less likely to unsubscribe if they have found content themselves.

References

1 Linda Address
24 July 2020
Best time to post on YouTube in 2021: how to net the biggest audience
HowSociable
https://howsociable.com/blog/best-time-to-post-on-youtube/ (archived at https://perma.cc/96ER-4E5Z)

2 Shai Danziger, Jonathan Levav and Liora Avnaim-Pesso
2011
Extraneous factors in judicial decisions
Proceedings of the National Academy of Sciences
DOI: 10.1073/pnas.1018033108

3 Geoff Weiss Here are the best months, days and times to publish YouTube videos
Entrepreneur
www.entrepreneur.com/article/241764 (archived at https://perma.cc/YMA5-UQB4)

4 Martin Hayward
11 March 2015
Irrelevant marketing from brands give rise to the 'deletist consumer'
Aimia
www.marketscreener.com/quote/stock/AIMIA-INC-1408916/news/Aimia-Irrelevant-Marketing-from-Brands-Gives-Rise-to-the-lsquo-Deletist-Consumer-20026296/ (archived at https://perma.cc/44CE-EJZK)

16

Step 4: building the perfect content hub

Way back in Chapter 4 I introduced the array of online video platforms (sometimes 'players' or OVPs) that are available. Now we've been through the planning process and learned a lot on the way we can start to look at OVPs not just as repositories of videos, but as hubs of content that drive engagement.

A content hub is more than somewhere that stores videos: it is a coherent channel that actively encourages engagement. It works as a destination on its own, entertaining, informing viewers and leading to ever-increasing viewing figures, subscribers and brand connections. The overarching principle of a good hub is to give viewers a great watching experience. It is about adapting the mindset of a TV channel controller, looking at content that keeps people engaged, scheduling that maximizes audiences, and structuring to help people easily find what they want. It's a logical conclusion to the idea of brands embracing the mindset of a publisher.

Inspiration for powerful non-brand-specific content hubs can be found on Netflix, the BBC iPlayer and even iTunes. The principle is to get people there, give them a warm welcome and keep them there. Great brands to look at are adidas Football and GE, both of which nail a hub as a destination:

adidas Football: ▶ **Video 98**

GE: ▶ **Video 99**

Video content hubs are simply well laid-out OVPs that curate content to be easy to follow. As covered in Chapter 4, not all OVPs are created equal, and they all have their own strengths and weaknesses. They come under one of two categories: 'Fixed' or 'Fluid':

- Fluid platforms are scrolled through at speed and are great for activating content with media spend, or for driving a media-sharing campaign. But once people have consumed a piece of content, they are on to the next thing. This is not the place to build your content future, so Facebook, Instagram and Twitter are pretty much out as hubs.

- Fixed platforms are where people scroll less and are in a 'view mode'. YouTube is an obvious choice but there are others in the public OVP space such as Vimeo, or in the owned space such as Brightcove and TwentyThree. No matter which platform you choose for housing your content collection, there are a number of rules to help you build it well. To make this easier I've constructed bad and good content hubs for comparison (Figure 16.1).

FIGURE 16.1   Bad and good content hub layout

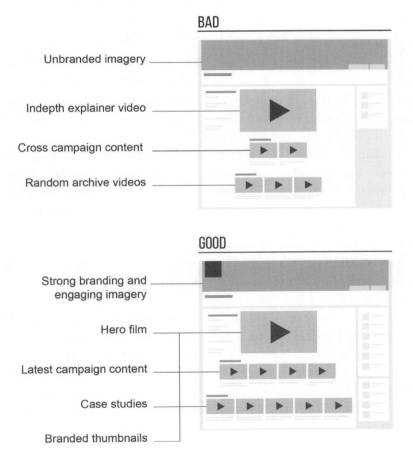

The goal of a hub is to keep people watching, thus driving engagement metrics and in turn people's feelings about a brand and the fluency with which it comes to mind. A good structure that is easy to follow is an excellent start, and actually having engaging content is also a given, but there are more specific things that can be done to drive engagement.

The first thing is to make people feel at home on the platform; if they feel welcomed, they will stay longer. A very good way of doing this is with a channel intro or channel positioning film. This can be a brand film or, even better, a platform-specific intro.

The second thing to do is to introduce a driver that is shown at the end of the video, which encourages people to watch further. This can be built into the film itself; maybe it's a presenter suggesting what to watch next or a piece of graphics naming other content. But these approaches are costly to change and can tie you into a specific structure. A much more flexible approach is to add a level of interactivity once the video is on the hub.

Interactivity on video content hubs

Almost every OVP has added some level of interactivity in recent years. From end frames and cards on YouTube, TwentyThree and Vimeo all the way to integration with shopping baskets on Wirewax, there are always new and exciting things to try. As with most things in this area, it is a case of trial and error until the best approach is clear.

YouTube's end frames are simple links to other resources and can be used to point viewers to other videos, playlists or channels on YouTube. This is a really useful tool if you have multiple layers of help content and you are looking to push viewers between playlists, otherwise your audience will be following multiple steps.

End frames can drive channel subscriptions and give links to a brand website. Adding them is worth a test and you will see engagement rates grow. Use the link below or search 'add end frames to YouTube video' to find our more: ▶ **Video 100**.

I do a fair amount of mountain bike riding (although it turns out that writing the second edition of a book does kind of get in the way of that) and I often watch technique videos to try to help myself fall off less. The Global Mountain Bike channel uses end frames really well and makes navigating hundreds of films much easier. They also integrate the presenters into the end frame process, making further engagement integral to the channel experience.

FIGURE 16.2   End frames to drive engagement

SOURCE Courtesy of Play Sports Network Ltd, Global Mountain Bike Network

How to ride slippy trails – mountain bike skills
29 November 2016, Global Mountain Bike Network YouTube channel
▶ **Video 101**

FIGURE 16.3   Interactivity within a YouTube video

SOURCE Courtesy of Play Sports Network Ltd, Global Mountain Bike Network

How much do pro mountain bikers get paid? Dirt Shed Show episode 114
12 May 2017, Global Mountain Bike Network YouTube channel
▶ **Video 102**

In a similar way, YouTube's interactive cards add interactivity throughout points in a video, not just at the end. Cards can point viewers to a specific URL and show customized images, titles and calls to action. They can also be used to add polls and surveys.

Again, looking at the GMB network, they make use of this in one of the films about how much professional bike riders get paid. Skip through to 02.11 to see how they use it. The nice thing about this is that when the survey pops up you don't see the results until you add your own vote.

If you'd like to learn more about adding links you can use this link or search 'add card to video': ▶ **Video 103**.

When these tests are in place you can see how well these are doing in your analytics: ▶ **Video 104**

Structuring and optimizing your video content hub

If people visiting your channel watch one video and leave, it's not working as a content hub. The way to avoid this is to make the navigation work in as clear a way as possible. So, simple titles that are clearly linked and a constant naming convention are the way to go. Look back at the discussion about optimizing video (page 126) for more on this. If you've chosen YouTube as your hub, it is essential to use playlists. Playlists ensure that viewers stay engaged in content and stop their eyes wandering over to the right-hand bar where they can be attracted to other content chosen by YouTube.

Further to this, just like individual videos, your entire channel should be optimized for organic search. This means making sure titles, thumbnails, channel art, descriptions, internal links, etc, are all there and up to date. This step alone will make an incremental difference to your channel's performance.

Here are some other channel tips:

- Choose descriptive titles for your playlists that help your channel SEO. Make sure these are consistent across playlists to improve the user experience.

- Ensure your channel's art matches your brand.

- Channel art appears differently on various devices, so make sure it works for everyone. Google answers that well and you can read it on this link: ▶ **Video 105**.

- Delete old content, and don't let your channel become a dumping ground. Be vigorous with this!

- Make sure there are no old channels left hanging around that people might find by mistake.

- Never organize by 'most recent uploads'.

- Don't forget the profile icon or other branding.

- Lay it out using a horizontal view if you have lots of content.

- Fill in all the boxes of descriptions – it's good for SEO and looks complete.

- A/B test different styles of thumbnail until you find the best type for you, and run this consistently across all videos.

And there we have it – a round-up of the key things you need to consider when building a multi-video hub. As with all things, it is a case of getting started, testing and adapting. It will take a while to get the hub performing beautifully, but you'll get there.

17

Step 5: create high-volume video content – easily

When content marketing first hit at full speed, the pressure was on for internal and external marketing teams to figure out a way of creating regular, accurate and informative written content. It took a while for some brands to achieve it, but most got there in the end… and then video came on the scene!

Video production is heavy on resources and skills; if it goes wrong it looks bad at best and unusable at worst… and when it goes wrong it can be sizeable budgets that go wrong with it. As you embark on the journey of putting video in your marketing plan, how do you avoid the pitfalls? How do you maintain a high-quality output? How do you develop great ideas? And how do you avoid your internal teams being broken by the workload?

There are a few things you can do, from prioritizing to up-skilling internal teams and sending the work out to external agencies. This chapter will give you the insight to decide how best to feed the content beast.

Do you need it, and when do you need it?

When you did your content-mapping exercise (back in Chapter 15) you may well have ended up with dozens of pieces of content that could be useful. This level of content can be daunting and expensive, but do you really need to do it all straight away? And do you need to even make it all? It's as important to get things started and test what works as it is to get all the content made. As long as there is enough content on your hub to keep people engaged you don't have to have vast volumes at the start. I talk to clients about this in terms of a simple cost/benefit chart, which helps them to decide what to create first. This tool identifies which films have easy, cost-effective wins and which films can be done when the pressure is off. Table 17.1 is fairly self-explanatory and will help you cut down on an ominous work-load. Mark each of the categories out of 10 and see what the score is.

You can see from the 'cost' column in Table 17.1 that two pieces of content are as affordable as each other, and they will both make the same impact on the brand, but they can still clearly be prioritized. Ease of implementation is the key difference here.

So, now you've decided in what order to make the content, you are faced with the big decision of whether to keep it in-house or send it out to a production agency. Even if you're working with a strategic partner that has production capabilities, you can still make some content yourself, and it can be very effective. When YouTube works with brands, they talk about growing the volume of content on social channels through the 'three Cs': Curate, Collaborate, Create.[1] It's a clear, common-sense approach that can also work away from Google's channels so it's worth understanding. I've put the three Cs in this order so we can talk about them in ascending order of how much work they involve.

Curate

The easiest way to add to your content portfolio is by linking to work already made by others (assuming here that you do it the correct way and don't just reuse it without permission). The 'curate' approach is really useful if you are taking a campaigning or content-rich approach that is light on brand messages, or if you want to get reviews from others. It can be as simple as collecting relevant links from around the web and including them on your channel, or as involved as asking your customers to make videos and submit them.

TABLE 17.1 Prioritizing content production

		Cost	Excepted effect on KPIs	Ease of implementation	Speed of implementation	TOTAL SCORE
Idea 1	Film 1	8	10	9	7	34
Idea 2	Film 2	8	10	5	5	28
Idea 3	Film 3	4	6	3	5	19
etc						

Be careful when curating the content of others, though, as you need to be aware of who they are and what they stand for. I was recently working with a brand that was curating reviews of its products but on a closer look we found that the videos also contained reviews of their competitors – which is not something that you really want nestled in your content hub.

At an advanced level, brands can generate content by running campaigns or competitions that encourage people to create videos. A campaign for the meat-based snack Peperami Roll did just this to good effect. The campaign created videos of a presenter rolling in comedic ways, then socialized these and asked viewers to send in their own 'rolling' videos around the tag #HowIPeperamiRoll. The prize for the best video was a classic Rolls Royce!

My favourite response was created by a chap called Leslie Wai who went above and beyond the call of duty to try to win the car, creating an animation about himself rolling off into space.[2]

Collaborate

The second way to get content onto your calendar is to collaborate with others. Influencers that know your market make brand videos such as reviews or sponsored pieces. The key thing here is to work with them to make content that broadens the reach of your messages. It's a great way of reducing the pressure to make content but can also get pricey if you are looking for high-profile influencers.

Create

The final method of content growth requires the biggest commitment and is also the most obvious one... you create it. Brand-created videos are the most closely controlled by the brand and they take on board all the planning around content type that we have been discussing up to this point. It can be any one of the content types from Hero to Go! (see page 73) and can be of any quality. You can either literally create it yourself or work with a production company to get exactly what you want. I certainly encourage brands to get involved if they can make content well and have a clear strategic framework in which to roll it out. Before looking at specific tips for working with agencies and making DIY content, remind yourself of the production process, which I covered in Chapter 7 (page 101).

Building your internal team

How do you take an internal team, up-skill them and empower them to make great videos? It's a big ask for anyone and (as with so many successful business functions) it boils down to playing to people's strengths and providing them with the right support and equipment.

The people

Start by holding some informal chats with your team. Who is up for the challenge? Who has hidden skills or untapped experience? The skills you will need to find are outlined below; they might be found in several individual people or one super hotshot that can do it all. Bear in mind that some people will see the creation of an internal video function as a chance to develop their careers, but others will see it as a burden. The main thing you have to do is to see through what they say in public and only involve team members that are actually supportive. Here is a list of the roles you need to fill:

- Writer: can they bring the brand message to life with a powerful story? This could be a copywriter but very often the written word is very different from something used in a video.

- Producer: who is going to make this whole thing happen, getting buy-in from team members and running the schedules?

- Director: who has the creative eye to make it look good and ask questions of everyone across the business?

- Camera op: who has a technical mind and is willing to spend their spare time looking at manuals and getting better at the skill? Of everyone on the team, these are the ones who will feel the heat most as their mistakes will be visible for everyone to see.

- Editor: look for someone with a technical mind and a good sense of the story you are trying to tell.

- Graphics: you might not need this, but if there is someone on the print or web team that can start to understand motion graphics it will lift the polish of what you do. There are loads of online training resources they can use to get up to speed, including LinkedIn Learning (www.linkedin.com/learning/me) and Video Copilot (www.videocopilot.net).

So, you've assembled your crack team and you are good to go. But remember the following – or you will quickly lose buy-in and enthusiasm:

- Give them time – to learn, to test and to make (see box below).

- Give them room to fail – don't start with high-profile projects straight away and make sure everyone in the company understands that things will not go perfectly while the team find their feet.

- Give praise – this is a creative process and if people don't feel valued the juices will dry up.

- Give training – if you can afford it, get in a paid expert to teach and your quality will go through the roof.

- Give them the best kit you can.

- Help them understand the overall business objectives of why they are all doing this in the first place.

TIME

If you don't properly allocate time to make videos, you'll put the whole experiment at risk, as you'll end up with a stressed, unmotivated team and bad output.

Creativity requires time
4 December 2013, rodgerwerkhoven YouTube channel
 Video 106

The IT and computer kit you will need

I'm keen to avoid getting technical in this book (although it is one of my favourite things) but we need to talk about data storage if you are going to create videos in-house. If you set up your own department, you are going to needs loads of it. And by loads, I mean the kind of storage requirements that will have the IT department breathing down your neck as soon as your first project starts – it will probably take up four times your department's total allocated space on its first day. A company that is used to handling spreadsheets, word documents and some publicity pictures will have to gear up substantially to deal with video. But don't panic – you can start low tech and build your way up… no need to install optical networks and offsite servers just yet.

When you shoot footage, it will initially be stored on a card in the camera (as rushes). Rushes are the most precious thing in the department as they are irreplaceable. With that in mind, the first thing after filming will be to take this card and store it somewhere, backing it up onto a mirror server so that you don't lose it if there is a drive fault. The mantra here is 'Until it's in two places it is in no place.' Mirroring is essential if you want to avoid disaster, even though it doubles your data requirements.

When you start editing, you may find that your network is not fast enough to handle video data, in which case the rushes should be stored on the machine that is being used for editing (called local storage). The best way to do this is with a locally connected hard drive that uses the fastest connection you can afford. Buy a good make and pay a bit more for speed and reliability.

So, taking these two things into account, the best way to get going is to have two large (as in 4 TB each) drives. One of these stores the rushes; the other is a mirror of it. Store projects over the network so you get all the benefits of the IT team's back-up systems but store rushes and large data files locally.

I'll stop there so I don't start boring you to tears with bit rates and write speeds!

Filming equipment

I've helped a number of companies to set up and grow internal departments and the first thing that gets discussed is always camera kit, as it's the largest visible cost of video creation. The fact is, it's training and learning that are the biggest investment, but as these are normally hidden in a different departmental budget they are less visible.

So how much should you budget for kit if you are making a high volume of videos? Clearly the equipment required will be directly related to the type of content you are creating, but here is a typical set-up. Note how this is a different equipment list to the one of DSLR and mobile phone based filming kits that I discussed in Chapter 6. You can spend way less and indeed way more than this, but the following costs are based on kits I've put together for in-house teams over the past couple of years, and balance value with quality.

CAMERA KIT

- HD camera with pro sound inputs: US $3,000–$6,000. Unless your team is super on it you really only need the basics but with cameras you really do get what you pay for. Consider getting a camera model that has been around for three years or so as it will still do the job for you and will be much better value than the latest big thing.

- Lenses: $500–$2,000. The quality of the glass in front of your camera will have a huge effect on the picture. Don't scrimp on this part of the purchasing decision.

- Tripod: $300–$600.

- Key light/soft lighting panel and fill light: $600–$2,000. The internet is full of advice on lighting but the 'softer' it is the better it will look. See page 169.

- Monitor: $400–$1,500. If your team can clearly see what the footage looks like, they are more likely to get things right.

- Anti-shine powder: $20. Everyone sweats, even the CEO.

- Cases and bags: $200–$500. You've spent a fair chunk of cash on kit; look after it and it will look after you.

SOUND KIT

- Boom pole and gun microphone: $400–$800.

- Radio microphone set: $450–$800. There are cheap radio sets out there, but don't spend less than this as they can sound awful.

- Headphones: $100.

- Microphone sticky pads: $25. Hiding the microphone inside shirts and jumpers is the worst part of recording sound. After decades of making do with clips, I now use the fabulous Rycote Stickies: ▶ **Video 107**.

BACKDROPS AND COLOURAMAS: $300

Go for paper, not cloth, as the results will be much better; just be prepared to replace them on a regular basis. If the room can fit it, I would always use something that is three to four metres wide. Anything less and you are restricted in the shot sizes that you will be able to do.

All this means that you are up and running for between $5,900 and $14,600. Remember that camera kit is a capital asset, and you will get about five years' life out of it before it is redundant. However, if you look after it well you will be able to resell it for a decent price (in the first two years at least) if you need to. I would plan to recoup costs over two years and build in depreciation over a five-year period.

Studio spaces

With the kit in place, we need to consider the physical space in which filming can happen. If you're looking to make a small number of basic talking heads, all you really need is a boardroom big enough to put lights up. If, however, you're looking for regular content creation with more advanced set-ups, it's time to consider converting some office space. Here are some top tips on making it happen:

- *Work closely with building managers.* To get this off the ground you will probably have to involve someone from facilities. I've had a number of conversations with these departments over the years and every time I've found them to be real allies; if anyone can get walls moved or power sockets added these are the people to do it. The key is to get them on board with the vision of what you are doing and why you are going all out on video. Once they see the business need they will get on board with making it happen.

- *Bigger is better.* You will need at least double the space you think if you want people's lives to be easy. The minimum for interviews with lights is 5 x 5 metres, and 8 x 6 and upwards will be even better. That broom cupboard isn't going to do the job. Choose a room with a view if you can, as it will look good without building a set or bringing in lots of props.

- *Power.* Often people worry that a studio will need massive power, but really just some extra plug points will do it. Modern cameras and LED lights draw fairly little power.

- *Sound.* Huge glass windows, uncontrollable air conditioning, noisy corridors and hand dryers in the toilets next door are all everyday issues that you will have to fight. If you can avoid them when you set up the room it will make your team's life much easier.

- *Storage.* Fairly large and lockable storage will have to go somewhere, the nearer to the filming the better.

- *Backgrounds.* Brands often get excited about green screen and my advice here is simple… don't do it! The last thing you need is to be keying footage and faffing about in the edit with tricky green screen footage. Buy background rolls and pole supports and you can change the backdrop as much as you like. There is also a temptation to use brand colours but this can go badly as video is not like print and matching exact brand colours is nigh-on impossible for non-specialists to achieve.

And there we have it: the cameras, lights, sound kit and studio you need for a DIY production department. It's exciting stuff. But what about outsourcing some or all of your production requirements? What are the pros and cons? And how do you get the best from the people that you use?

> Over the past few years, I have been working with UK-based solicitors Osborne Clarke to enable them to create a high volume of marketing videos internally. Hurricane designed and installed two studio spaces, in both their London and Bristol offices. This included multi-camera setups, an edit suite and sound kit. The key to success proved to be the creation of simple workflows and training. On both sites we were lucky to have enthusiastic, capable people that could be trained up on high-volume, high-quality video production and were supported by forward-thinking senior leaders. At the last count the internal team had created over 600 videos in two years, all at speed and a low cost.
>
> It's worth taking a look at the output from both studios on the OC.TV YouTube channel: (▶) **Video 108**.

Outsourcing your video and strategy

Lead agency

Traditionally, brands have used their lead agency as the source of video production. The lead agency handles strategy and planning, and then brings in a video production partner to get the filming and graphics done. This model works well for fully integrated campaigns that take in the entire ecosystem of marketing such as print, TV, digital and content, as all the thinking is in one place. If it is a more stand-alone campaign or is video-specific, this model may be overkill. Lead agencies charge somewhere between 20 and 50 per cent on top of production fees, so you can find budgets don't go as far.

Video marketing agency

The world is a fast-moving place and the agency landscape is always developing. As video has grown into a marketing discipline all of its own, specialist agencies (like my agency Hurricane) have evolved to offer a full-service video package. These hybrid agencies sit between full-service agencies and production companies, offering a range of services from strategic thinking and planning through to production, PR/social activation and media buying. They can work alongside a lead agency or take on some of the roles that they would traditionally have done. The only word of caution here is that it is fairly rare to have this skillset in one place; there are lots of video production companies saying they offer planning and activation services, but not as many who actually have the staff to do it. The best bet when looking for someone like this is to make sure that some of their team have worked outside of the video niche and look for them to prove they have marketing credentials and campaign experience as well as production know-how.

Video production company

Production companies range from one-man teams to multi-million dollar behemoths. Here are the key points to consider if you want to work with one:

- You will need to shoulder more responsibility for campaign strategy with this approach than with an agency. You will also need to activate the campaign yourself or bring in a separate partner.

- Production companies often have a speciality (eg 'hand-drawn animation') so make sure they can offer the right solution for your brief, not just a solution that they know how to make. Companies that have a wide range of creative styles in their showreel will be more flexible than a one-trick pony.

- The success of the output will be directly tied to the quality and insight of your brief, as these companies may well not have the in-house skills to offer insight if your strategy or brief is slightly off-target.

- You get what you pay for, so don't simply go for the cheapest.

- Focus on getting a cultural fit as much as you do on credentials and experience.

- There is a new wave of websites offering highly cost-effective online production partners. Known as crowdstudios, these can offer content creation at low prices and are offering better service levels all the time. There are lots of bad sites out there with results that can be hit and miss, but there are also good ones like Tongal (www.tongal.com).

Freelancers

One-person operations are highly cost-effective solutions to getting videos made, although there are a few things to consider:

- They won't have been involved in your strategic thinking so brief them very precisely on what you need and manage the edit process closely from the start.
- If they are ill or get another shoot booked in they probably will not have the backup to get the work done – so don't use them if the film is very time-sensitive.
- Communications and feedback can be very hard with this approach as you are relying on one person who is doing many jobs. You won't have the production managers and resources to hand that you would have with a larger outfit, so don't expect anyone to get back to you quickly.
- If you get a good one it is worth giving them as much work as possible, so you become their preferred client and they are willing to work around your needs, rather than the other way around.

Summary

And there we have it. You now have the skills to build an internal production team, or to use external resources to get the work done. As with all these things, start small and test, then scale up what works and interrogate your approach and results. Out of this activity you will end up with some great content. Now it's time to get the world to sit up and watch, and that's exactly what we will be looking at in the next chapter.

References

1 Kim Larson
   July 2015
   Building a YouTube content strategy: lessons from Google BrandLab
   Google
   www.thinkwithgoogle.com/marketing-resources/building-youtube-content-
   strategy-lessons-from-google-brandlab/ (archived at https://perma.cc/
   UCH4-LL2V)
2 Leslie Wai
   2 December 2015
   This is #HowIPeperamiRoll around town,
   Vine
   https://vine.co/v/iWn0LALmQdO (archived at https://perma.cc/838V-2YYX)

18

Step 6: activate your multi-video campaign and test

In Section Two we went over the range of video activation techniques available and considered how these techniques can be used for a single piece of content. In this chapter we move on and scale this approach for multi-video campaigns, introducing analysis and testing to create a rolling strategy with the results of one video forming feedback into the next. We will also be covering the key steps you should take before, during and after campaign launch. If you take a while to read books like this, it might be worth skimming back over Chapter 8 to refresh yourself before pushing ahead.

Pre-launch prep

Assuming that you have a great piece of video content ready to go, there are a few things that need to be done before launching a campaign around it:

1 Make sure that the goals of the campaign are clear with specific mentions of success established (referring back to the vision and mission statements constructed earlier).

2 Confirm what tests are to be conducted and on what channels.

3 Optimize for search and engagement growth.

4 Prepare networks for launch.

5 Compile a media plan.

6 Create interactivity across the campaign.

1 Clarifying KPIs and goals before your campaign

The fundamental difference with multiple video campaigns over single videos is that you will be looking at how to build engagement with viewers over longer periods. So, it is highly unlikely that you are going to look at single metrics such as views and shares; it is more likely that you will consider signs of interest building over time, such as subscriptions, follows, click-throughs to other content and total watch time.

As the campaign launches, there will be KPIs set for each video that you launch, which will directly relate to the part of the sales funnel that needs to be activated. But before launch, it is worth marking out overall KPIs that directly relate to the vision and mission statement.

2 Plan testing

Testing different edits, openings and messages as well as media, channels and audiences is not purely for those with huge media and production budgets. Even a modest campaign can be improved with a testing process. Before buying up all the media you can afford or sticking to one version of a film, plan some testing into your process. Look at test results early and make changes quickly; the joy of having a multi-video campaign is that you have plenty of content to test with.

Exactly what tests you conduct will depend on budgets, audiences and goals; here are a few things to put in place to make your testing more efficient:

- Platform types. Plan to try a variety of platforms that relate to your strategy, spending small amounts until you see what works. Remember that different platforms will be seen in different ways; fixed social platforms such as YouTube will give a longer tail of activity but fluid ones such as Twitter and Facebook will get attention quicker. Which platform is having the biggest impact – five-second cuts on Instagram or in-depth conversations on YouTube?

- Plan to test as many things as you can handle, but also make it methodical so you can work out what is actually working. Better to test one or two things at a time than to throw everything open, as you won't be able to analyze the results.

- Build in a comparison of results across paid social and programmatic sites to see where ROI is greatest.

- Put in steps to look at results of A/B testing that you may have conducted on thumbnails, etc. Small changes can make a real difference.

- Agree who on the team will decide if the activation strategies are working, if they need adapting or if the campaign would benefit from increased media spend.

- Play with platforms before the main launch. The middle of a big media spend is not the time to be finding out how technologies work.

3 Optimize video campaigns for search, tracking and lead generation

Ensure all content has been optimized for search and for engagement growth. I covered a wide range of optimization techniques in Chapter 8, so now we just have to expand these approaches to a multi-video campaign:

- Descriptions and titles should provide consistency across links. This will help people navigate clearly around content and related works. Make sure that when you plan a series people can identify all the episodes easily – this is especially important if they work as a single linear whole, as viewers may well come across a middle episode first and you have to help them to get them in order quickly. This is less significant if each episode stands alone.

- Brand, channel and series identity also come into play at this stage. A consistency of look and feel in thumbnails should show through on all your content, and indeed across the content hub that it is placed on.

- How are the campaign and its constituent videos going to be tracked? Do you have the right approaches in place to allow that? Things like watch time and shares will be easy, but if your metrics are CTRs or visits to a landing page you will need to consider tracking tools. Bring in your SEO or web team at this point, as they will help you put measurement techniques in place. Consider using a link shortener such as Bitly or Stumble-Upon that will enable the tracking of click-through rates, etc, and will allow you to set up different platforms and ads with different links – so you can track what is working.

- The use of social OVPs that link into analytics (for example YouTube and Google) will allow you to see which users have clicked through to your content, so make sure someone is ready to dig down across all available data.

- If you are using advanced techniques such as personalization, remarketing and automation, now is the time to figure out how viewers will be directed to further content, and how you will adapt for second-time visitors to content hubs and social sites.

4 Get your network on standby

Part of the pre-launch is working on the buzz. If you have a PR agency or department on this you will of course be well briefed on whom they are talking to and how they will get it noticed. But if you don't have the luxury of external or in-house PR resources you will have to take a few steps yourself.

5 Media plan and set-up

You may be relying purely on social (earned) activations but to make a real impact the campaign will need at least some priming with paid placements. Buying paid ad space (media buying) is an entire discipline in itself, and it's likely that you will have an agency in place to do this. However, if you don't have that luxury, or you like to keep on top of what's going on, here are a few pointers on multi-video campaigns, to go in conjunction with the insights of Chapter 8:

- Scale is crucial. You can be clever with your budget and you can have great content, but at the end of the day it is the brands that have the biggest media behind them that will get into people's brains. Consider your media budget across all videos; where can you make the most impact for the lowest cost? The old TV model was that media spend would be 10x the production budget (so a $100,000 ad would be backed up with a million dollar spend). This is changing as adverts become more targeted, but you should be looking to spend at least the same again on media as you do on production, if not more. Spend much more on awareness-raising videos than on retention films. To maximize the effectiveness of your spend, be precise about the audience you are targeting and make sure to have sufficient media budget to reach them.
- Should you be doing it yourself or outsourcing? A media or video marketing agency will cost a bit extra but will add a massive amount of value to the process. Make sure you at least consider this before going it alone.

- Use the right tools for your budget. Some activation platforms (such as Google's Double Click) take a lot of effort and budget to get working at full steam but are best for wide-ranging, complex campaigns. Other tools (such as Google Display Network) on the other hand are cheaper and easier to get started with but are less scalable. As a rule of thumb for these examples I would say that if you have less than $10,000–$40,000 to play with you should be looking at GDN, and once you are above that budget you should be moving to Double Click (although it's not set in stone and it really depends on your goals and audience).

- People are more likely to watch video ads if they see them more than once, so look to serve multiple times and make sure media spend isn't spread too thinly. Targeting a small audience with multiple servings will have better results than spreading resources thinly over a large audience.

- Consider carefully the frequency caps that you put in place on ads. A big awareness campaign will aim to serve ads to viewers multiple times but don't get annoying. Videos that appear in feeds several times a day will attract negative comments and risk brand overload, leading to poor campaign results. As a rule of thumb, look to cap ads at no more than three impressions per viewer per day. Also consider whether you really want to serve the same ad again more than three times to one viewer, as your budget could be used better elsewhere.

- Target your ads at the light buyers of your product, as the ROI will be better than wasting media on loyalists that are already engaged.

- If you are using paid placements, you should put videos onto the system at least two days before the launch to give time for approvals. You don't want your go-live date to tick past only to find that your YouTube pre-rolls are in the approval process and not being served.

6 Adding interactivity to a campaign

Interactive video is becoming increasingly important in marketing, as it moves video from the linear delivery of information to an experience that viewers control and shape. The key value is that interactive video more effectively drives the behaviour of viewers, as they cannot passively view the content; they must literally engage in order to progress. It's a massive area that could easily fill a book on its own but here I'm going to run through some of the ways that interactive can be used, as well as give some insights from interactive video experts and users.

Interactive video takes many forms but here are some of the main approaches: branching, hotspots, text annotations, playlists, email gates and personalized.

- *Branching* shows content in small chunks that users can navigate themselves rather than one long video. This creates a non-linear narrative that people can self-discover and drives up engagement rates. Branching often happens at the end of a video when viewers are given a choice of what to watch next.

Newton Running from Boulder in Colorado used branching in a series of videos to raise engagement across their range of running shoes. Every runner has different attitudes and requirements, so it makes sense for viewers to choose their own route through a video. The video allows viewers to choose options that apply to them, from 'male/female' to 'foot type'. The brand benefited from a 90 per cent completion rate and a reduction in the time spent by call centre reps explaining the product to shoppers. The system also provided important insights into customer preferences that could be used in later campaigns.

Newton Running's 'Choose a shoe' interactive product selector experience
▶ **Video 109**

- Branching doesn't always require a specialist video player like the example above. In fact it can be achieved with something as simple as YouTube. In the example below an anti-knife-crime charity has used branching to help young people understand how choices they make can affect their entire life.

Choose a different ending: start
3 March 2009, adifferentending YouTube channel
▶ **Video 110**

- *Hot spots* are mouse-over elements that add detail to content. They also allow viewers to break out to websites or add items directly into a shopping basket (see the Wirewax interview below).
- *Text annotations* are visual elements that reinforce key messages with on-screen text. They can typically be clicked in the same way as hot spots with a text box appearing on screen.

- *Playlists* offer up other videos to watch, either during or at the end of the current video being played. This interactivity is typical in owned players such as Vidyard and Brightcove, although social OVPs like Vimeo and YouTube do have a limited functionality in this area. YouTube playlists share this name but are not really interactive as they are not within the video that is being watched.

- *Email gates* are forms that appear at points within a video to encourage viewers to enter their contact details. They are typically placed at the end of a video to try to attract people to give up their details or before content to create a gate that has to be completed before people can watch.

- *Personalized videos* use personal data (such as email and name) and integrates this into a video. The video is typically sent to the viewer's email a few minutes after they sign up with their details or can be sent to a database of existing email users. Personalized videos offer really high engagement rates as everyone likes to receive something personal to them. You can go directly to the personalized tech providers (like Idomoo) but it is easier to go through video marketing agencies that will offer this as a service and manage the whole process.

CASE STUDY
Wirewax: A chat with Steve Callanan

To gain a full insight on interactive, I chatted to Steve Callanan, MD at leading interactive video company Wirewax. Wirewax know their stuff, including a project with Guy Ritchie to help fashion brand Ted Baker boost online sales by 32 per cent across a 19-week campaign.

JM: What do you see as the benefits for brands using interactive video?

SC: There is no doubt that conventional video is an incredibly powerful, booming and engaging medium but it is costly, complex, difficult to produce and, most disturbingly, a digital dead end for audiences. Viewers can't take action on emotional impulse, communicate back in return or glean more when desired. For brands, this is a wasted opportunity. Simply allowing audiences to find out more, book a test drive for that car, buy what they can see or take part in what they're engaged with turns a matrix of coloured pixels into a uniquely powerful, multi-billion-dollar opportunity. With the overwhelming majority of audiences interacting (average 67 per cent) doing so many times over in the same session (average four times) and spending 3.5 times longer with an interactive video than the conventional alternative, it is clear that brands should embrace interactive video or risk losing out to competitors already embracing this technology.

JM: What do brands need to think about if they want to implement this?

SC: Interactive video is no longer a painful and expensive exercise. The technology has advanced significantly over the last few years so that enriching video content can be executed in minutes and with machine learning applications that process is almost entirely automated. While retrofitting existing content is an easy win, creating content especially for this type of lean-forward viewing experience is where this is going to get really exciting.

View the Ted Baker film mentioned in this case study at:

 Video 111

Launch day

After all the prep, it's actually launch day. For me it's preferable to get going with paid activations such as pre-rolls or Facebook ads and programmatic as soon as possible. Consider doing this before pushing out to your owned (already engaged) audience. This will ensure that you have some decent viewing figures before people find it organically through social. The only caveat to this is that your super-influencers should be getting preview copies to share, as it's important that they feel special.

With the paid activation under way (see Chapter 8 for details) you can turn your effort towards owned audiences, launching the PR offensive and getting the influencers going. Your owned audiences will be keen to hear about new campaigns, videos or products; they are easy to reach and open to what you have to say. To reiterate a point made throughout this book, though, just talking to current engaged fans is not going to grow your brand (as they already know who you are). It's good for maintaining relationships and building engagement but you have to put this within an outreach context.

With videos live and pushed out, be ready to engage with the audience and to point them to other connected content. The whole point of a multi-video campaign is to get people watching more than one thing. Recognize your community and as engagements start coming in, shout people out by name, engage with comments and generally take part in the conversations.

As the campaign builds up a head of steam, keep an eye on the analytics and be prepared to adapt your content for better results.

Post-launch: the four Rs – review, renew, refresh, reiterate

So, it's done. We've planned, crafted, created, optimized and launched an awesome video – it's time for tea, cake and medals! Ah, if only it were that easy. Although much of the heavy lifting is done, you need to squeeze every last drop of value from it and to make sure everything has worked as it should. It's time to move into the post-launch phase that I call the 'four Rs'. First, we will review the project, then we can renew, refresh or reiterate our way to success.

Review

The video is out in the world and the social noise is gathering. But is it working? And how do you demonstrate to others that there was real ROI? The key here is to record and analyze every metric available using the best tools you can get hold of. Paid players (such as TwentyThree and Brightcove) will have lots of data to dig into and they will provide support to get the data you need. Social channels will also have a lot of metrics, but these can be limited or scattered so I've outlined some tools that will help interrogate the success of videos on the main social platforms. The main social players all have built-in tools and measurement services, from self-serve tools like YouTube and Facebook analytics to more powerful (paid for) tools like Google Brand Lift, which will run tests on a live audience to see if your brand messages are cutting through. I've put a link to this tool, along with some other third-party tools, below:

- Brand Lift: Think with Google. ▶ **Video 112**
- Iconosquare: Instagram speciality measurement. ▶ **Video 113**
- Conviva: official Facebook media solutions partner for video and Facebook Live analytics. ▶ **Video 114**
- Sprout Social: reimagine how social media can grow your business. ▶ **Video 115**

When using these tools, there are huge numbers of KPIs to look at (as we discussed in Chapter 6). However, where you are thinking like a publisher rather than an advertiser, it's important to look at metrics that measure the overall growth in attention, as well as just cold views and click-throughs. My key metrics would be:

- Total watch time: 'The amount of time in aggregate that your viewers are watching your videos.' This is important across all channels, especially on YouTube, as 'YouTube optimizes search and discovery for videos that increase watch time on the site'.[1]

- Audience retention is a measurement of how many viewers stay on your content channel. Think like a publisher and look to retain people as long as you can.

- Engagement rates are key to campaigns as the highs and lows in engagement rates across your videos will tell you which parts were most viewed and which led to a 'drop-off'. Use this metric to figure out which content is resonating with your viewers. It's really useful when testing content as it gives valuable insight into what to do next.

- Brand lift is a wide-ranging metric that measures how many people know about a brand before and after a campaign. If you are building an awareness campaign at the top of the sales funnel this is a key KPI to measure. It won't tell you if the video is any good, but it will tell you if it's working. Most social channels have ways to measure this, and they often involve samples of the audience being shown different things and brand awareness between the groups being compared.[2]

- A key method of checking the success of your content is to send it out for external review. There are many systems available, from focus groups to high-tech eye-tracking studies that monitor subconscious behaviour. One popular solution for testing content is to use an agency called System 1 Group (formerly known as Brain Juicer PLC) (▶ **Video 116**). They offer a range of packages to test content on real people, and can give brands feedback within 24 hours. This speed of insight allows teams to quickly adapt what they are doing. You can expect to find out which messages have created an emotional response as well as insights on what can be improved. System 1 also creates a score for emotional impact. Measured out of 5, my agency (Hurricane Media) has made it to up to 4.8 for one of our films (created for Aptamil baby milk) so we are pretty pleased with that!

Renew, refresh, reiterate

When you know what's working, you can decide what to do next. This is where we can get going with testing and the ROI of your content will go through the roof. Testing and adapting ad campaigns is an entire book in itself, but in general the principle is to come up with a best guess (or hypothesis), run the campaign, see if you were right and adapt accordingly. If you have sent the video for focus-grouping or online analysis you will get a really clear idea of what is working and what is not. And even if you are looking at more mathematical metrics you will be able to figure out areas of improvement.

- *Renew.* If the content is working well and media spend is delivering results, it's time to renew the activation of what you are doing. Put the video in more paid placements until you hit your goals or can't justify the media spend any more. It's like renewing a library book. If you like the book, keep renewing it until you've read it from cover to cover.

- *Refresh.* If interest in the video is dipping, or performance is not as good as expected, it's worth refreshing what you have. This normally involves a re-edit, changes to start and end messages, activation on alternative channels or adding in other ingredients. It's worth rolling the dice a few more times before writing off a piece of content. Videos are typically refreshed following feedback from focus groups that highlights a part of the film that's putting people off. It's a simple job to remove or refocus that one part, thus lifting the overall success of the film. Just make sure you track what you're doing so you have good learning for the next campaign.

- *Reiterate.* This is taking the central idea of a film and doing something similar another time around. There are two main reasons to reiterate content, and they come into play if the video has done really well or really badly. First, if the concept is resonating well with audiences, but for some reason the video is not doing the job, it is time to do it again but differently. Take the basic principles and do them in a new way. This might be changing the execution (for example doing an interview instead of an animation) or changing the activation strategy. Second, at the other end of the scale the video may have done really well, in which case hitting the same messaging but in a slightly different way is an easy win.

Activation key points

Video campaign activation is a massive topic, but my purpose was to give you the knowledge needed to start building a multi-video campaign. Whether that is to totally go it alone or to understand what your social and video agency is up to, here is a brief rundown of the key points:

- Take the skills and tools used to activate a single film (Chapter 8) and scale these up across the whole content plan.
- Introduce a system to test your theories and adapt to new findings.
- Pre-launch, clarify your KPIs and test against these as soon as you can.
- Decide on the tests you will conduct before the campaign launch.
- Optimize all content consistently so it works coherently.
- Get a media plan together as soon as you can, tie it to the plan and use the right tools for the job.
- On launch day, activate owned channels first (although you may choose to do this days or weeks before so they are primed and ready).
- After launch, run the four Rs: review, then renew, refresh or reiterate.

Section Four summary

If this were tennis it would now be game, set and match. Over the last 18 chapters we have looked at the psychology of why online video works so well, how to build engaging creative content, how to activate single films and then how to build and launch multi-video campaigns. Each section has ended with a summary of key takeaways, and before I finally sign off here is a run-down of learning from Section Four:

- Before starting on a campaign, run an audit of existing content so you have a starting point as a reference.
- Create a vision statement to clarify what you want video to do for the brand.
- Create a mission statement of how you will get there.
- Use the content tree model to frame the types of content you can use.
- Create videos to drive specific stages of the digital sales funnel, from Awareness through Consideration to Conversion and Retention.

- Use the HHHG model to create the right content for the business need.

- Run a simple content-mapping exercise to help decide when and where to use content.

- Prioritize video creation and get something out quickly to run tests, rather than creating a large volume of videos before seeing how they will work.

- Schedule your content around the best time of day and day of the week for your audience.

- Maximize the impact of your content hubs by understanding how they each work and accommodating if they are 'fixed' or 'fluid'.

- Increase engagement with interactivity.

- Make high-volume content creation less formidable by approaching it through the curate, collaborate, create model.

- Add testing and adaptation into the release schedule to maximize ROI.

References

1 Think with Google
Playbook for creative advertising
www.thinkwithgoogle.com/features/youtube-playbook/ (archived at https://perma.cc/V3RE-98B2)
2 Think with Google
Brand lift
www.thinkwithgoogle.com/marketing-strategies/video/brand-lift/ (archived at https://perma.cc/5QRV-J45T)

19

Live video: online events and webinars

Back in the distant mists of 2015, an upstart company called Meerkat launched a live broadcast app onto a hungry world. They released the app just before the South by Southwest Festival and the music and media crowd went crazy for it. It had a sudden launch to fame, but like many start-ups it was to be short-lived. The attention of the big players was focused onto live and within months Twitter released the far better, less glitchy and more intuitive Periscope. But in what is indicative of the marketplace, it wasn't long before a larger rival in turn squashed this new player. The launch of Facebook Live took its turn in drawing audiences and their associated advertising revenue. This Greek tragedy of growth and burnout is indicative of live video in contemporary marketing and brands need to be aware of underlying best practice about the media, as much as which platform is currently the favourite. With that in mind, in this chapter I'm going to run through key features of live video whilst avoiding ephemeral details. It's worth understanding live video as it has now grown to be a cornerstone of business communication. The Covid-19 pandemic cemented video calls for all of us, and brands have been quick to adopt it; indeed the live video industry value is expected to generate \$184.3 billion by 2027.[1]

Without getting too deep and philosophical about it, let's ask, 'What makes live, well... live?' Clearly, it's the transmission of what's happening right now to somewhere else, with the viewer watching at (more or less) the same time as it happens. But is this enough? Is actual timing the only thing that is necessary for us to say it is live? Surely it not only has to 'be' live, but it has to 'feel' live. In fact, if what we are watching does not embrace the moment it might as well not be live. In a past life making radio shows we used the phrase 'as live' when something was pre-recorded as a non-stop episode and later broadcast to viewers as though it was happening at that moment. It sounded live as it was a single take, and we never told them it was pre-recorded, so as a far as the listener was concerned it *was* live. But these shows always lacked something and were never as successful as truly live shows, and that's because they lacked the sense of immediacy and audience participation that must come across for a live show to work. It is the sense that the chaos of the world could burst in at any point that makes live so exciting.

What makes live video so impactful is the idea that viewers, contributors and brands share in a moment at the exact same time. Watching Felix Baumgartner jump off a hot air balloon at the edge of space was amazing. But watching the same event on catch-up the next day when you knew he had survived was just not the same. So, great content needs to not only *be* live, but to *feel* live. The beauty of live is that it does not have to be perfect, and in fact it is the lack of perfection that gives it its realness and excitement.

Felix Baumgartner's supersonic freefall from 128k – mission highlights
15 October 2012, Red Bull YouTube channel
▶ **Video 117**

Live video really comes into its own when the audience is encouraged to take part. I don't know if you have ever had a 'shout out' on a radio station. It's just a comment you made being read out, or even just a track you requested being played, but it's exciting and it makes you feel connected. Live surveys, competitions, reading out social media and a shared sense of immediacy are all ways to make live work harder and allow brands to turn viewers into engaged advocates. Facebook's Zuckerberg is a big fan of live video for exactly this reason and on the launch of his own platform's live offering said: 'When you interact live, you feel connected in a more personal way.'[2] Live video has a positive impact on rates of engagement on Facebook. People comment 10 times more on Facebook Live videos than on regular videos, and Live video is more likely to show up in people's timelines.[3]

But while making things feel 'in the moment' is key to engagement it's not actually the way that brands are building huge audiences with live. In fact, most audiences are engaged when the event has passed, not during it. An event to note at this point was when a Texan called Candace Payne brought the internet to its knees with a Facebook Live review of a Chewbacca mask she had bought for her son. A true phenomenon, it made her a global star and received over 165 million views in just a few months.[4] Payne's video was live and reflects the reality of how live videos grow attention over time. For although the video was broadcast live, the overwhelming majority of its viewers came long after she had put the phone down and stopped broadcasting; the difference from pre-recorded videos was evolutionary, not revolutionary.

Live video formats

Just like traditional video, live can be presented in many different formats. Here's a quick run-down of content types to explore... and some examples of brands getting it right.

Demos

British chef Jamie Oliver advertises his new cookbook, *Veg*, by live streaming recipes:

Veg BBQ was live – Jamie and Gennaro
6 August 2019, Jamie Oliver YouTube channel
 Video 118

Q & A

Even LinkedIn has live video, and it's a great place to drive depth of conversations with customers. This example was a campaign run by social listening tool Hootsuite:

Hootsuite
 Video 119

Live product launch

Fenty Beauty launched their makeup line with global mega star (and co-owner Rihanna) hosting the event, which is a bit of an unfair advantage!

> Fenty Beauty Launch Rihanna Takesover Sephora (FB Live) High Quality 720 HD – Fenty Review
> 10 September 2017, Miss Iconique YouTube channel
> ▶ **Video 120**

Conferences and other traditional offline events

It makes perfect sense to stream live events for those that can't make it. In my opinion, though, if you want to maximize impact you should be creating content specifically for the online audience rather than rehashing a weaker experience of the live event.

> VidSummit 2019 live!
> 17 October 2019, Derral Eves YouTube channel
> ▶ **Video 121**

Webinars

If you want to engage an audience and deepen conversations, you really should be considering webinars. A feature of marketing activity for years, their use was traditionally limited, and they were overlooked (wrongly) by marketers. Covid-19 changed all that, and 41 per cent of companies had a team in place responsible for webinar creation by the end of 2020.[5] Webinars have proven themselves to be an incredibly powerful tool for creating leads, deepening conversations and driving conversions. Mid-funnel 'education' and top of funnel 'lead generation' are the major focus areas for this highly versatile tool.

Webinars are truly unlike anything else; they position you as an 'expert in your field' and, if done right, can keep audiences engaged for hours.

Why webinars?

- Webinars generate new leads. A business with more than enough leads will never struggle to grow. Unfortunately, most businesses lack high-quality lead-generation, and webinars are a great way to attract new eyes, generate new leads, and ultimately convert new customers. With webinars, some kind of registration is expected. People are familiar with submitting their name, email, and sometimes other information in order to register for an upcoming webinar event. They've highlighted themselves as a lead that is interested in whatever you're teaching, and they've opted in to hear more about it.

- Your audience can ask questions and get real-time feedback. Even better, you can ask your audience questions and tailor your content in real time to better serve your audience.

- Just because a webinar is 'free' it doesn't mean people are not exchanging anything for the content. To attend a webinar, your prospect has to register, put the date in a calendar, set aside time for the event, show up at the right time, and then give you 1–3 hours of their time. They do all of this just to listen to you talk about a certain subject; this positions you as an expert before you even start teaching the content.

- You can qualify new leads and build relationships. There's no better way to build a relationship than by giving value first. Generally, the first step in making a sale is related to education. Webinars give us the opportunity to teach our leads and help them understand why our product is valuable in the first place.

- Webinars allow your audience to place a name with a face and a voice with a name, building personal relationships and creating real-time conversations. Just short of visiting your prospect in person or jumping on a personal phone call, webinars are the best way to build personal relationships with your leads. The best part is that it works with new leads just as well as it works with 'seasoned' leads. You can leave a great first impression on people who are hearing from you for the first time.

- Companies live and die by cash flow, so, the faster you can convert a lead into a customer, the better off you'll be. Webinars can really help speed up this process. Why? Simply because they take all of the initial funnel steps and merge them together; they build trust, deliver value, and kill objections in a small period of time.

CASE STUDY
Conversation with Thomas Madsen-Mygdal, TwentyThree

To really dig into the topic of webinars I interviewed Thomas Madsen-Mygdal, CEO and co-founder of video marketing and webinar platform TwentyThree. TwentyThree empowers organizations to relate and communicate with the world through video. They've seen just how fundamentally video has changed our world over the past 15 years and are working with customers to design, develop and deliver some of the best video tools on the market.

JM: So, Thomas, tell me about the scale of webinars in the market-place.

TMM: Well, webinars have grown so much that they now touch every team in a business, from sales and account managers to marketing, product teams and internal comms. They are invitation-only events for existing customers, the CEO hosting a round table with 20 clients, account-based marketing events (where you might have a bank with 250 bank advisors, who run a webinar every quarter for their clients) and much more. It's everything across the whole spectrum of what brands were already doing in the physical world but now in a virtual world.

JM: Why are webinars such a big deal at the moment?

TMM: Marketing has been steadily moving to an always-on model – people can access all the information they need in the world whenever they need it. It's a flat engagement model. But human beings need orchestration and storytelling. In the real world, we want to have some drama. It could be that big launch or that quarterly meeting... all orchestration that creates human engagement and understanding. If everything is always the same then nothing is interesting. We're entering this era of digital event marketing that creates drama and an orchestration of events to drive the marketing cycle. Webinars mean you can create events that build a narrative.

JM: Are videos calls and webinars the same thing?

TMM: There is a confusion between video meeting software and webinar software. And, in some ways, you could say the categories are merging a little bit together, but they are still very different.

Webinars have a lot more of a one-way presentation style and you have control of the production values over and above a video call. Video calls are a free-for-all that you don't really control. In webinars you are producing an experience, but you can still have participation and it's really important that you do – you just get to control when it happens. Webinars also give you the ability to play in other video content, feeds from video mixers and everything you need to create a brand experience, from graphics overlays to prerolls. They will also tie in with your CMS and other marketing tools so you can really focus on getting people involved and tracking results. The other thing is video quality; the quality of a Zoom call could be super cool if there's 10 people on the call, but if it's 2,000 people loads of them will get a terrible picture.

JM: What mistakes do people make with webinars?

TMM: There are three big ones. One is about the lifecycle, the planning and running of the programme. Second is creating the experience, and third is how you use the content afterwards. People often fail at one of these points.

First, in terms of planning and running the webinar programme, some people create amazing response and have 10,000 people on webinars. And some people struggle to even get 100 people on. This is because of the planning around the event. I think the key thing is organizational setup, which is having someone acting as a webinar programme manager or webinar team leader. I see it as sort of webinar programme manager (like the webmaster in the 1990s, the head of digital in the 2000s and the social media manager in the 2010s). One thing to think about if you are working at scale is starting to have webinar teams. It's people that can create formats for the organization and roll them out, get them produced, get them orchestrated, get people comfortable, train people internally.

Second, people fail to create engaging experiences, from the event host to relevant presentations, energy and setup. This is not all about money... a little bit of lighting and a microphone will get you far. It's about content and storytelling. People have to focus on stories that are entertaining, and this is often where they go wrong. Two years ago (when we ran our webinar survey the first time) a lot of people were running slides and audio as a webinar, a lot of which was pre-recorded. But our latest data shows that successful webinars are real faces, real time, authentic, live, not pre-recorded... If you're trying to make it live and participatory, why fake it! Inside this live element we can see that people might have three or four pre-recorded videos, like a product demo or CEO saying something, or a visiting expert, and so on.

This all goes back to meeting facilitation and a lot of other crafts that have been around for a long time. I mean, you can do four hours that are very meaningful if you're actually involving people and giving them tasks and can get them to brainstorm. You can do a lot of things even in a basic chat. It's about learning from the thousands of years of facilitation and meeting design that we use offline. You need to start thinking like a broadcaster of content rather than a PowerPoint presenter. You need to ask, 'How do we make this worth doing?'

Third, what you do after the event is really important. You have invested a considerable amount of time in doing this video and you have a 45 minute recording that you could actually use for a lot of stuff, but people fail to do that. Think about how you maximize the effect of the asset you have created.

JM: What should people be looking for in their webinar platforms?

TMM: They should be looking for the least friction possible. The audience doesn't want to download software, and some companies are not even allowed to download and install software. Your platform should just work right in the browser, because there's no reason to give the audience a barrier of downloading specific software. After that, find tools to create a professional experience by adding graphics, multiple cameras, polls, quality and quantity, all that. It's all about the experience. Finally, make sure you get a platform that can handle the data that you generate, If you're going to run 1,000 webinars a year, you need to have everyone in your organization able to do it and the whole data attribution side nailed down. You need to know who is on your webinars and that everything goes into your CRM system. So you can say, 'Okay, somebody joined the webinar for 45 minutes and asked five questions.' This isn't designed to be some kind of surveillance economy, but it is understanding what the client's attention is so you can service them better.

When we look at the data on what people are tracking, they're tracking how many sign-ups they get for the webinar... but they're not tracking time-based engagement. They're not tracking the quality of the people that are participating in the webinar. A 20-person webinar might be the most valuable one if it's the right people who are there for two hours and get a great experience, as opposed to having 1,000 people on a webinar where it's the wrong people and it's the wrong experience. People using webinars need to measure the right success metrics or they won't be able to improve ROI.

Building an audience for your live video output

1 Building an audience: before broadcast

At the risk of teaching you to suck eggs, it's worth saying that the more effort that goes into building awareness of the broadcast before the live date, the more successful it will be. Ideally, put out news of the event with posts two weeks, one week and one day beforehand. Also, don't forget that people do forget; even engaged viewers can be distracted by life so a count-down to the show is a good call – maybe at two hours, one hour and 30 minutes. Don't overdo it, though, as you don't want viewers to be fed up with the content before you've even started to broadcast. Also, ensure coherent tagging, consistent URLs, titling and graphics across all your platforms.

The key to planning is to think about why you are broadcasting in the first place; does it tie into tent-pole events or other parts of your campaign? Classic examples of live content tied to dates are sports events, public holidays and news stories.

You will also find that regular live streams make the conversation easier to have, as regular contact with people will get the message through.

Here's a brief checklist to make sure you are squeezing every bit of awareness out of your live stream activity.

EMAIL CAMPAIGN

- Create an email campaign with three pre-event and one post-event touch points.
- Segment your campaign (if possible) to allow better tacking and data interpretation.
- Include registration or where-to-watch links in event newsletters.
- If you are using webinar software such as TwentyThree, you will be able to send these emails directly from the platform automatically and they will all tie into a single analytics platform.

SOCIAL

- Plan a social campaign with multiple touch points, starting as far before the event as possible.
- Use an event hashtag on everything you do.
- Provide highlights reels of previous events or interviews with speakers from the event discussing how good it will be.

INFLUENCERS

- Write a press release that specifically highlights the live stream portion of your event to attract media attention.
- Develop a toolkit that includes email templates, graphics and social messaging for influencers of your event.
- Ask everyone speaking at the event to amplify it across their social networks.

SPONSORS AND ALLIANCES

- Provide a promo toolkit to sponsors and other partners with sample messaging and graphics for email and social channels.

If you're after platform-specific advice that is bang up to date, it is worth taking a look at these pages from the big four social platforms:

YouTube: ▶ **Video 122**

Facebook: ▶ **Video 123**

Twitter: ▶ **Video 124**

Instagram: ▶ **Video 125**

2 Building an audience: during broadcast

The general principles to maximizing viewers during broadcasts are the same no matter what channel you are using. The big one, and apologies if this seems obvious, is to have highly engaging content that is actually worth watching and sharing. No amount of social activity will build your audience if they are dropping off as fast as you can put them in.

If you can build a series of live videos that connect to each other, you will also find that your audience builds over time. At Hurricane we created a live Halloween quiz show for a UK brewery company. It broadcast four times on the night of Halloween and the audience built up from one to the next. If you are going to the expense of setting up a studio or live event you may as well grow hits across the day.

Beyond content, here are some other pointers.

- Find out if it is possible for your chosen platform to 'feature' the event in some way, whether on a front page or sub-page.
- During transmission, create highlight clips and push these out to other social channels with links as a teaser (these could just be screen grabs through Twitter for speed).
- Identify your key opinion leaders and influencers and reach out to them directly from the live video so that they spread the word for you.

3 Building an audience: after broadcast

As seen in the Chewbacca mask story mentioned earlier, you're likely to pick up a high proportion of views after the event. Yes, you can tweet that it's on, but if it's only a 30-minute stream the response will be limited. The key is to use organic and paid seeding to get the live stream watched afterwards. The perfect solution would be to post a full version and a cut-down version of what happened so viewers can choose to consume the whole thing or just the highlights. Ideally, both of these would point to a future live stream so that you can build your audience over time.

If you're using Facebook Live, there is actually no direct way to boost a live broadcast like you would with a normal post. However, once the broadcast stops and the video has been added to a page timeline, you can interact with it as you would any other post, including boosting and sharing from your page. This is one of the only ways to get organic reach on Facebook without any ad spend whatsoever, so it has got to be worth a try.

Moderating live content

The moderation of live content is becoming increasingly contentious. As hundreds of thousands of people start to live broadcast, how can the social networks keep up? Hate speech, assaults and all manner of other vile activities can now be broadcast instantly; for instance, in March 2017, an attack on a 15-year-old was broadcast live on Facebook.[6] The volume of live content outpaces the ability of social platforms to moderate it. While videos can be reported for spam or offensive content, just like other posts, the real-time nature of the events means that reported videos are only taken down well after the event has ended.

Facebook has been under the microscope for many things, including for its handling of extremist and terrorist material when their guidelines for moderation were leaked to a newspaper. Along with normal posts, live video was identified as difficult to moderate. In the *Guardian* article, an unnamed integral Facebook source said that the volume of material in the system meant moderators had 'less than 10 seconds' to make a decision that might require intimate knowledge of a terrorist organization and its leaders: 'It's a mission impossible.'[7]

But how does this impact on brands? Well, the answer is that when streaming live video, brands need to be aware of who else is using that platform and what the platform is doing to maximize the quality of moderation. While your own live feed will not be a problem, the issue is what is positioned alongside it and around it. The same goes for running adverts alongside live content. You need to be aware of the digital real estate on which your ads are running, and who is placed alongside your messaging. For more on this, see Chapter 9 where I talk about brand safety.

Although the moderation of third-party broadcasts presents a challenge, you shouldn't forget that issues might come from your own broadcasts. It's easy for swear words to come out of people's mouths by mistake, and in an interview situation you can never be certain that people will not go off-piste with an answer. To minimize risk, clearly brief contributors before going on air about what language is and is not acceptable. And if there is doubt over someone's ability to regulate their language or opinions, it may be best simply to not use them, or to pre-record their section.

Moving away from some of the challenges of live video, we can return to the fact that it is a powerful medium, and it can be very positive for brands to take part in. But when creating live broadcasts at scale, how do you maximize return? Well, the answer is that it's pretty hard to get live viewers in significant numbers once the film is in motion. However, there are things you can to do maximize interest, and a lot of activity you can undertake before and after the broadcast to drive success.

Live-streamed video examples

Live video needs to be part of a wider campaign and integrated into wider activities. It can be a way of spreading the message about the campaign, for example broadcasting from behind the scenes of something you are doing, or from the event that is the basis of the campaign itself. Below I've put together a selection of examples that could come in handy.

- Global Citizen is a non-profit organization with a mission to end extreme poverty by 2030. The brand used Instagram Live to promote their #TogetherAtHome campaign — an effort to encourage social distancing in order to slow the spread of coronavirus. In this livestream, H.E.R. advocated for quarantine, performed a few songs, and responded to live comments to lift spirits during difficult times.

H.E.R. - #TogetherAtHome concert series
26 May 2020, H.E.R. YouTube channel
▶ **Video 126**

- ASOS created a buzz about the extent of their range by recruiting a model to try on 100 different items in 30 minutes. With its warm, supportive presenters, this format reached the Gen Z and young millennial audiences perfectly.

100 layers of ASOS
23 August 2016, ASOS Facebook page
(▶) **Video 127**

- adidas Football has nailed a near-perfect YouTube channel, so it's no surprise that they got live video right as well. In June 2011 they created 'The dugout', a series of live broadcasts to engage football fans before the World Cup. Regular, insightful content with football stars and match insight added a massive amount to the conversation around the sports events and meant that adidas was in the same space as the major sports broadcasters.

David Beckham in the dugout with KickTV trailer adidas football
20 June 2016, new video YouTube channel
(▶) **Video 128**

- Streaming from an event allows people that can't attend in person to connect with the story and the brand. Tough Mudder have tapped into this by allowing people who can't make it to a training event to engage online and train at home. Low production values and lots of enthusiasm are all that are needed here. They also remember to include the watching audience so it feels like a single community, and to name other social channels to broaden the conversation.

Tough Mudder: training with coach T Mud
11 June 2014, Tough Mudder Facebook page
(▶) **Video 129**

Summary

Live video is effective and is here to stay, but like all formats it requires careful consideration of how its effects can be maximized and what risks surround it. The great news is that it is cheap to start, and no one expects perfection. The main thing to take from this chapter is to have a go, start testing, prove what works and grow from there. You won't know until you try.

References

1 Grand View Research
   June 2020
   Video streaming market worth $223.98 billion by 2028 – CAGR: 21.0%
   www.grandviewresearch.com/press-release/global-video-streaming-market
   (archived at https://perma.cc/YUZ3-7E3D)

2 Mark Zuckerberg
   6 April 2016
   Facebook
   www.facebook.com/zuck/posts/10102764095821611 (archived at https://
   perma.cc/3CU8-Q7GK)

3 Facebook
   6 April 2016
   Introducing new ways to create, share and discover live video on Facebook
   https://newsroom.fb.com/news/2016/04/introducing-new-ways-to-create-share-
   and-discover-live-video-on-facebook/ (archived at https://perma.cc/
   A4TD-PVVQ)

4 Candace Payne
   19 May 2016
   Laughing Chewbacca mask lady (full video)
   Jon Deak YouTube channel
   www.youtube.com/watch?v=y3yRv5Jg5TI (archived at https://perma.cc/
   2QBJ-NF36)

5 Twenty Three
   Annual benchmarking survey: State of webinars 2020
   www.twentythree.net/stateofwebinars (archived at https://perma.cc/R423-SDBC)

6 Associated Press
   22 March 2017
   Chicago girl allegedly sexually assaulted on Facebook Live as 40 watched
   Guardian
   www.theguardian.com/technology/2017/mar/22/chicago-girl-allegedly-sexually-
   assaulted-on-facebook-live-as-40-watched (archived at https://perma.cc/
   Z2EN-F4LD)

7 Nick Hopkins
   24 May 2017
   Facebook struggles with 'mission impossible' to stop online extremism
   Guardian
   www.theguardian.com/news/2017/may/24/facebook-struggles-with-mission-
   impossible-to-stop-online-extremism (archived at https://perma.cc/
   H6WQ-RWGB)

INDEX